THE PUMP ROOM ORCHESTRA BATH

Olivia Hyman, *The Colonnade, Bath*

The Pump Room Orchestra
BATH

*Three Centuries of Music
and Social History*

ROBERT HYMAN

AND

NICOLA HYMAN

First published in the United Kingdom in 2011
by The Hobnob Press, PO Box 1838, East Knoyle, Salisbury, SP3 6FA
www.hobnobpress.co.uk

British Library Cataloguing in Publication Data
A catalogue record for this book is available from the British Library

ISBN 978-0-946418-74-9

Typeset in Scala 11/12.5 pt. Typesetting and origination by John Chandler
Printed and bound by CPI Group (UK) Ltd, Croydon, CR0 4YY

Contents

Colour plates will be found between pages 114 and 115

Foreword

by Tom Conti

I WELCOME this most interesting history of the Pump Room Orchestra in Bath and I recommend it to you.

During my many visits to Bath, either to film or play in the beautiful Theatre Royal, I look forward to spending time in one of my favourite rooms in the world, and enjoy the music of the Pump Room Trio.

I am delighted always by the quality of the playing of the trio and the warm and historic atmosphere it creates in this most beautiful space, conjuring visions of the exhilarating, naughty and elegant life in this carefully preserved eighteenth century town.

Now to know more, that Handel took the waters in the Pump Room and Haydn enthused over this 'splendid room' for example, only adds to the pleasure of visiting it.

We wish to dedicate this book to our daughters,
Olivia and Antonia,
in thanks for their support and forbearance

Robert's Preface

THE Pump Room is a unique hub in the centre of Bath. For over three centuries the Pump Room Band and the room that houses it have been inseparable.

I am originally from New York, and it was on a short tour as Leader of the London based NCOS training orchestra that I had my first fleeting glimpse of Bath's lustrous stone buildings and undulating roofs. Years later Nicola and I decided to move to this spa city where I hoped to join or start a string quartet. One day, not long after our arrival, it was with some surprise that we fell upon a piano trio playing in the atmospheric Pump Room with its magnificent Georgian architecture.

Today I am privileged to be a member of that trio, and to play a small part in its long and rich history.

Hardly a day passes that an inquisitive visitor fails to approach the Pump Room stage with a question for a member of the Pump Room Trio. It might be to ask something specific about one of the instruments, the name of a piece that was played or, rather irritatingly, are we amateur or professional and even who pays us! He or she may simply wish to ruminate over the acoustics in the room or let trio members know that they themselves play an instrument. Occasionally the person just informs us on how fortunate we are – 'doing something you must love, and in such a magnificent setting'! But mostly it is to let us know how much the music is appreciated and how fine the playing has been.

It was early in my sojourn in the trio that tantalising anecdotes of its unique past began to surface. I might hear tales of the eccentric early days of the band, its Master(s) of Ceremonies, its importance to many of Bath's physicians and to the people who came to the Roman Baths and Pump Room for the cure, to seek entertainment and to hear the band.

I felt compelled to assemble its three hundred year old history and was astounded that no dedicated work existed on the Pump Room Band. The more I delved the more captivated I became.

Nicola joined me in the project when time constraints and other commitments became an obstacle. Her painstaking care in researching, discovering and authenticating many more figures of the past; her retrieval of stories, passions and legacies became almost 'Salander'-like as her investigations proved indispensable. This book would not be as expansive or complete without her dedication. I look forward to jointly divulging the many revelations discovered in the making of this book.

To pursue the wider subject of the room's music in general would be exhaustive and beyond the realm of this book. This history is a personal tribute to the hundreds of musicians who have played in the Pump Room Band, Orchestra or Trio over the centuries, to their families and to those whom it owes its survival. It pays homage to those Bathonians and visitors from all over the world who came or now come especially to hear and see the 'orchestra', and to those who have discovered it as they wandered through.

Robert Hyman

Nicola's Preface

THE Pump Room is a public space, a theatrical setting built in Bath over an ancient spring. But little is known of the players on the stage who, for more than three centuries, have been branded with the Pump Room name. Who were the men, and relatively more recently the women, who played in the Pump Room Band, Orchestra or Trio? What did their time in Bath lead to and what trace did they leave behind? The trail has led to South Africa, New Zealand, Canada, Tanzania, Swaziland, South America and the United States.

Wilfred Wade, a pianist with the Pump Room Orchestra before the Second World War, ended his article *Some Bath Musicians*[1] with the admission that it took 'no account of the many famous musicians who visited the Pump Room during the great days – but that, perhaps, is another story'. But it *is* part of the story we tell here over half a century later and which dovetails with this book's central theme – that of the musicians who played *in* the Pump Room Orchestra, whether famous or not, and of those who struggled to survive the impact of wars, poverty, economic stringency, ill health, municipal philistinism, and partisanship.

I thank my husband and co-author Robert Hyman, a violinist in the Pump Room Trio for eighteen years, for entrusting me to share in this project. Without his thoroughness and conviction this book would not exist.

Nicola Hyman

Acknowledgements

IN writing this book we are indebted to the effusive violinist Frances Fleming for recording his legendary life and the manoeuvrings among the Pump Room musicians during the 1760s. Trevor Fawcett's sharply focussed lens on eighteenth century Bath and the elegant and concise articulacy of his social histories guided us through this rich period. We thank him for his kind advice and gentle steering. Kenneth James's seminal work, his monumental thesis, *Concert Life in Eighteenth-century Bath*, earned biblical significance. To Ian Woodfield for his musical monolith *The Celebrated Quarrel between Thomas Linley (senior) and William Herschel*. We joined the 'cult' readership of the late Kenneth Young's nostalgic and affectionate study – *Music's Great Days in the Spas and Watering Places*. Over tea in the Pump Room the late Kenneth Gregory offered a journalistic view of the last orchestra, sprinkled with sporting metaphors! We were delighted and honoured to be invited into the lives of Pump Room Orchestra musicians past, whether by a widow, child or grandchild. For sharing their memories, photos, anecdotes and letters we sincerely thank the late Noel Wade, Tony Hatton, Shirley George, Vivien Griffiths, Ann Somerset Miles, Julie Walker, Mary Syms and Pam Hawker. For his interest and input, Nicholas Roberts, 'cellist with the Coull Quartet and great grandson of Pump Room Orchestra cornet player Joseph Russell. And to John Chandler, our publisher, whose commitment to the book was sealed over a coffee at Bonghi Bo's in Bath, a good place to meet.

We would especially like to thank Stephen Bird, Head of Bath & North East Somerset Council's Heritage Services for his advice, support and patience. Also thanks go to Stephen Clews, Romans Baths and Pump Room Manager, and to Pat Dunlop, the Roman Baths and Pump Room Commercial Marketing Manager. Much appreciated for giving their valuable time and their expertise are Colin Johnston and his professionally efficient staff at the City Archives in the Guildhall. The Georgian Newspaper Project became a valuable research tool – thanks go to its editor, Dr Donald Straughan.

Alistair Hinton, composer and ex Pump Room Trio pianist, never wavered from delving into his records and responding with speedy emails. Grateful thanks especially go to him and Shena Power; also Lorna Osbon, Edna Blackwell, Dennis Cole; Matthew Taylor, Steve Buck, Mike Evans, Keith Tempest, Derek Stuart-Clark, Sarah Lovell, Geoff Ditcham and Katy Rowe for sharing their personal experiences of playing in the Pump Room. Thanks to Martin Salter (the last of the Pumpers) and Ken Ritchie for their views from the front of house. David Lord was very generous with his time revisiting the early recordings and supplying us with photos and newspaper cuttings. For inviting us to share her annual pilgrimage to the Pump Room, we thank Janet Mancini Billson.

Much admired are the clever watercolours of the Pump Room evoked by artists David Paskett and Michael Aubrey and the album cover from photographer Gregory Kynaston. For support with source material and information we thank: Katherine Wall and Helen Daniels (Victoria Art Gallery); Jeff Walden (BBC Written Archives Centre); the British Library; Rachel Bowers and Jenni Wagstaff (Bath Film Office); Gladys Powney and Sarah Fox (Bath Heritage Services), Julien Chilcot-Monk; Ann Meddings (Theatre Royal); Ann Buchanan (Local History, Bath Central Library); the staff at Bristol Central Reference Library; Lucy Rutherford (Bath Abbey Archivist); Paul Westwell (Musicians Union); Jon Overton (Sally Lunn's); light music researchers and writers Philip Scowcroft and Brian Reynolds; Tim Bullamore; Brian Preston; Richard Barnard; Steffen Nowak (violin and 'cello maker); Lynette Erwin (Anne Storace researcher); Peter Sheppard Skæved (RAM); Eleanor Roberts (Hallé Archives); Stephen Walker (Scarborough Spa Orchestra); Robin Gordon-Powell; Dick Trafford; John Madigan for his wartime dancing memories; Bob Bennett; Tony Griffiths and Donna Griffiths. Thanks to Jill Warrener for her assiduous proofreading.

Present Pump Room aficionados: the distinguished Leonard Pearcey, Peter Child, Godfrey and Frances Abbott, Anne and Gordon Spurrell, Brian and Angela Skinner, Ivy and Malcolm Brown – the 'Sleepy Lagoon couple', Philip and Marie Ennis, Susan and Martin Tomes, Shirley Allan, Patrick Michallat-Cox and Kay Yeoman. Your familiar presence offers continuity between the Pump Room's past and its future.

During the writing of this book, accuracy has been our primary objective. Any errors or misunderstandings are entirely unintentional.

Introduction

BATH has the only natural hot springs in Britain, which in medieval times were believed to have curative powers. By the time of Elizabeth I's visit to Bath in 1574, attempts to explain these properties scientifically were underway. People came to Bath, a watering-place and English Spa, to bathe 'in the hot water for ailments such as leprosy . . . gout, palsy and colic'.[2] Bathing was the 'chief use of the various springs . . . even though a drinking fountain to quench bathers' thirsts had been installed in the King's Bath before 1600 . . . '.[3] Crucially, the addition of a drinking-pump in 1661 pre-empted new medical theories and marketing prospects, but bathing still prevailed over imbibing. Spa water was also available from a pump in the Pump-yard with two Sergeants-at-Arms in charge of its distribution. As a garrison town during the civil war, Bath's spa trade suffered.[4] Samuel Pepys, the famous English diarist, visiting Bath in 1668 described the bathing ritual in which he and his wife indulged.

> Up at four o'clock, being by appointment called up to the Cross Bath where we were carried one after another, myself and wife . . . though we designed to have done before Company come, much Company come; very fine ladies; and the manner pretty enough, only methinks it cannot be clean to go so many bodies together in the same water. Good conversation among them that are acquainted here, and stay together. Strange to see how hot the water is; and in some places, though this is the most temperate bath, the springs so hot as the feet not able to endure. But strange to see, when women and men herein, that live all the season in these waters, that cannot but be parboiled, and look like the creatures of the bath! Carried away, wrapped in a sheet, and in a chair, home; and there one after another thus carried, I staying above two hours in the water, home to bed, sweating for an hour; and by and by, comes soft musick to play to me, extraordinary good as ever I heard at London almost, or anywhere.[5]

'Soft Musick' was likely to have been offered courtesy of a group of wind players known as the City Waits. There was also music in the Cross Bath, often amplified by enthusiastic gentlemen bathers joining in song, and thus eventually discouraged.

Bath was still a long way from the fashionable and cultural spa town it later became. There were occasional concerts in the Abbey and other social events – banquets, balls and public meetings took place in a room above the Market House in the new Guildhall, the headquarters for city administration. A fiddler and oboist accompanied the country-dances on the outdoor bowling green where 'clapper boys' were employed to chase off the birds.

In 1670 a 'band of musick' could be observed performing under large sycamore trees in the Gravel Walks, the communal gardens where visiting gentry would parade and socialize. 'Surrounded by much good company, [many] found drinking the waters more beneficial than bathing'.[6] Joseph Gilmore's Bath plan of 1694 shows three figures, possibly entertainers, on a green adjacent to the Walks. Groups of strolling players were a colourful feature of Bath's street life[7] despite the Corporation's attempts to regulate their numbers. In *The Image of Georgian Bath* Peter Borsay cites the market place, Guildhall, Abbey, the Gravel Walks and the King's Bath as the principal landmarks in 1700, confined within the 'area of the medieval city'.

Bath's ceremonious welcome of Queen Anne in 1702, following in the wake of earlier royal visits to the city, drew a swell of fashionable social aspirants. One such person was Richard Nash Esquire. After being sent down from Oxford, he became disaffected with the Army and then over-indulged as a law student in London's 'Middle Temple'. The delights of Bath's gaming tables, in a city suddenly so popular as a health and pleasure resort, were irresistible. Nash was nicknamed Beau after the *Beau Monde*, an 'elite' group who were drawn to his charisma and style, although he 'had not a foot of land, and never realised a single hundred'.[8] Assistant to self-appointed Master of Ceremonies Captain Webster, a notorious gambler, Nash was the obvious successor when Webster was killed in a duel by a losing card player. Thus began a reign lasting over fifty years as the undisputed 'King of Bath'.

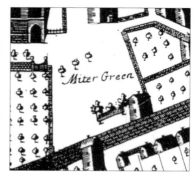

Three Figures (possibly performers) on Miter Green. Joseph Gilmore's Bath plan of 1694 (courtesy of Bath Record Office (B&NES Council)

The Pump Room adjoining the King's Bath, John Fayram, 1739 (courtesy of the Victoria Art Gallery, Bath & North East Somerset Council)

Water is Best[9]

THE growing medical trend in drinking spa water to cure internal complaints led to an increasing throng of drinkers around the outdoor King's Bath pump. The need for shelter, especially in inclement weather, justified the decision to build what would be 'a rather elegant Pump Room'.[10] Designed by John Harvey in the style of an orangery, it was funded entirely by the Corporation and completed in 1706. Attendance continued to escalate, with drinkers often prescribed a pint or two of spa water in the morning (consumed while still wearing bonnets and dressing gowns) and up to a gallon a day. Water was dispensed by a pumper, a function which later became officiated and was to carry a particular status.[11]

The Physicians, whose interest it was to allay their clients' boredom, 'solicited Nash to let the band [from the Gravel Walks] perform in the

Pump Room'.[12] Conceivably driven by altruistic motives, the Physicians maintained that

> . . . the least stroke imaginable upon any musical instrument has such an effect on the human body as to move its component machinulae in all their parts, giving the fibres of the whole body more or less, according to their degree of tension, correspondent concussions; and consequently the spirits are not only raised, or made finer, but the other animal fluids are also briefly agitated, and their preternatural cohesions and viscidities destroyed.[13]

Nash 'acquiesced', **and this is where our story begins** . . .

The five musicians from the Gravel Walks were invited into the Pump Room to entertain the visitors in the long intervals between drinking the water.

Visitors to Bath arrived at the city gates and, if coming from London, were stopped at the Walcot Northgate. Runners were sent to the Abbey and welcoming bells were rung. The Waits would already be lingering outside their lodgings, ready to play 'in the confident expectation of a handsome tip – if only to send them away.'[14] The first stop on the visitors' itinerary would be the Pump Room where the payment of a guinea was noted in the Subscription Book. This covered admission to the Pump Room and two tickets for the balls. Guests would leave their card with their contact details, which would then be copied into a Visitors Book, enabling others to locate them while in Bath.

It is claimed that the cantankerous royal physician Dr John Radcliffe, unhappy with the unhygienic conditions of the baths, threatened he would place a toad in the water. Its toxic secretions would likely compound the fear of infection and ultimately force the baths closure. Nash allegedly responded by announcing that the Pump Room Band would coax the amphibious creature out of the hot water (drawing from the Parisian theory that music could arrest the poison of a tarantula's bite). Another account was that Nash's '*hautboy* [oboe] was offered to match against the Doctor's head'.[15]

To raise the stature of the first group 'most of whom [he] disapproved, being very indifferent performers',[16] Beau Nash added seven professional musicians from London. This decision was significant according to Kenneth James who, in his extensive thesis 'Concert Life in Eighteenth Century Bath', wrote that this early Pump Room Band, 'though initially few in number . . . formed the nucleus of Bath's various orchestras througfhout that period'.

Beau Nash's Early Pump Room Band

ONE side of the Pump Room was dignified by the presentation in 1709 of a long case clock built by Thomas Tompion. The London maker possibly felt 'that the honour of Freeman accorded him by the city called for some such gift'.[17] Its built-in equation, showing the difference between 'solar' and 'mean' time, was rare even then. For members of the band, however, its function would more likely have been to shed some light on when to begin and end their session. (To this day, just over three hundred years later, it remains not only a focal point for the room, but also a useful tool for musicians in the Pump Room.) Two guineas were paid each year to the person entrusted with looking after the clock.

Balls became a regular weekly event at Harrison's Assembly Rooms on Terrace Walk (later Simpson's Rooms). Noted in the Pump Room Visitors Book was an increased charge for 'subscriptions to the balls at two guineas a week'. Any reference to the cost of maintaining the band's music had been (conveniently) omitted, leading subscribers to believe that 'the subscription was for the balls only'.[18] Nash now paid the musicians one guinea a week for playing 'morning mood music'[19] in the Pump Room and one guinea for playing at the Balls.

During the winter season the band played in the Pump Room daily, excluding Sundays, from half past eight to ten in the morning. In the spring season music began half an hour earlier. Known to many as Nash's Band, the musicians moved around the Pump Room using portable wooden music stands. It is probable that Abbey organist Thomas Dean and his successor Josias Priest played harpsichord in the Pump Room Band, as would Thomas Chilcot.[20] The music served as a backdrop in a socially diverse venue where people went to take the waters and met for conversation and gossip. The Pump Room Band is believed to be the country's first *resident seasonal* orchestra to play in a room where the public assembled.

> Nash never suffered any of the company to make innovations in the amusements, nor the band of music to be under their awe and direction . . . **They** were **his** servants; **he** was **their** patron; nor

would he ever suffer any of them to enter into articles with those who had diversions out of the rooms. Yet he never restrained them from pursuing any business that might be to their advantage.[21]

Much of the music in coffee houses, gardens, private houses and breakfast concerts also fell under the auspices of Nash. But the Corporation's Waits were independent of Nash's Band and played all over Bath, publicly and privately.[22] Benefit concerts were promoted and celebrated guest musicians from London and elsewhere were invited to play. Visiting in 1714, Alexander Pope wrote of Bath's emerging sophistication in a letter

From the window where I am seated I command the prospect of twenty or thirty of the finest promenades in the world . . . My whole day is shared by the Pump assemblies, the walks, the chocolate house, the raffleing shops, medleys, etc.

While a certain Mrs Bradshaw in 1721 described Bath in a letter to a friend as 'nothing but noise and nonsense'. Daniel Defoe, writing in 1724, was more favourably disposed

We may now say it is the resort of the sound rather than the sick. Morning began with bathing in the Hot Baths followed by drinking the tepid mineral water and gossiping in the Pump Room or listening to the small group of players who formed Nash's Pump Room Band. Breakfast at the Assembly Rooms was followed by a concert. On other days ladies breakfasted in their lodgings while gentleman met in the coffee houses to discuss the affairs of state and to read newspapers. Dinner at four o'clock was followed by further visits to the Pump Room. The day ended with drinking tea in the Assembly Rooms, evening visits to each other's lodgings or attending the Balls theatre or concerts.

Bath's summer social season gradually evolved into one long season that lasted from September to May, expanding investment opportunities in amenities and entertainment. This allowed Nash during the relatively quiet summers to preside in Tunbridge Wells as MC, a role he held for several years.

John Gay's *The Beggar's Opera* came to Bath following its huge success in London in 1728. It is likely that for the orchestra 'the Pump Room musicians must have been co-opted, for they certainly took part in the subsequent staging at Bristol'.[23]

In 1730 the New Assembly Rooms or Thayer's Rooms opened opposite the Lower Assembly Rooms on Terrace Walk, sharing the popular twice-weekly balls. Nash scrupulously coordinated the strict protocol of dances at these balls, 'where every nicety of dress was observed' and rank and privilege were given 'their fullest expression'.[24] A band played French dances, minuets and English country dances. Not even royalty were exempt from the rules of decorum at the assemblies, or the eleven o'clock halt to dancing as ordained by Nash's watch 'itself set by the Pump Room's Tompion clock'.[25]

The Arrival of Francis Fleming

'**A** TURN for wandering, artistic faculties, a generous heart, and a shallow purse'[26] were the attributes of Irish violinist Francis Fleming, who arrived in Bristol off the boat from Dublin in 1732. Writing later in the third person, under the pseudonym Timothy Ginnadrake, Fleming recalls his anticipation that Bath would be 'fine, rich and opulent'. But he was disappointed with the 'scarcely half-peopled' city where 'the houses were very indifferent, there being only one with a sash window'. Fleming admitted that 'although he did not apply so assiduously as he ought to his music..' his improvement was such that when introduced to Beau Nash that year he was

> admitted into the band of music, where he acquitted himself to the satisfaction of the company, being remarked for the fine and loud tone he brought out of his violin . . . [27]

Two members in the band 'were lame and two very much afflicted with the gout'.[28] When the band's cache of wine was substituted with water and tincture, Fleming, already resented for the ease in which he befriended 'persons of distinction', was the suspect prankster. The band players, stricken with diarrhoea after drinking the liquor, and caught short in their rush to the 'temple of Cloacina', fell over each other in a series of undignified tumbles. Hilarity of the whole company[29] witnessing this debâcle stopped the dancing and Fleming was left playing the violin by himself!

A music society in Bath existed 'where good amateur players took part alongside resident professionals (from the Pump/Assembly Rooms band, the theatre, and perhaps the City Waits).'[30] The latter were still perceived by some as Bath's municipal band and were placed 'on an official footing in 1733 and henceforth received four guineas a year'.[31]

Some physicians considered the Pump Room unsuitable for their clients with its large arched windows, too hot in the summer and too cool in the winter. The rooms were also cramped for space. Architect John Wood the Elder in 1733 declared that 'there is no place belonging to it for the invalids to retire into, when the waters begin to operate'.[32] However, Wood's plans to add another storey to the Pump Room were foiled by the objections of a local coffee house owner who feared the expanded facilities would reduce his trade. But, in 1734 the Pump Room Band was finally relieved of performing in cramped conditions by the addition of 'a gallery built for the musick'.[33]

Jonathan Pinchbeck's fan etching shows fashionably dressed ladies and gentlemen, the fountain and a five-piece Pump Room Band. Two viol players, an oboist and bassoonist, led by a trumpeter, play in a semi-circular gallery that is precipitously accessed by ladder.

Fleming could flatter himself that his 'flashes of merriment and effusions of fancy . . . often sent the tables at the Pump Room in a roar'.[34] His engaging personality earned him the role of leader, intensifying the irritation of some band members. (He held the position, at times precariously, until his death over forty years later). Fleming became the first director of Bath's subscription concerts in the Lower Rooms, but still managed to travel widely. He played for a season at Scarborough in 1736 and with his French wife Anne (née Roland), a dance teacher, he would visit Paris to keep up with the latest dance fashions.

Methodism was gaining some sympathy in the city and on one particular day in 1739, while preaching in Bath, John Wesley became involved in a public spat with Beau Nash. 'Satan took it ill to be attacked in his headquarters, Sodom of our land, Bath'[35] the preacher sniped. To drown out Wesley's harangues, Nash had the Pump Room Band play the national anthem with the addition of 'french horns and kettledrums'.[36] The influential Countess of Huntingdon, Selina Hastings, resident in Bath part of the year, was persuaded in her religious zeal that Nash was 'a monument of irreligion, folly and vice'. She prompted satirical verses on the Master of Ceremonies' 'conversion' which were mischievously displayed on the Pump Room and Assembly Room walls.

Fleming's close friend and collaborator for many years was Thomas Chilcot, composer and Bath Abbey organist. Their Pump Room Band colleague Charles Love, who played trumpet, oboe and horn, subscribed to Chilcot's set of Twelve Songs. Love's versatility on more than one instrument was not untypical of the time.

By 1747 musical life in Bath was flourishing. There were popular breakfast concerts, usually sponsored by 'some leading figure among the spa visitors, occasionally by Nash or the proprietor of the Rooms'.[37] Meticulously organised, tickets were one and a half shillings 'but the cost did cover the band of music'.[38] The gentry held concerts and 'soirées' in their own homes inviting celebrated musicians who might compose or dedicate pieces to their hosts. George Frederic Handel visited Bath in the summer of 1749, staying with his friend the famous actor James Quin. Musical skills were preferred in ladies companions, valets and governesses who formed the entourage of wealthy families. Beau Nash himself owned a harpsichord that he purchased in Bath, adding to the violin and oboe it is acknowledged he played.

An expensive fifth bay extension to the west side of the Pump Room was added in 1751 to alleviate overcrowding.

> The expense of compensation, demolition, and building of a costly extension exceeded many times the Pumper's rental and shows how much the Pump Room was then valued. [39]

Friends and supporters funded a monument that year to Nash, 'to perpetuate the memory of this great man'. His statue proudly holds the plan of the General Hospital he had so actively supported. Scrutinising the visitors today, the statue presides from its central niche at the back of the Pump Room.

Lady Luxborough Goes to Bath chronicles the visit of a lady who, due to an earlier indiscretion, 'was forbidden to go to London or on the Bath Road where her friends lived'.[40] Poor health brought Lady Luxborough, a lover of music, to the Pump Room – 'the animation of the scene pleased her'.[41] Marjorie Williams, the author of *Lady Luxborough Goes to Bath*, intimates that compositions likely to have been played by the band were songs by Arne and Purcell, a concerto grosso by Corelli,[42] (a composer much admired by Fleming), a piece by Tartini and some of Handel's works. 'The popularity of Handel dominated Bath.'[43] His four oratorios were performed at Wiltshire's Rooms on Terrace Walks. The concert was organised by Thomas Chilcot whose 'Six Suites of lessons for the Harpsichord' had been subscribed to by Handel years earlier. It is possible that Handel made more visits to the city than were chronicled. Handel's name appearing in the *Advertiser and Journal*'s list of Arrivals in April 1758 'just a few days before the first known large scale performance of his music at the Abbey would seem a curious coincidence'.[44]

Nash had single-handedly regulated and managed the band in its early years with complete authority, but by the 1750s he had lost his monopoly over the provision of music in Bath. Pump Room Band string players Thomas Shaw and David Richards promoted the first performance in Bath of Boyce's serenata, *Solomon* in 1758 'as it was originally composed for the Philharmonic Society in Dublin'.[45] However, the high fees commanded by singers Passerini and his wife substantially limited any profits. Conversely, David Richards was doubly compensated for playing both violin and 'cello solos at the Italian maestro's own concerts, illustrating the interdependence of well-known guest soloists and local musicians. The latter formed the bedrock of musical life in the city, albeit a bedrock with its own pecking order. It is likely that 'as a rank and file member of the Pump Room Orchestra'[46] Richards played the 'cello. But 'while Francis Fleming retained his position as leader of Nash's band at the Pump Room and for the balls . . . he lost his position as Bath's foremost violinist, to David Richards'.[47] A much greater loss was to befall Fleming that year when his wife Anne died suddenly. With three young daughters to support, he was propelled into a new role as Dance Master in the city.

On the 7th April, 1759 the *Whitehall Evening Post* announced that 'on this day Handel proposed setting out for Bath, to try the Benefit of the Waters, having been for some Time past in a bad State of Health'.[48] The same paper reported that his illness had prevented him making the journey, and his death a week later at the age of seventy four. Nine years earlier Handel had been 'at the summit of his wealth and popularity'.[49] Handel's Will included a legacy of 'one thousand pounds to the decayed musicians and their children'.[50]

An ambitious young Thomas Linley joined the Pump Room Band at this time. Born in Wells the son of a carpenter, he was apprenticed to the composer and Bath Abbey organist, Thomas Chilcot, and later studied with Paradies. Chilcot's last solo concert in 1760 featured Fleming's eldest daughter Anne, possibly one of his pupils. Fleming ended the year refuting charges that he was 'indifferent about following his business' and reassured the public 'that for his family's sake he would continue to be as diligent as ever'.[51]

Abel had been in Bath that year performing harpsichord and *viola de gamba* solos in addition to two of his own overtures. Returning a year later with composer and violinist Felici Giardini, Abel cultivated a lifelong friendship with the portrait painter Thomas Gainsborough, and became one of his subjects. Gainsborough was also a family friend of the Linleys and painted several of Linley's children, especially Elizabeth, Anne and Thomas Linley the Younger, all of whom showed exceptional musical talent. David Richards may have been one of the young Thomas's violin teachers.

On the 3rd February 1762 at the venerable age of 87 Beau Nash died in poverty. His poor state of affairs was largely due to gambling debts, lawsuits and his personal donations to many good causes. Crowds turned out for the magnificent funeral organised by the Corporation, who as a gesture of kindness had given Nash a small pension when he retired. Chief mourners were the proprietors of the two Assembly Rooms, Simpson and Wiltshire. Six city aldermen carried the coffin in the procession to the Abbey. The City Waits 'marched alongside the Pump Room musicians'[52] who played a dirge at appropriate intervals. Beneficiaries of Nash's charitable efforts – the invalids from the hospital, brought up the rear. Nash's life had lacked neither theatricality nor frivolity. 'Profligate and extravagant though he seemed, Nash was also Bath's finest publicist.'[53] His eccentric persona may have been regarded as ridiculous by some, but his achievements were substantial and he well deserved the bestowal of the honorary freedom of the city.

After Beau Nash

BATH's dynamic musical life did little to enhance the prosperity of musicians in the Pump Room Band as their pay remained poor. Like other Bath musicians who played in more than one musical group, Samuel Eve, an oboist in the band for many years, also played at the theatre. Teaching, repairing and making of instruments, property speculation and retail offered essential supplements to band members' meagre wages. String player Thomas Shaw was a grocer in Chapel Row near the prestigious Queen Square. Thomas Underwood, 'Musical Instrument Maker and Music Seller', announced in the *Bath Chronicle and Weekly Gazette* of October 14, 1762 that he had 'quitted business in favour of [other local musicians] Messrs Benjamin Milgrove and John Brooks'. The business rented out 'Harpsichords, spinets and all sorts of musical instruments . . . by the week . . . tun'd, made and mended in the neatest Manner'.

Benjamin Milgrove, a French horn, violin and clarinet player in the Pump Room Band, also composed hymns and was precentor and organist at the Countess of Huntingdon's chapel. After completing seven years apprenticeship to Underwood he inherited the Stall Street business. With his partner, Pump Room Band 'cellist John Brooks, he later relocated to Abbey Green where they also let property. John Brooks's father, an eminent comedian in the theatre, had also been a 'cellist in the Pump Room Band. (John Brooks's son James would become one of Bath's leading violinists.)

William Rogers the Younger was a string, trumpet and horn player in the Pump Room Band. His father, William Rogers the Elder, had relocated from London several years earlier to open a toy and jewellery shop in Abbey Churchyard. A craftsman but also vendor of articles made outside Bath,[54] he was able to secure financial stability for his son.

Remuneration for teaching varied according to one's place in the pecking order of musical esteem. Harpsichordist Thomas Orpin charged up to ten guineas a year for a couple of lessons a week, his reputation enhanced by the accomplishments of one of his pupils. Jane (Jenny) Mary Guest was a tradesman's daughter. Her performances in concerts at the age of six prompted these anonymous lines

> With envy, Orpin, you may view
> Your pupil – soon she'll tutor you.[55]

After Nash's death, his former assistant Monsieur Jacques Caulet became his immediate successor. Keen on physical exercise, Caulet (Collett) regularly walked to London and back. When in Bath he

> glided smoothly through [rather] than cut a great figure in his sovereignty [and was] . . . possessed of much agility, and very fond of exercising it in dancing with children publicly in the rooms. Among other antics which he shewed, he would in dancing with them spring from the ground several feet, and at falling, by a very sudden transition, contract his height in such a manner as to appear a little boy, leading one of the children to the bottom couple, rising to his usual stature gradually till he elevated the child in his arms extended . . . [56]

Monsieur Caulet resigned after only a couple of years, blaming inadequate earnings. Francis Fleming implied that a pursuance of cards rather than shuttlecock might have extended his occupancy in the post of MC (Master of Ceremonies).

A casual joke and a flattering poem to a lady of influence catapulted Irish writer Samuel Derrick to the post. Anxious for acceptance by the company, he resolved 'to have the band of Music compleat'[57] at the first concert of the season. Scottish writer Tobias Smollett, a former colleague of Derrick, compares him to Tom Thumb in his later novel *Humphry Clinker*. Smollett spent the winter of 1765 in Bath and describes the effect of the Pump Room, 'which is crowded like a Welsh fair', on his character, the young Lydia Melford

> The noise of the music playing in the gallery, the heat and flavour of such a crowd, and the hum and buzz of their conversation, gave one the headache and vertigo.

Lydia considers Derrick 'a pretty little gentleman', but a coffee house spat with a drama critic ended when the latter declared 'he would fight him when he had washed his feet and got clean stockings on'. Though donning a white hat in imitation of Beau Nash, Derrick was unable to match Nash's flair for collecting subscriptions. 'None of Nash's successors had anything like [his] clout or charisma.'[58] Staunchly loyal to his late respected employer of nearly thirty years, violinist Fleming mourned the departure from the code of behaviour established by Beau Nash. Fleming regarded Derrick as a mere 'apology of a man'[59] and regretted that Nash's 'rules were innovated, and many of his precedents disregarded'. The role of MC was still a profitable and sought after position, but unlike Beau Nash in his early years, Derrick was not granted exclusive monopoly of music provision in the city.

Thomas Linley and a Crisis in the Band

A WATERSHED in the history of the Pump Room Band was now looming. Disharmony prevailed and dissatisfactions within the band were allowed to fester. Members organised the odd concert or concert series and occasionally formed their own orchestras. A rift in the band was exposed when string player David Richards, frustrated with his prospects in Bath, resolved to leave and try his luck in London. Richards had been unable to guarantee the company's attendance even when one of his concerts was led by violinist Felice Giardini and Abel was playing 'cello. According to Fleming, Richards, an outstanding violinist and 'cellist, was 'incapable of wearing a mask to deceive [and] never met with the patronage of the company'.[60] This distinction was reserved for the young Pump Room Band musician Thomas Linley, whose 'plea of a young family to maintain'[61] often evoked its members' sympathies. With his wife Mary, he would have twelve children, of which three daughters became outstanding soprano soloists. Ozias Humphry, a painter who lodged with the family between 1762 and 1764, remarked that Linley was 'engaged almost continually at the Pump Room, the Theatre, or in teaching his numerous scholars'.[62] As a singing teacher the platform Linley gave his talented children enhanced his concert promotions in Bath. Elizabeth, his eldest child, was a soprano and her brother Tom was studying violin with the celebrated William Boyce. Such were their musical attributes that 'instead of impoverishing their parents [they] began to enrich them . . . '[63]. Beguilingly, as a little girl, Elizabeth would

> with such looks and features as prevailed upon the motley visitors to Bath . . . gracefully [hold] up her little basket with her father's benefit tickets at the door as they passed in and out of the Pump Room.[64]

Passing Elizabeth might be 'a great Number of Gentlemen and Ladies who [had] kept such a Prating that the Pleasure of the music was lost'. So complained the Reverend John Penrose in a letter in which he described the 'Tweedle-dum and Tweedle-dee of ten musicians, seated in a Music Gallery at the West End of the Room.'[65]

Thomas Chilcot died in November 1766. Linley 'failed to secure his position at the Abbey [and] was left without any real influence on Bath's music-making'.[66] Richards, one of the most valued Pump Room musicians, was still determined to leave the band for London, but was offered a substantial pay increase of a guinea a week to remain. He subsequently learned however that Linley had demanded the same. Funds would have to come 'from the salaries of some of the performers who could very ill afford it . . . '. From the Parade Coffee-House on Monday, January 9th 1767 Richards wrote a letter of resignation to the Gentlemen Subscribers to the Concerts, Rooms, Pump Room etc declining the offer and stating that he could not

> seem to oppress any person in my own possession, or cause any uneasiness, or even seem to carry any thing with a high hand towards any individual, I must beg to be excused accepting those proffer'd favours, and purpose pursuing my London scheme.[67]

Richards' departure for London (where he eventually led the Drury Lane Theatre Orchestra) meant that 'the only musician between Linley and the control he sought was Fleming'.[68]

Recognising that a semblance of order was required, a management meeting shortly followed. The issue of pay for band members, whose age and health at times indisposed them, was also raised.

> Whereas, upon examination into the state of the band of Music, it appears that about two years ago there were three persons who from age, infirmity, and long service in the band, appealed to the Master of Ceremonies deserving some support, and other persons were admitted as their deputies on that consideration; but as the allowance then made of one guinea and a half a week seems too disproportionate, we the under-written gentlemen take the liberty, on behalf of the Company, to adjust the above, and reduce that allowance to one guinea to each of those aged or infirm persons, and do agree that any persons doing their duty in the band, do each of them have one guinea per week.[69]

Funds for elderly band members and the deputy fee were to be reduced by a management prepared to pay only two guineas a week for regular members 'as little as a proper performer can be procured for'.[70] The management decided

That Mr. Brooks can be admitted to play the violoncello, in the place of Mr. Richards, and be allowed full pay.

That Messrs. Rogers, Grant, and Milgrove, be continued as deputies to Messrs. Philips, Glass, and George [presumably, the three appellants], at one guinea per week.

Further manoeuvring took place behind closed doors, when a certain

Mr. Fr—e, who assumed an authority over the band of music at the instigation of Jack Dilettanti prevailed on Derrick to dismiss Fleming, without assigning any reason . . . to make room for a Tewkesbury [a violinist from Wincanton].[71]

Francis Fleming, while preparing to play his morning session in the Pump Room on Tuesday, 24th February 1767, received a note from the Master of Ceremonies

Fleming, Sir, Mr. Fr—e sent me a note last night, in which he desires me to tell you, that you are no longer one of the band of the Pump and Ball Room in Bath. I hereby comply with that desire in his name. And am Sir, Your friend and humble Servant, S. Derrick.

Fleming. who 'had presided in the band upwards of thirty-five years [and] nobly disdained to be the instrument of such injustice . . . ',[72] was incensed. Comparing this catalogue of confusion to Hell in Milton's *Paradise Lost*, Fleming appealed to the company to revoke this decision. Of nearly five hundred members present at the hearing, only a handful supported the motion to sack Fleming, for 'the singular reason . . . that when he performed he did it by mere memory, and not by books as others do'.[73] Fleming describes the insidious atmosphere at this seemingly kangaroo court

Such were the shifts his adversaries were drove to for matter to accuse him; – and thus in attempting to deprecate him, they made his merit the more conspicuous. The remorseful Derrick was the cat's-paw in the affair, the mysterious Fr—e, no more than an agent, but . . . fed on by Jack Dilettanti.[74]

Frère was a member of the concert management committee, and Kenneth James is in no doubt that the mysterious Jack Dilettanti

Gainsborough, *Thomas Linley, Senior* (courtesy of the Dulwich Picture Gallery)

was none other than Thomas Linley. James attests 'that Linley attempted to have Fleming, his former master's colleague and friend, removed as Leader of the Pump Room musicians' soon after the death of Thomas Chilcot, and that Linley's earlier demand for an increase in pay, knowing it would have to come from the wages of other band members, 'betrays a ruthlessness quite sufficient for him to have been the initiator of the plan to remove Fleming'.[75]

On 24 March 1767 the newspaper maintained that the 'Band of Music [at the Pump Room] being full' and its list of members confirmed that Fleming's appeal was upheld:

Thomas Linley [violin]
John Grant [violin]
Benjamin Milgrove [French horn]
William Rogers [Trumpet/horn]
John Brooks ['cello]
Thomas Shaw [clarinet/viola/violin]
Robert Peck [harpsichord]
Francis Fleming [violin]

The apparent manipulation of Derrick by Fr—e and the mysterious Jack Dilettanti, not only damaged Fleming, but also compromised the reputation of his potential replacement, Tewkesbury. With Fleming reinstated, Tewkesbury was forced to circulate a notice in order to protect his reputation. Maintaining that, though initially employed to replace Fleming, some members in the company understood he was filling the role of departing string player David Richards. It was with the unanimous approval of the company that Tewkesbury had confidently resigned his first violin position in Salisbury under the patronage of Harris . . .'[76] However, with 'cellist John Brooks taking David Richards' place in the band and Fleming reinstated as leader, there was no position after all for the so recently appointed Tewkesbury. Having relinquished two successful dance schools in Wincanton, Tewkesbury petitioned that he was left unable to support his 'aged mother and her family'.

The Pump Room Band clarified the sequence of events with their own petition signed by John Grant, Benjamin Milgrove, William Rogers, John Brooks, Thomas Shaw, Robert Peck and Francis Fleming but [significantly] 'with Linley excepted'

> Mr. Brooks was put into the Pump and Ball-Room band of music, in the room of Mr. Richards, who retired to London.

> Mr. Richards then went away absolutely; and Brooks was again put into his place, which he now holds.

> Mr. Fleming was absolutely turned out to make room for Mr. Tewkesbury, the band being otherwise full.

> Mr. Fleming never did play in the Pump or Ball Rooms in Bath with Mr. Tewkesbury.

[Mr. Eve, the Hautboy, was on his death-bed at that time and Herschel was not in the band.][77]

Herschel & Linley

THE offer of the post of organist and choirmaster at the Octagon Chapel brought William Herschel to Bath. He left behind a busy musical life in Yorkshire as performer, composer and teacher. Herschel wrote that his father, an *hautboy* player in the Hanoverian Foot-Guards, 'taught me to play on the violin as soon as I was able to hold a small one made on purpose for me'.[78] Construction of the chapel's Swiss Snetzler organ not yet complete, Herschel prepared the chapel choir to perform the *Messiah* for its inauguration the following year. A newcomer to Bath, he advertised himself as a teacher of 'Guitar as well as the Harpsichord, singing and the Violin'. His versatility on a variety of instruments was demonstrated at his first benefit concert on New Year's Day 1767 at the lower Assembly Rooms where 'I had but little Company but it was select'.[79] Word had reached Samuel Derrick, who invited Herschel to join the 'established Band of Musicians that played at the Public Subscription Concerts, the Pump Room, the Balls, the Play-House etc'.[80] Herschel's initial caution gave way

> when I found that Linley the first musician in the place was one
> of this band and that like him I might be allowed to send a deputy
> when not convenient to attend personally[81]

As a deputy Herschel was not included in the March 1767 list of regular band members 'perhaps out of delicacy while Samuel Eve, the previous oboist was still alive – he died three months later'[82].

The campaign to remove Francis Fleming had failed. Music in Bath, according to Fleming, was now in 'a state of anarchy rather than a monarch or aristocracy . . . '. [83] However, within eight months Derrick 're-established his control over all Bath's diversions, including the concerts'.[84] Demanding the musicians' full availability, the MC's exercise of authority was reported in the newspaper shortly after.

> Derrick, between the two Acts of the Concert last Night, addressed
> himself to the band of Music and ordered them, at their Peril, not

to refuse to attend any musical Gentlemen who might wish to employ them on such Nights as were not engrossed by the Public.

This provoked a sonnet in the *Bath Chronicle* on 19th November 1767

> Derrick whose arbitrary nod decides
> beyond appeal what's right, and fit,
> Whose hand directs the motion of the cat-gut band
> Where their own Fleming comus son presides . . .

Bath was heralded a city of culture in 1768 when the theatre on Orchard Street was granted a royal patent – the first outside London. Over the next decade, from a pool of twenty-six musicians named in the theatre logbook, including 'outstanding players in Brooks, Ashley, Cantelo, and Alexander Herschel',[85] ten were from the Pump Room Band. Bath's social pulse was gravitating north away from the two Lower Assembly Rooms to the growing upper town, determined by the development of the fashionable Circus and the Royal Crescent. A site for John Wood the Younger's Upper Assembly Rooms was chosen nearby and the foundation stone was laid on 24 May, 1769 when 'a band of music attended and great ceremony was observed'.[86]

Samuel Derrick's will vindicated the gossip surrounding the cause of his death earlier in the year, leaving his 'essence of cantharides, [aphrodisiacs] which has hitherto proved so effectual to me, but now my destruction . . . '. His obituary in the *Gentleman's Magazine* rather unkindly described him

> of diminutive size, with reddish hair and a vacant countenance;
> and he required no small amount of perfume to predominate
> over some odours that were not of the most fragrant kind.

The Riot Act was read three times by the deputy Town Clerk at a violent disturbance created by opposing factions in the fight for Derrick's successor. A youthful Richard Brinsley Sheridan in his comic poem *The Ridotto of Bath* alludes to the fray, largely feminine . . .

> Off fly their tuckers, caps and têtes;
> Pins and pomatums strew the room

Finally . . .

In heaps confus'd the Heroines lie,
With horrid shrieks they piece the sky . . .

Besieged with poems and presentations in the intense political campaign for the throne of 'the King of Bath', the visiting company and resident gentry voted for William Wade, (nephew to General Wade, distinguished Member of Parliament for Bath). The role was eventually split between the new Upper Assembly Rooms and the one remaining Lower Rooms but political wrangling and jealous competition characterised the appointments for many decades to come.

At that time Herschel's arrival posed a potential threat to Linley who featured so prominently on Bath's musical landscape. His favouring by Derrick would have likely irked Linley and repercussions followed. Herschel and Linley's joint direction of the *Messiah* at the Octagon Chapel[87] the following year was a precedent not repeated. Popular benefit concerts continued to be monopolised by Linley and his young family members, especially his talented daughter Elizabeth. Enriched by these performances in the city the Linleys lived for some years in the Royal Crescent. 'The earnings of Elizabeth alone were sufficient to have supported the whole household in affluence.'[88] Owning property on Milsom Street and a one third share in Margaret's Chapel in Bath, Thomas Linley could afford to send twelve year old Tom to study with Pietro Nardini in Florence. This is where a warm friendship developed in 1770 between 'The Tommasino' and his exact contemporary – Mozart.

By the age of sixteen Elizabeth Linley was 'a well known and greatly admired public singer and also one of the acknowledged beauties, if not the beauty of Bath'.[89] One of many obsessive admirers was Walter Long, said to be worth over ten thousand pounds a year and over thirty years her senior. Her parents sanctioned their engagement, but such was Elizabeth's distress that Long graciously withdrew from the contract, gifting Elizabeth with a handsome payment and family jewels.[90] Samuel Foote parodied the events in a play *The Maid of Bath* published in 1771. Meanwhile Smollett's Jeremy Melford satirised the Pump Room clients in his final novel *Humphry Clinker* published the same year, Smollett satirises the Pump Room's clients through his character Jeremy Melford

> Yesterday morning at the pump room, I saw a broken-winded Wapping landlady squeeze through a circle of peers to salute her brandy-merchant, who stood by the window, propped on crutches; and a paralytic attorney of Shoe Lane, in shuffling up to the bar, kicked the shins of the Chancellor of England, while his lordship in a cut bob drank a glass of water at the pump.

Joining these auspicious publications was Francis Fleming's *The Life and Extraordinary Adventures, the Perils and Critical Escapes of Timothy Ginnadrake (That Child of Chequer'd Fortune)*. The three gold-leafed, leather-bound volumes were printed in Pall Mall, London as well as in Bath. No bigger than a violinist's hand, they are semi autobiographical. Humorous escapades of Fleming's youth, with their frequent episodes of over indulgence, are darkened by the Machiavellian events of the final volume. Of the books' two hundred or so subscribers, one was William Herschel. Another was a Mr. Linley, perhaps insuring against any discomfiting revelations. Other subscribers, many of whom did not live to see the final volume, were Ralph Allen, the John Wood Esquires, Thomas Chilcot, John Grant (from the Pump Room Band), Thomas Orpin, the entire Bowdler family and Captain Wade, Master of Ceremonies. Offering us a glimpse of the younger Fleming's cosmopolitanism and extravagant tastes, a Mr. Vandeneloofter, a Brussels banker, was also on the list.

Through the words of 'our hero' Tim, Fleming charges with hypocrisy those easily impressed by an 'Italianised' name. Frustrated with poor audiences at previous benefit concerts, Fleming creates a stage name, 'Signor Turko Francisco Fleminiani', drawing such a large audience that people 'who were dying the week before, were brought in litters to hear this famous Italiano'.

Presided over by William Wade, the new Master of Ceremonies, the grand opening of the new, Upper Assembly Rooms in 1771 was a lavish affair celebrated with a ridotto. Thomas Linley was appointed Director of Concerts at the New Rooms; his domination of Bath's musical life was now incontestable. The old Lower (Gyde) Rooms' solvency was now under threat and Morning Music in the Pump Room ceased due to a dispute over contributions from both Assembly Rooms. 'Deprived of a great part of their former income',[91] Thomas Shaw and the other Pump Room musicians, whose allegiance had been to the old rooms, were offered a benefit concert as compensation. Shaw and Benjamin Milgrove, friends of Herschel and strong supporters of Fleming, 'repeatedly refused to play under the direction but that of the Master of Ceremonies',[92] implying their refusal to play under Linley's baton. Other Pump Room Band players, John Brooks and the recently married John Grant, could ill afford such scruples, while unsurprisingly Francis Fleming was absent from the New Assembly Room band.

Pump Room Band places were highly valued, but for the band to survive in this competitive climate, subsidies from both Rooms were essential. On October 5th 1771 the New Rooms committee resolved that the five Musicians of the band engaged for the Balls that formerly played at the Pump Room be paid, one Guinea each per Week, for playing at the Pump Room, to commence on Monday next and to continue as long as the old Rooms supply the same number of Hands or til such time as the Committee shall see Reason to alter it.[93]

Balls took place on Monday and Thursday evenings at the New Assembly Rooms with concerts on Wednesday evenings requiring additional players. Competing for the same audience, the Lower Rooms also needed to engage musicians for its concerts. This almost forced the Orchard Theatre in turn to abandon its mid week concerts. Musicians had to pick their way through restrictive practices designed by the various management committees. New Rooms band members were told not to 'play at any other Publick concert in Bath, without the consent of the Proprietors' and were contracted to play 'as often as we shall be called upon on the Wednesday in the next ensuing Season'. Such an imposition proved unworkable, but it was three years before a compromise was reached which released players to perform at other venues.

Linley's orchestra at the New Rooms included Herschel in a deputising role on occasional Wednesday evenings. Was it an affront to Herschel's dignity to play in an orchestra led by a fifteen-year-old – Thomas Linley the Younger? If so, the regular engagement of Herschel's younger 'cellist brother Alexander, with whom he lived, may have offered him some consolation. A well-publicised quarrel, fuelled by Linley's failure on two successive nights to provide Herschel with a music stand, set 1772 in motion. Herschel 'on Account of that Deficiency . . . [placed his] Books upon the Ground' and walked out. A notice in the *Bath Chronicle* blamed Linley for this 'ungenteel treatment'.[94] The accused dryly retorted that being without a music stand 'must violently agitate the tender Sensibility of his Frame' obliging Herschel 'with great reluctance' to respond further. The music stand incident actually diverted attention away from a more serious issue. Had Linley broken a gentleman's agreement and deliberately fixed Elizabeth's concerts to clash with Herschel's more recent rival series at the Lower (Old) Rooms? In 'The Celebrated Quarrel between Thomas Linley (the Elder) and William Herschel: an episode in the musical life of 18th Century Bath' [unpublished], Ian Woodfield is inclined to blame Linley for not allowing Elizabeth to sing at Herschel's concerts, earning Linley the label the 'Monopoliser of Benefits'. The *Bath Chronicle* printed the following

> . . . it is but evident to every Connoisseur in Music, or impartial person that Linley's views are entirely selfish and envious. Herschel hopes the Public will not throw any Odium on him if for the Future he renounces all Connections with a Character so totally opposite to his own.

Linley retorted by describing Herschel's disposition as 'mean and contemptible', his attacks, the 'Malice of a Slanderer' and how 'very sincerely he despised him'. Herschel accused Linley of having a 'Bitterness of Temper which is the general Attendant on low Cunning and dark Envy, when they are drawn out of their lurking Place and exposed to Public View'.[95] The *Bath Chronicle*'s exposure of this spat only served to swell audiences. It then appealed to the nobility not to give their tickets 'to improper persons whose dress and situations in life did not entitle them to associate with people of distinction'. During the controversy a certain Mr Brimble took the liberty of proposing that, for a one and a half guinea fee, he and his men would 'put up and take away the Platform and Orchestra for the Balls, and Concerts'.[96]

While ensnared in this high profile conflict, William was diverted by arrangements he was making for his sister Caroline to join him and Alexander in Bath. Rescued from a life of drudgery under her mother in Hanover, Caroline came to Bath to keep house for her brothers. Her retrospective accounts recall the bleakness of her early life in Bath, with little knowledge of English and limited companionship.

> I never was allowed to form any acquaintance with any other but such as was agreeable to my eldest Brother.[97]

One such acquaintance was Francis Fleming's daughter Anne, 'Bath's most renowned dancing mistress'[98] who William engaged to prepare Caroline for society. She was tasked with drilling Caroline 'for a Gentlewoman'[99] twice weekly, with ten guineas made available for Caroline to buy suitable clothes.

Billed with solo singer Signora Farinelli from the Berlin Opera, Thomas Shaw the Younger was the leader and soloist at one of the rival concerts promoted by William Herschel in opposition to Linley's in 1772. In March that year Thomas Linley and his family were thrown into a distressing family crisis – the elopement of eighteen-year old Elizabeth and Richard Brinsley Sheridan.

The young writer first met Elizabeth when his father Thomas Sheridan, a freelance actor, playwright and elocutionist moved his family to Bath. The couple fled to France where Elizabeth could escape the unwanted attentions of the married Captain Thomas Mathews. Later, back in Bath and severely wounded in a duel with Mathews, Sheridan was cared for by Elizabeth and on his recovery they remarried on April 13th 1773. The affair inspired Sheridan's first play *The Rivals* whose heroine, the idealistic Lydia Languish, resembles the beautiful and gifted Elizabeth Linley with the dictatorial Sir Anthony Absolute modelled on his own father. Sheridan's draft for a later play was first called *The Slanderers, a Pump Room Scene*. Rivalry continued to contaminate Bath's musical life. In a letter to his father, Sheridan describes the combatant platform of two oratorio concert series promoted by his father-in-law and rival Herschel.

> Linley and his whole family, down to the seven year olds are to support one set at the new Rooms, and a band and singers from London another at the old.[100]

The campaign spread to Bristol with more rival concerts, dividing subscribers, backers and critics; all partisans in the conflict. Both factions in the next rival concert series in Bristol in 1773 were led by the sons of old adversaries, the two young Thomases. Thomas Shaw's (the Younger) playing was said to be endowed with 'Force and Command'[101] while the seventeen-year-old Tom Linley played with 'Spirit and Fire'.[102] But

> upon the whole, the one (Shaw) is certainly the most perfect Master of the Fingerboard, but the other has a Polish of Tone and Manner which renders him the most pleasing musician.[103]

Fate further divided the fortunes of both these young men. Over the next two years Tom Linley wrote twenty violin concertos. Many were performed during the oratorio season at Drury Lane and Tom went on to lead the Drury Lane Theatre orchestra when his father and brother-in-law took over its direction. But tragically, five years after the Bristol concert, this 'pleasing musician' was drowned in a boating accident. (Linley's life was marred by the early deaths of many of his other children but this incident devastated the whole family.)

Thomas Shaw married a 'Miss Smith of Bath' whom he took to London where, seven years after the death of his young Bath rival, he too would become leader of the Drury Lane Theatre orchestra, under the man his father had so resolutely opposed, the indomitable Thomas Linley.

By 1774 Herschel was relieved of the demands of promoting and performing in public concerts by a lucrative private teaching practice, as well as concert engagements in the homes of the nobility. Rival concert series ceased, as did competition between the New Rooms and Lower Rooms. An agreement to share the band under Linley and arrange the oratorios on an alternating programme was reached. The years of rivalry were largely over but Linley's dominance was not. Even Linley's most stalwart mutineers had little option but to agree to play in the band at the New Rooms, their resolve weakened by work shortages. Its powerful management committee even curbed how William Wade ran assemblies in both Rooms,[104] creating further tension among subscribers. Complaints were aired in the *Bath Chronicle* that Thomas Shaw the Elder and Benjamin Milgrove had been 'smuggled into the band of music, at no less expense than thirty guineas an annum',[105] both playing the violin. Achieved with the help of Wade, to the irritation of Thomas Linley, implicit in the criticism was that two younger players had been displaced in favour of these Bath veterans.

When Thomas Linley resigned his position as Director of Concerts in the New Assembly Rooms in 1776 in order to devote more time to his London commitments, William Herschel was the obvious replacement. Violinist James Brooks, son of Pump Room 'cellist John Brooks (who had replaced the departed Richards a decade earlier), was appointed leader under Herschel's direction. Both father and son had played under Linley in earlier Assembly Room concerts. James, 'possibly only sixteen, had succeeded Linley's son as Bath's leading violinist . . . '[106] But whether due to the absence of Linley's brilliant children, the introduction of too innovative a programme, inadequate publicity or Herschel being diverted by astronomical pursuits, the concerts that year at the New Rooms were not popular.

With the city's musical life in crisis, the New Rooms management committee appealed to Linley to return. Not even the popular performances of guest singer and composer Venanzio Rauzzini during the autumn concerts could abate the financial losses. (Rauzzini's castrato voice had inspired the young Mozart to write for him the motet, *Exultate Jubilate*, and the opera *Lucio Silla*). Linley reinstated his son Thomas to the leader position at the New Rooms concerts. However, old rivalries re-emerged when Flemish composer and violinist Franz Lamotte was engaged by the managers of the Lower Rooms to co-direct its concerts with Rauzzini. Thomas Linley interpreted this action by the Lower Rooms as a conspiracy 'deliberately opposing' concerts at the Upper Rooms. This latest crisis in Bath was weathered, and perennial divisions were ultimately resolved. In 1771 the last paupers' concert Linley directed in Bath united all of the main musical protagonists.

Linley, his family, Rauzzini were the principal performers, supported by Linley's band . . . Messrs. Herschel . . . the Pump Room Band . . . part of the theatre orchestra and many other performers.[107]

Lamotte's death was reported at the Hague in 1780 and Thomas Linley had finally left Bath for London. Bitterness over Linley's ambitious practices in Bath had undeniably existed, but as a result of his influence

the most renowned musicians of the age were attracted to the city, and the reputation of Bath's musical life was raised from a position of mere local acclaim to one of national interest and importance.[108]

In the wake of Linley and Lamotte, Herschel regained full control of concerts in Bath and Bristol. However, his increasing commitment to astronomy led to a catastrophic *Messiah* in 1782. Caroline later wrote 'William used to go to bed with a bason [basin] of milk or tea and Smiths Harmonies, Optics, Ferguson's Astronomy . . .'

Caroline had hoped for more musical tuition from her brother, but as William devoted even more attention to building telescopes and observing the night sky, his reliance on her as an assistant became unequivocal. One of Caroline's most promising vocal performances led to an offer as a soloist in Birmingham, which she declined due to her dedication to her brother. Herschel's concerts showcased the talents of his pupils – children of his wealthier patrons, some of whom, according to him, preferred 'astronomical instead of music lessons'. Income derived from this teaching helped fund his astronomical expenses.

Although Linley's musical career in the theatre flourished in London, his great fortune was eroded in later life, partially attributable to funds owed to him by the Drury Lane Theatre which he part owned with his son-in-law Richard Brinsley Sheridan. Thomas Linley was broken by a further loss, that of his beloved daughter Elizabeth to tuberculosis when only thirty-eight. Both are buried at Wells Cathedral.

Herschel composed six sonatas for harpsichord, violin and violoncello, seven violin concertos, three oboe concertos, one viola concerto, five symphonies, eleven organ sonatas, thirty-two organ voluntaries, and many vocal works as well as church music for the Octagon Chapel. In 1781, with a powerful telescope he built himself, Herschel discovered Uranus from his abode at 19 New King Street (now the Herschel Museum of Astronomy). '. . . Herschel's fame was spreading fast and within a few months it had come to the notice of George

Thomas Ryder's engraving of William Herschel (courtesy of the Herschel Museum of Astronomy)

III', (wrote astronomer Patrick Moore two hundred years later). Herschel initially named the planet, previously classified a star, *Georgium Sidus,* in honour of the King. Royal patronage followed, but not without conditions. Herschel's increased work load and enhanced prospects more than likely account for his gradual neglect of the Assembly Room concerts, and the fact that a *Messiah* he directed in Bristol was one of the worst ever reported in the West Country. Moore informs us the money would have been 'sufficient to enable him to abandon music as a profession and devote himself wholly to astronomy'.

Of Alexander Herschel, Caroline described his 'cello solos as 'divine'. A diary entry of Italian astronomer Barnaba Oriani[109] refers to Alexander building 'telescopes for sale when not engaged as a musician in Bath', while Caroline's own astronomical work led to the discovery of her first comet in 1786. Alexander was a principal 'cellist in Bath and Bristol for forty-seven years before returning to live out his days in Hanover.

William Herschel and Thomas Linley were distinguished harpsichordists, organists, composers and highly esteemed vocal and instrumental teachers. The latter's singing instruction was described by tenor Michael Kelly as 'masterly'. It was to Herschel that Linley sent his son Ozias for mathematics and violin lessons, his regard for Herschel's tuition eclipsing the bitterness of earlier disputes. From as early as 1760 Linley played the harpsichord or the violin in the Pump Room Band, with Herschel joining in 1767.

'Survival of the Fittest'

A MUSIC festival concert at the Chippenham Assembly Rooms in September 1773 advertised a 'large band of the most capital players from Bath' including harpsichordist Thomas Orpin, Thomas Shaw the Elder on double bass, Benjamin Milgrove playing second violin, horn and clarinet and 'cellist Alexander Herschel, all under the direction of the latter's brother William. Milgrove was now successfully selling toys and fancy goods from his Bond Street premises – the musical instruments, musical accessories and sheet music side of his business now less prolific. Author of *Forty Easy Lessons for One or Two Guitars,* he had also acquired sole selling rights to MC William Wade's publication *The Dancer's Guide.* Proficient on the guitar and keyboard, it was his compositions which earned Milgrove his musical reputation in the city. These included his pastoral opera *Echo and Narcissus* (in which Rauzzini was principal vocalist), harpsichord sonatas and church hymns.

Morning music in the Pump Room could engage band members for up to thirty-two weeks of the year. However, a dependency on concerts, if cancelled, could prove financially ruinous. The welfare of band members was unlikely to be high on the directors' agenda, whether at the Rooms or the Theatre. Success of concerts was often determined by the whims of the subscribers, who superficially ricocheted between one luminary and another, whether it be the director, soloist or leader. Scurrilous and manipulative marketing tactics were deployed by backers of concerts, to the frustration of the musicians who were powerless over whether the event was ever going to happen. This unstable situation was not confined to the city of Bath – 'particularly in Bristol the musicians seem to have been little more than pawns manoeuvred about by competing cliques of gentlemen'.[110]

The occasional benefit concert was another source of potential revenue, but competition for an audience was intense. Elderly and less dynamic musicians, with perhaps little flare for self-promotion and publicity, were at risk of being outshone by newly arrived, younger and often higher profile musicians from abroad. Ian Woodfield summarises the plight of the Bath musician, whose 'success and failure on a provincial concert platform might well mean the difference between moderate affluence and real poverty'.[111]

One of Fleming's former colleagues was the veteran keyboard musician Robert Peck. (His son, also Robert, was possibly tutored by William Herschel.) Rival musicians collaborated in a benefit concert for him, a 'member of the Pump Room Band for almost forty years then ninety-six years old . . .'[112]. Peck had also played at the theatre with both John and James Brooks and with Thomas Shaw the Younger. Annual concerts were staged on behalf of Robert Peck the Elder until his death at the age of one hundred. With the proverbial luck of the Irish, Fleming had survived the 'slings and arrows' and retained the 'first violin' position in the Pump Room Band until he died in 1778.

Grand balls in the new Guildhall banqueting room were funded by the Corporation, and at the Pump Room, in deference to the more fastidious visitors, separate compartments for Ladies and Gentlemen were installed. Meanwhile world events were leaving their mark, and the Pump Room Band's survival was in jeopardy. . The *Bath Chronicle* of 2nd December 1779, reported that with the American Revolutionary War depleting the nations funds, London opera singers were starving.

The Pump Room Band's new leader, violinist James Brooks could not have married his sweetheart Anne Whale at a more precarious time. His father, Pump Room Band 'cellist John Brooks, was facing increasing financial difficulties and unable to support his large family. The company's reluctance to 'acknowledge excellence in one of their own countrymen . . . caused John Brooks to sell all he owned and leave his home in October 1782'.[113]

One of Brooks's colleagues was the highly respected Pump Room Band violinist John Grant, who supplemented his earnings by running a lodging house where many outstanding visiting musicians stayed. Grant played at the Theatre and at the New Rooms. He was also one of a quartet of violinists performing in the *Messiah,* under the direction of Herschel, for the launch of the new organ at St James's Church in 1782. In the audience was composer and violinist John Marsh from Salisbury. Marsh's overtures were played by the Pump Room Band who lent him copies of Haydn's symphonies during his visit. Another musician in the quartet was William Rogers the Younger, a second violinist in the Pump Room Band and grandson of the toy and jewellery shop owner.

In 1783 James Brooks was forced to sell the 'entire contents of his home in River Street'[114] which he re-let, but was powerless to abate his father's bankruptcy. He had been leader of the Pump Room Band 'probably since Fleming's death five years earlier'.[115] Although James Brooks's compositions and virtuosity on the violin were acclaimed, he swayed between one financial crisis and another. This contrasted with the band's second violinist, William Rogers the Younger, whose family legacy promised a more secure future for him when he married Miss Webb in Bristol that year.

Brooks's annual income from playing in the Pump Room Band would not have exceeded forty guineas. For this he would perform every morning over twenty weeks and each Wednesday night in a concert at the New Assembly Rooms during the season. The 1783/84 season ended prematurely due to a 'dispute between the man who presently holds the pump and the musicians, so they will not play any longer'. Lack of music at the Pump Room, 'the most pleasing of entertainment for a refined mind',[116] was lamented in a letter to the *Chronicle*.

By March the following year the *Chronicle* reported a lack of support for music in the Pump Room and poor encouragement of young musicians. It partly blamed the system which allowed the old, Lower Rooms to contribute only half that of the New Rooms. In April 1784 the MC opened subscriptions 'for music continuing at the Pump Room during the season'.[117] In May the band played a breakfast concert 'gratis' in the Spring Gardens.

The Fleming legacy was carried on through Francis's daughter Anne whose dancing skill he had so nurtured that she would 'attain that ease and proficiency in the French style for which Bath would henceforth admire her'.[118] Exhorting her pupils to 'do credit to Bath',[119] she showcased their talent with her sister Kitty in the glittering balls held at the latter end of the century. The *Bristol Gazette* paid tribute to her as 'a complete proficient in this elegant accomplishment . . . whose exemplary virtues in society' were matched by her 'shrewd and vigorous intellect'. After her death, at the age of 76, Anne's obituary honoured her father Francis as

> one of the most excellent musicians in his day [who] led the Pump Room Band during the memorable supremacy of Beau Nash and was a conductor of the earliest Bath Subscription concerts [and] as a wit and humourist . . . was equally distinguished.[120]

In the Shadow of Rauzzini

S UCCEEDING William Herschel as Director of Concerts at the Assembly
Rooms in 1781, Rauzzini settled permanently in Bath. His abode in
Gay Street, overlooking Queen Square, was his main residence. But
it was at his 'country home', Perrymead Villa in Widcombe, where he
entertained friends and well known musicians, holding musical fêtes
and soirées in summer. His earlier pupils had included Nancy Storace,
(the famous opera singer and sister to Stephen Storace – the popular
comic operetta composer); tenors John Braham and Michael Kelly; and
also Jane Mary Guest (later Mrs Miles) – arguably the most accomplished
keyboard player of the time.

Bath's prosperity in the 1780s was signalled by a massive building
boom and an unprecedented volume of annual visitors. All three hot
baths – the King's, Queen's and
Cross Baths, had been improved
around that time by a confident
Bath Corporation. At the back
of the Pump Room, along with
the newspapers, lay the 'Book
of Intelligence' in which new
arrivals inscribed their names,
gossip and news.

Meanwhile   Rauzzini's
musical   events   progressed
and his Christmas fundraising
concert of 1784 featured works
by composer Stephen Storace
who had visited Bath a couple
of   years   earlier.   (Storace's
Piano trio in G is occasionally
performed   by   today's   Pump
Room Trio).

Tragedy   befell   James
Brooks when his new young wife

Joseph Hutchinson, *Signor Venanzio Rauzzini*
(courtesy of the Victoria Art Gallery, Bath &
North East Somerset Council)

died only fifteen months after their marriage. His father John Brooks, with veteran Pump Room Band colleague Thomas Shaw the Elder, were the co-beneficiaries of a concert of Handel's Sacred Music at the New Rooms in 1786. The occasion was

> particularly poignant as both of whom were nearing the end of their lives, [and] had given many years of service to Bath's concerts and the theatre.[121]

John Brooks died a year later, a loss the *Chronicle* acknowledged would be 'universally regretted'.

Benjamin Milgrove's Villa Gardens summer concert that year, in which his composition *Acasto and Thyrsis* was to be performed in honour of the Prince of Wales' visit to Bath, unfortunately clashed with one to be held in the Spring Gardens. His rival wrote to the *Chronicle* claiming three of his musicians were equal to 'three and twenty [of Milgrove's] though not selected by Milgrove'.[122]

Violinist John Loder was 'a respectable member of the Pump Room Band' and played 'tenor' (viola) in chamber groups with James Brooks and William Rogers the Younger (both fellow Band members). One of a Bath musical dynasty with links to the Cantelo family, John Loder's older brother Andrew was versatile on the horn, clarinet and 'cello. He was a member of the Theatre Royal band, a singer and composer of church music and later would go on to organise concerts at the New Assembly Rooms.

Rauzzini was still at the helm of the main concert series in Bath, but its financial solvency was an ever-present challenge. In the 1780s Richter's and Stamitz's visits impacted on the local musicians' earning potential. However, James Brooks' 'Academy Concerts' at the Bear Inn (modelled on those organised by Thomas Orpin years earlier), stood up to the glamour and higher profile of such musicians.

The young Anne Cantelo had been articled to J C Bach, but upon his death returned to her native Bath. Madam Mara's unexpected appearance in Bath forced Anne to give up her first benefit performance scheduled for December 1787. It was to mark the completion of her apprenticeship. But with Rauzzini's help, Anne, a great friend of Jane (Guest) Miles, eventually became a successful oratorio singer.[123] The company's partiality for foreign performers exacerbated Bath musicians' anger and frustration.[124] Such provincial issues would unlikely have concerned the sixty-six year old Thomas Orpin, who was now in London and about to marry a Miss Alderwick. (Ten years later the widow of this eminent Bath harpsichordist, organist and inventor of the 'celestina', married a cheesemonger). Rauzzini's financial problems continued. Engaging the 'Bath Band'[125] in 1788 at twelve guineas was the major expense in a large production of the *Messiah* during Passion Week. Attended by only two hundred people, the profit was a disappointing eleven shillings.

Visiting that year from Birmingham, nine year old Mary Ann Galton's first impression of Bath and the Pump Room was blissfully unaffected by such matters.

> Bath was a new world to me . . . The Pump Room, with its statue of Beau Nash, the waters sending up their columns of steam, the band of music . . . and the vast ever-shifting throng of gaily dressed company, was to me a scene of constant enchantment. The beautiful green-house plants or artificial flowers at all the doors of approach to the Pump Room, and the silver balls to attract the flies, completely dazzled my view.
>
> [The ladies] wore huge balloon bonnets with magnificent ostrich feathers . . . ample muffs and long tippets, and fur linings, of the silken Agora goats' hair . . . The music, too, I felt most heart-stirring . . . [126]

This clever child would eventually, under her married name of Mary Ann Schimmelpenninck, become an influential theologian and abolitionist.

Two years later John Williams's satirical *Observations in the Pump Room* was published. Writing under a pseudonym he notes that the band comprised 'about twenty musicianers.'[127]

Haydn's Visit to Bath

IN London's musical circles, talk centred on a legendary composer recently arrived from Austria. When first in the capital, Haydn wrote of feeling 'a victim' under the burden of so much attention. Although an invitation to dine at the London home of Thomas Shaw the Younger, who had left Bath six years earlier, was accepted

On 14th Sept. [1791] I dined for the first time at Shaw's. He received me downstairs at the door, and then led me to his wife, who was surrounded by her 2 daughters and other ladies. As I was bowing round the circle, all at once I became aware of the fact that not only the lady of the house but also her daughters and the other women each wore on their headdress *a part* over the front a most charming curved pearl-coloured band of 3 fingers' breadth, with the name Haydn embroidered therein in gold; and Shaw wore this name on his coat, worked into the very ends of both his collars in the finest steel beads. The coat was made of the finest cloth, and with elegant steel buttons. The Mistress is the most beautiful woman I ever saw.

N.B. Her husband wanted a souvenir from me, and I gave him a tobacco-box which I had just bought brand new for a guinea; he gave me his instead. Several days later I visited him, and saw that he had had a silver case put over my box, on the cover of which was very elegantly engraved Apollo's harp and the following words: *Ex dono celeberrimi Josephi Haydn.* N.B. The Mistress gave me a stick-pin as a souvenir.[128]

Haydn's music had been popular in Bath, and it is likely that his *Symphony No 53 in D major* was played in the Pump Room.[129] One would hope that Thomas Shaw wasted no time in relaying details of this exciting visit to his father in Bath, whose death only four months later was reported in the *Chronicle.*

Died in a very advanced age, Mr. Shaw, a superannuated musician of the Ball and Pump-room band; many years keeper of a lodging-house [one tenant being the oboist Fischer] in Duke Street; and father of Mr. T Shaw, Leader of Drury-lane Orchestra. [130]

In his *London Notebooks*,[131] Haydn enthused over his visit to William Herschel's residence 'where I saw the great telescope'.[132] Haydn details Herschel's fortunes in Slough where his landlady

> fell in love with him, married him, and gave him a [large] dowry . . . Besides this he has a yearly pension for life of £500 from the King, and his wife, at the age of 45, presented him with a son this year, 1792.[133]

Chaos, indulgence and eccentricity characterise John Nixon's satirical painting 'Interior of the Pump Room', completed in 1792, in which patrons jostle around the huge pump under Nash's watchful stone eye.

The dilemma of low attendance at local musicians' concerts was well chronicled in the press, echoing events of forty years earlier when Francis Fleming assumed an Italian name to attract a sizeable audience. That said, the entire Bath Band helped the Bath City Infirmary and Dispensary raise fifteen hundred pounds in 1793. Supplemented with musicians from Oxford, London and Bristol, neither Rauzzini nor foreign soloists were involved. Vocalist Sarah Second, having relocated to Bath but initially overlooked by Rauzzini, relied on the Pump Room Band when forming a complete orchestra for her concert that year.

The impact of the French Revolutionary Wars triggered a national financial crisis. Two Bath banks collapsed, bankrupting several local property developers and leaving new terraces unfinished for years. Rauzzini's generous hospitality continued regardless. In the summer of 1794 he entertained Irish flautist Andrew Ashe, the young Venetian violinist Giovanni Battista Cimador and the great Haydn himself. Haydn wrote

> On 2nd August 1794, I left at 5 o'clock in the morning for Bath, with Ashe and Cimador, and arrived there at 8 o'clock in the evening. It's 107 miles from London. The Mail Coach does this distance in 12 hours. I lived at the house of Herr Rauzzini, a Musicus who is very famous, and who in his time was one of the greatest singers. He has lived there 19 years, supports himself by the Subscription Concerts which are given in the Winter, and by giving lessons. He is a very nice and hospitable man. His summer

house, where I stayed, is situated on a rise in the middle of a most beautiful neighbourhood, from which you can see the whole city. Bath is one of the most beautiful cities in Europe.[134]

'Oh had I Jubals lyre', wrote one admirer to the *Bath Herald*, inspired by Haydn's presence in the city, 'I would sweep the strings, till Echo tired with repeating, – Haydn treads upon the Bathonian ground! And had this place – previous to his arrival – been the seat of discord, it must now be lull'd into Peace by the God Harmony . . . '

Haydn noted on this visit that 'the city is now building a most splendid room for guests taking the cure'.

Music in the New Grand Pump Room

ROMAN and Celtic remains of the temple of Sulis Minerva were discovered during excavations prior to the building of this 'most splendid room', the new Grand Pump Room. It was initially designed by the city architect Thomas Baldwin but completed by John Palmer after Baldwin resigned due to bankruptcy. 'Some augmentation to the Musicians at the Pump Room . . .' was suggested and where previously they had been 'plac'd in an obscure nook . . . [the musicians] were to play in a spacious lofty recess with a coved ceiling'.[135] A central curve in the balustrade was designed to accommodate a conductor. The Corporation agreed to a subsidy of three guineas a week over sixteen weeks to support the struggling band.[136] Against a backdrop of financial gloom the new Grand Pump Room was opened soon after Christmas in 1795.

One musician deprived of the use of this new facility was John Loder. His death in Weymouth that year at the age of thirty-eight prompted his Pump Room Band colleagues to organise a benefit concert for his widow and seven young children. Poignantly, the eight-year old John David Loder (possibly a pupil of James Brooks) played a violin concerto, sharing a platform with pianist Mrs Miles and his uncle, David Richards, an esteemed violinist. (This was not the same David Richards who played in the Pump Room Band during the Fleming years). Loder's widow Bathsheba despaired that 'the utmost fruits of his profession were barely sufficient to provide his numerous family (members) with decent subsistence'.[137] Prospects were also looking bleak for the late John Loder's colleagues in the Pump Room, Diminishing contributions from the Old Rooms reduced the band's season in the Pump Room to just twelve weeks. Twenty years earlier Morning Music had been played over thirty-two weeks of the year.

Aiming to offset losses from concerts in the city, a special committee from within the company was set up to relieve Rauzzini of the administrative aspect of his duties. Despite an announcement in early 1796 that any surplus funds from subscriptions would be used 'for the benefit of the disabled and decayed musicians, widows and orphans of the established band at the Rooms and the Pump Room',[138] the interests of the Upper Rooms still took precedence. Any such 'surplus' was 'totally inadequate . . . to support such of the Musicians as might, by age or infirmity become incapable of following their profession'. A plea to Bath's 'trading inhabitants' to support the band's annual benefit concert that year 'for the continuance of the Musick at the Pump Room'[139] failed.

Aged sixty-six years old, string and brass player William Rogers the Elder died. He had been in the Pump Room Band for over thirty years. Three years later his son also died not long after moving to London. As a violinist in Bath's chamber ensembles and second violinist in the band, William Rogers the Younger had emulated his father. So beautiful was the tone of the violin he left behind, the *Bath Chronicle* wrote that it was 'scarcely to be equalled and not to be excelled'.[140] Records from the sale of the contents of Rogers' home reflected a legacy in the family jewellery business.

Private rival subscription concerts so rigorously controlled by Beau Nash now posed a threat to Rauzzini's programme. One such series was promoted by David Richards, now known by many in Bath as the maternal uncle and teacher of the young prodigy John David Loder. Richards had relinquished his role as Director of the highly esteemed Norwich Theatre orchestra in 1795[141] to support his widowed sister and her family. James Brooks's wavering position was now in real jeopardy. In a descending spiral of financial decline, his unsuccessful benefit concerts were compounded by the familiar burden of a large family to support.

It was doubtful Brooks gained any consolation from his role in the Pump Room. Some considered the music was in need of 'improvement',[142] which forced the Corporation to announce publicly its commitment to the band. Despite a well-attended annual benefit concert for the band, directed by Rauzzini in March 1797, funds were apparently so depleted that the *Herald* announced that 'the music at the Pump Room would be discontinued for the season'.[143] This was not the outcome envisaged for the new Grand Pump Room.

Two months later, the more desperate plight of the family of Robert Deacon, 'musick porter' in Bath for thirty years, who had died from a fall down the Guildhall stairs, called for the band to perform without pay under Rauzzini's direction. Hard times for many, but perhaps not so for the entrepreneurial Benjamin Milgrove, busy promoting his new invention, the 'comma', an aid to tuning the horn while maintaining the tone.

Tavernor Wilkey, the oldest member of the Pump Room Band, died in 1798. He had played in Linley's orchestra with John Brooks,

William Rogers and Alexander Herschel at the famous opening of the Assembly Rooms in 1771, and at the theatre as well as in the Pump Room. To supplement his meagre wages as a musician he had run the Beef Steak House in the market.

When Jane Austen came to Bath

MUSIC was probably absent at Jane Austen's first visit to the new Grand Pump Room in 1797. Her companion then was her Uncle James Leigh-Perrot 'who drank the hot spring water here to relieve his gout'.[144] Also attending the Pump Room for the same complaint is Austen's fictional character Mr. Allen, guardian to the young Catherine Morland in *Northanger Abbey*. Austen's early impressions of Bath are reflected in those of her heroine on her first visit to the city, 'Oh! Who can ever be tired of Bath?'

> Every morning now brought its regular duties – shops were to be visited; some new part of the town to be looked at; and the pump-room to be attended, where they paraded up and down for an hour, looking at everybody and speaking to no one.

It is in the Pump Room where Catherine endures private agonies.

> With more than usual eagerness did Catherine hasten to the pump-room the next day, secure within herself of seeing Mr. Tilney there before the morning were over, and ready to meet him with a smile; but no smile was demanded – Mr. Tilney did not appear. Every creature in Bath except himself, was to be seen in the room at different periods of the fashionable hours; crowds of people were every moment passing in and out, up the steps and down; people whom nobody cared about, and nobody wanted to see; and he only was absent . . .

Catherine resigns herself to the fact that as

> His name was not in the pump-room book, and curiosity could do no more. He must be gone from Bath.

But it was the Pump Room that Catherine

had already found so favourable for the discovery of female excellence, and the completion of female intimacy, so admirably adapted for secret discourses and unlimited confidence.

Jane Austen was intrigued by the functions and fashionable foibles of the Pump Room

> Mr. Allen, after drinking his glass of water, joined some gentlemen to talk over the politics of the day and compare the accounts of their newspapers; and the ladies walked about together, noticing every new face, and almost every new bonnet in the room.

Jane Austen's uncle Mr Leigh-Perrot was in the Pump Room taking the waters when his wife was being set up for shoplifting at Smith's Haberdasher's, in what was believed to be a blackmail attempt. Jane's aunt endured seven months of incarceration and crippling costs before eventually being acquitted.

The new Bath Harmonic Society founded by the popular leading composer and physician Dr Henry Harington achieved 'a zenith of polite acceptability'[145] when the future King George IV joined in 1799. However, Bath failed to make an impression on the Prince Regent who reportedly said that 'of all his dull sojourns, Bath was certainly the dullest'.[146] The seven hundred people that attended the first concert of the season, led by James Brooks, may have begged to differ. Rauzzini's concerts were described by the company 'as the most elegant entertainment which this city can boast..!'[147]

With Bath's most glorious period drawing to a close, the press reminds the city traders of its obligation to support the Pump Room Band as a new era dawns

> The Pump Room Band is one of the oldest and best establishments of this place; it draws visitor and inhabitant to one general place of morning rendezvous; there long-parted friends indulge in unexpected meetings, whilst the inspiring melody of the orchestra spreads a general glow of happiness around . . . Perhaps none are more interested in the Pump-Room Band, than the Tradesmen in the lower parts of the city; and as it undoubtedly draws the Company down to their shops, it particularly behoves them to give it every assistance and support by their subscriptions and recommendations.[148]

Pump Room leader and composer James Brooks 'remained

unrivalled as the city's foremost violinist'[149] for over two decades, but still had to fund the publication of his own violin concerto.[150] He ended the century performing in London . . . and serving as Governor of the Fund for Decayed Musicians.[151]

After Rauzzini

By 1800 Bath, with a population of thirty thousand, was 'among the dozen largest cities in England and the greatest health and holiday resort in Europe'. [152] When sea bathing became the new health and social trend, however, many of the well-off were drawn to Brighton, the favoured resort of the Prince Regent. 'What a rage this dipping is become . . .' wrote William, husband of the famous actress Sarah Siddons to a friend.[153] But Bath's inland position meant little risk of attack during the French Revolutionary Wars, persuading some families from south-east coastal towns to relocate. However, living conditions in Bath among the working population were poor. Severe food shortages and employment disputes induced riots; troops were needed to disperse three hundred 'hungry Timsbury colliers'.[154]

John Nixon's drawing in 1800 shows a notice board in the Pump Room advertising concerts and balls while, in a letter to a friend, William Siddons warned of laughing at the Room's patrons – 'don't laugh too soon. Who knows who is to be plac'd in the Pump Room'.[155] Outdoors, Sydney Gardens' recreational attractions included swings (not permitted on Sundays), bowling, a maze and occasional fireworks. There, people could eat and drink while listening to music. Excited by her family's impending move to nearby Sydney Place, Jane Austen wrote 'It would be pleasant to be near the Gardens. We could go into the Labyrinth everyday.'

Residing at this exclusive address between 1801 and 1804, then lodging at Gay Street, before moving to a much poorer abode on Trim Street in 1806, afforded Jane a close scrutiny of Bath's morals and mores. Her intolerance of Bath's social conventions is vented in her novel *Persuasion* through the sober Anne Elliot who 'disliked Bath' as 'it did not agree' with her. Opulent drawing rooms and the 'elegant stupidity of private parties' so admired by Anne's sister and father, are suggested in Rowlandson's aquatint 'The Private Concert'. The Austens' lodgings at 25 Gay Street was only a few doors away from the residence of Bath's Director of Music, Venanzio Rauzzini. Admired by the ladies, music historian Charles Burney's daughter Fanny described him as an angel. Rauzzini would have directed the New Assembly Room concert series to which the Austens subscribed.

In 1805 a new Theatre Royal on Beaufort Square replaced the one on Orchard Street. The same year, the Wiltshire Rooms were demolished as York Street was formed to improve access to the Lower Rooms.

Benjamin Milgrove was now mostly preoccupied with musical composition up until his death in 1808. His obituary described him as an 'eminent musician of this city'.[156] (Inheriting her father's business acumen, Milgrove's daughter opened a French school in Bath.) Two years later music in the city suffered a further monumental loss. While preparing for the Bath June Music Festival at his home in Gay Street, Venanzio Rauzzini died. The *Bath Herald* paid homage

> In private life few men were more esteemed; none more generally beloved. A polished suavity of manners, a mild and cheerful disposition, and a copious fund of general and polite information, rendered him an attractive and agreeable companion . . . in Rauzzini, this city has sustained a public loss.

Buried in Bath Abbey, where his pupils Nancy Storace and John Braham erected a memorial stone in his honour, he is immortalized in portraits by Joseph Hutchinson, one of which hangs in the Sun Lounge adjacent to the Pump Room today.

Virtuoso flautist Andrew Ashe was elected to fill Rauzzini's role as Director of the Bath Concerts and in the first few years 'managed to engage some star performers to add lustre to his programmes'.[157] Soprano Angelica Catalani, pianist Ferdinand Ries and the violinist Madame Gautherot were among them.

Trade and commerce in early nineteenth century Bath were relatively healthy, and in 1813, in anticipation of the coming season, the Water Committee arranged for the Pump Room to be redecorated. Two years later the orchestra was presented as 'a nursery for good musicians which encourages professors of superior merit to settle here'.[158]

In his study of music in the writings of Jane Austen, Patrick Piggott suggests that Wednesday, 22nd February 1815 was 'almost certainly the date of the concert' in the New Assembly Rooms, which bore witness to the uncomfortable frisson between Anne Elliot and Captain Wentworth in Jane Austen's *Persuasion*.[159] Whether or not the case, the concert that evening was organised by Andrew Loder; Alexander Herschel led the 'cello section and the wife of Andrew Ashe, the former Miss Comer 'whose sweet plaintive tones had delighted Catherine Morland'[160] in Austen's earlier novel *Northanger Abbey*, sang. In *Persuasion*, Mary

Musgrove spots Mr Elliot's and Mrs Clay's clandestine liaison from 'her station at a window [of The White Hart] overlooking the entrance to the Pump Room'.

Dogs were now banned from the Pump Room by the Corporation, 'being often attended with great inconvenience to the invalids and others'.[161] One elderly invalid was Queen Charlotte, a one-time pupil of Johann Christian Bach and patron of music, whose philanthropy extended to the Royal Mineral Water Hospital. A year before her death Queen Charlotte stayed quietly for a month on Sydney Place. Fanny Burney, a former employee of the Queen, recorded their rendezvous at the Pump Room in her diary. 'Just before Christmas 1817 we went together between seven and eight in the morning, in chairs to the pump-room.' Of the Pump Room, Queen Charlotte wrote that it

> was built for the invalids, in which they might be supplied with water from a covered pump and afterward to take the exercise prescribed to them, sheltered from the inclemency of the weather.

Andrew Ashe was unable to match his predecessor's ability to 'lure a wonderful galaxy of metropolitan and international talents to Bath'.[162] Failing to stabilise the fragile financial situation he had inherited from Rauzzini, Ashe's last four concerts in 1822 resulted in a loss. Sir

George Smart (whose parents were Bathonians) with John David Loder accepted the posts as Managers of the Concerts. Now thirty-five years old, Loder was still remembered for his childhood violin performance at the funeral of his father. Under Smart and Loder's partnership, the success of the concerts led to the Bath and Somerset First Triennial Grand Music Festival in 1824.[163] John David Loder's *General and Comprehensive Instruction Book for the Violin* had been published ten years earlier. It was distinguished as the first non-French manual to incorporate the stylistic and technical innovations of Paganini.

Charles Foote Taylor, *John David Loder* (courtesy of the Victoria Art Gallery, Bath & North East Somerset Council)

Thomas Rowlandson, *The Fish Market* (courtesy of the Victoria Art Gallery, Bath & North East Somerset Council)

Seventeen years later Loder was privileged to lead the orchestra when his mentor appeared in Bath.

Bath's first Assembly Rooms, the Lower Rooms (situated below The Walks), had been gutted by fire and reconstructed as the Bath Literary and Scientific Institution. By 1825 the New Assembly Rooms and the Guildhall were the main venues for popular balls and concerts in a city becoming more sober and respectable. Though Reverend John Skinner of Camerton, a village seven miles outside Bath, reveals a converse image of the city in his diary – 'the streets are so crowded with prostitutes, some of them apparently not above fourteen or fifteen years of age'.[164] Cholera was endemic, especially in the overcrowded, unsanitary housing along the river on Avon Street. This area was most unlikely to have been on the tour of the eleven year old Princess Victoria when she came to Bath to open the new Victoria Park in 1830. But the Pump Room, where the livelihoods of its musicians continued to be threatened by lack of support and low funds, was on the Princess's itinerary. On their behalf, that year, the Mayor and Corporation appealed

> . . . in aid of the funds of the band . . . as a means of protracting its performances to a more advanced period in the Season. The Pump Room music is justly entitled to be classed among the most attractive objects of our city, the prolongation of its performances is on every account desirable.

'Entirely on one string',[165] Paganini performed 'a Grand Concerto, an 'Allegro Maestoso' and a Sonata Militaire'[166] in the first of three concerts in Bath at the end of 1831. John David Loder led the orchestra for 'Signor Paganini's Grand Concerts' at the Theatre Royal with his eighteen year old son, Edward James Loder, playing the pianoforte. Sadly John David was denied the pleasure of his father, the late John Loder, seeing them perform at this historic occasion. (In gratitude Paganini later sent John David the gift of 'a very valuable diamond ring' from Paris.[167]) Members of the Pump Room Orchestra often performed at the Theatre Royal, and it is very likely that some played in the pit for these concerts. John David also maintained the family music publishing tradition, established by his Uncle Andrew's business on the Orange Grove, with his own successful one on Milsom Street. He later became a Professor at the Royal Academy of Music.

The next generation of Loders continued the family musical dynasty. John David's son, Edward, composed the romantic opera *Raymond and Agnes* as well as numerous popular songs such as *The Brave old Oak*. Edward's twin brother, John Fawcett, was a violinist and led the Bath Choral Society concerts at the Assembly Rooms, as had his father before him. Evocative of the Flemings a century earlier, John Fawcett's wife became a professor of dancing and established an academy at the family 'music warehouse' on Milsom Street. But 'the most remarkable of all of them was Kate',[168] granddaughter of Pump Room Band violinist John Loder. She studied at the RAM from the age of thirteen and in 1844 'distinguished herself as the piano soloist in Mendelssohn's *G minor Concerto* [and] performed before the composer'.[169] The *Musical Times* described the 'galaxy of talent on that brilliant and fashionable occasion'.[170] The first private performance in England of the Brahms' *Requiem* was at Kate's home nearly thirty years later when, despite the onset of paralysis, she played the orchestral part as a piano duet with Cipriani Potter. Kate's portrait watches over the boardroom at the RAM today, not far from that of her uncle John David Loder.

The Pump Room Orchestra in Victorian Times

By 1833 the Pump Room Band's reputation was such that when one of its members, John White of George Street, died, the news was reported over fifty miles away in Bridgwater.[171] Subscribers to Charles Dickens's *Pickwick Papers*, published in 1835/37, read that the Pump Room was

> . . . a spacious salon, ornamented with Corinthian pillars, and a music-gallery . . . and a Tompion clock, and a statue of Nash . . . There are baths near at hand, in which a part of the Company wash themselves; and a band plays afterwards, to congratulate the remainder on their having done so.

Dickens's character Mr Pickwick lodges at the Royal Crescent and embarks on a treatment regime at the baths. Dickens found the spa water distasteful, but it was the music which was not to the taste of Italian born Dr Augustus Granville who visited two years later

> Formerly, the Bath Orchestra and pump room musical performances were the theme of good commendation in England. With the decline, however, of the renown of the Spa, its musical attractions declined likewise; until at length the mere semblance of an orchestra remained, such as I myself heard as late as 1839, to scrape upon a few sorry cremonas the same eternal bars of Corelli and Handel every day at two o'clock.[172]

Returning a year later, Granville was much more impressed by the popularity of the Pump Room Promenade Concerts, which ' . . . at the noontide hours of fashion, is become *une affaire de rigueur* for the elite and elegant of this beautiful city'.[173] Among the guest musicians who came to Bath in those years were Franz Liszt, Johann Strauss the Elder and Charles Hallé. In 1848 Hallé declined a permanent position in Bath

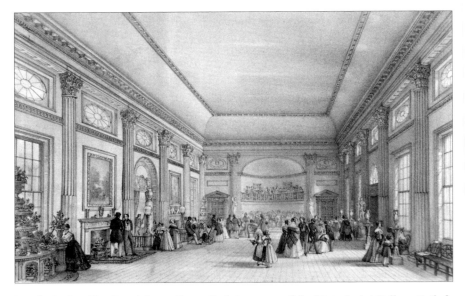

Day & Haghe, *The Grand Pump Room, Bath* (courtesy of the Victoria Art Gallery, Bath & North East Somerset Council)

as Musical Director, in favour of the conductorship of the Gentlemen's Concerts in Manchester. A letter dated September 19th of that year from his first wife Desirée to her sister in New Orleans reads

> Meanwhile let me tell you that we have been at Manchester since the 6th of this month; Mathilde's last letter informed you that Charles, having received proposals from this town more advantageous than those from Bath, had decided to establish himself here, where, moreover he finds such immense musical resources that he could not hesitate between the two towns.[174]

The 1855 season began with recommendations from the Baths and Pump Room Committee to the Council that the Pump Room Band offer promenade concerts three times a week with a Saturday vocal concert 'without prejudice to the water drinkers'. Corporation Minutes in the late 1850s indicate that a Mr Rainey and a John Henry Macfarlane conducted the Pump Room Orchestra. The latter, a 'Professor of Music', founded the short-lived Bath City Choral Society in 1859 and was commended for the direction of its concerts.[175] Macfarlane's Musical Depot dealt in pianos, harmoniums and sheet music.

Intent on reviving the spa industry, the Corporation proposed the rebuilding of the White Hart Hotel on Stall Street. But it was ten years before the new hotel was built and renamed the Grand Pump Room Hotel. In the interim, catastrophe struck another prominent Bath building only a couple of streets away. On Good Friday in 1862 the Theatre Royal was gutted by fire. *The Times* reported that

> The magnificent wardrobe and valuable library are utterly consumed. . . Chute, the lessee, who is not insured, loses about £500, and members of the Company and the orchestra are also sufferers by the fire. The origin of the fire is a mystery.

The Theatre was re-opened in 1863 at a cost 'rather over £11,000'. In 1865 despondency prevailed within the Baths and Pump Room Committee who reported, 'the receipts had not been equal to the previous season'.[176] Subscribers paid five shillings for a series of sixty winter concerts with admission tickets just sixpence each. A review was ominously suggested 'in order to avoid any more expenditure in excess of the Corporation grant' of eighty pounds a year. Although the band survived, some members of the Council failed to recognise the Pump Room Orchestra as an important resource and believed the sum of nearly two thousand pounds to support thirteen musicians (at the Pump Room) 'who only have to saw and blow' as excessive.[177]

A possible solution to this impasse presented itself in September 1867 in the form of Horatio Nelson King, the lessee and manager of the newly built Theatre Royal. Tendering a bid to manage the concerts in the theatre and the Pump Room to the 'great advantage to both places', he wrote to the Chairman of the Pump Room Committee proposing

> to negotiate for the Pump Room Concerts this Season. Bath and Bristol Theatres having now separated and I find great difficulty in getting first class talent for my orchestra at the Theatre and wishing to make that a feature . . . by engaging and retaining at a certain salary competent artistes, with a first class leader enabling me by these means to give music of the highest class. I shall if the Concerts come under my management engage for the Season a full band and give at least six Special Concerts (no evening ones) producing talent of the highest order. Being personally known to most of the best artistes of the day I shall 'avail' myself of their services, taking into consideration the advantages I should gain by a permanent band for both places. If the Corporation will allow me a grant of £75 I will do my utmost to render the concerts worthy of the support of the citizens of Bath and keep up the former prestige of the Concerts which are I believe essential to

the benefit of the city. I shall be pleased to meet your committee and consult with them on matters of detail if they wish it. If I find at the termination that my success in a pecuniary point of view has been such as will allow me to make a reduction in the amount granted I shall with pleasure reduce the same. It is essential to me to have the matter settled at the earliest moment on account of my making arrangements with artistes in London. I shall be glad of an early decision.

An early decision was unlikely to have been forthcoming. The orchestra at the time was in the middle of a crisis concerning its director T H Salmon 'who for several years past had had the conduct of the [band], but was prevented by ill health'[178] from recommencing his duties. He was relieved at the start of the 1867 season by the temporary engagement of William Duck,[179] the proprietor of Duck's Musical Repository on Pulteney Bridge.

Thomas Henry Salmon died that year at the age of fifty-four. His brother William Edward, a violinist, a teacher of the piano and 'cello, and father of three young children, wrote to the Committee from his home on Kingsmead Terrace begging to be considered

> for the 'Music director and Leadership of the Pump Room Concerts on the same principle as carried on for you by my late Brother (T H Salmon) for whom I did the working part and regarded the accounts and made out the programmes for the last three seasons he held the situation.
>
> I humbly urge my application as I have had practical experience in concert business having been with the late Alfred Mellow five seasons and have played in all the principal London and Provincial Orchestras and am well known in the Musical profession for ability and steady Business habits. [180]

Thomas Joseph Pinker, a 'householder residing at 38 River Street'[181] and Mr Duck's assistant for many years, was a rival bidder. His request for a hundred pound grant from the Baths and Pump Room Committee exceeded Salmon's by twenty pounds. Salmon's tender was enhanced by a 'large orchestral library of standard works adapted to small bands – formerly the property of the late Alfred Mellow, T H Salmon, J. D Loder and others'.[182] On the 12th October, 1868 twelve Pump Room Band members signed a letter confirming their confidence in Salmon and that they would 'most Cordially cooperate with him'.[183]

Salmon's Displacement as Director

OVER the next few years William Salmon presided over the orchestra. Its instruments were stipulated by the Corporation to be 'mixed, wind and stringed'.[184] Obliged to reapply for the post annually, Salmon was eventually forced to defend his candidacy to which 'detrimental allusion had been made'.[185] He invoked the testimonials of well-known soloists procured during his management, including those of sopranos Helen Lemmens-Sherrington, Edith Wynne and Louise Liebhart.

But in October 1876 an appointed Music Committee gravely reported that several of its 'competent members' were dissatisfied with the 'music heretofore provided at the Pump Room . . . appealing as it does to a refined audience'. This 'refined' audience, under Salmon's baton, would have listened to Mendelssohn's *Italian Symphony*, overtures by Sterndale Bennett and Brull, Schumann's *Schlummerlied* and a selection from Lumby's *Traumbilder*. A voluntary four man quango, the 'Committee of Citizens' was tasked with improving the management of the music and inspiring public confidence with a view to 'increase [the] prosperity' of the facilities.[186] The Corporation however was not persuaded by the committee's recommendation that 'having music at the Pump Room daily [would] prove beneficial'. By 1880 it was resigned to the 'gratuitous daily and evening performances' and to the hard fact that the 'primary object of the Pump Room music was to provide amusement for those persons taking the waters'.[187] At risk of doubling its costs, the Corporation considered engaging the Hanoverian Music Committee 'a public body labouring equally with the Council' for the provision of 'higher quality' music and to generate more revenue.

In September that year, with his position now hanging by a thread, Salmon wrote to His Worship the Mayor, the Aldermen and Gentlemen of the Council

> Having had the honor of several seasons of being your Music director and Manager of the Grand Pump Room Concerts I would beg most respectfully to state that the concerts while under my management, when they were three days a week, for which I

received your kind grant of Eighty pounds a week, was successful as the Balance I rendered at the termination of each season will show.

The last two seasons when they became daily, and especially when held at 11.30 am, there was a great decrease of subscriptions and attendance of non subscribers altho' I employ the best instrumental and vocal artists at a considerable outlay.

I would merely add that I am ready and anxious to meet your views and wishes either as Music director or Manager.

My chief object is an artistic desire to add to the Musical reputation of the city

I am Gentlemen
Your obedient servant
William Edward Salmon
Music Director and Professor of the Violin

The letter diverted the Corporation away from its mission to generate more profits. Nothing further was heard of the Hanoverian Band.

Three years later, Herr van Praag, a German violin teacher at Cheltenham Ladies College advertised in the *Bath and Cheltenham Gazette* that he was now 'at liberty to arrange for lessons in Bath'. This 'young pretender' would before long pose a significant threat to the Music Director's already precarious position. Salmon's 'Full Orchestra consisting of First Class Artists'[188] went on to perform in a Grand Pump Room Concert in November 1883 in honour of the Prince of Wales' birthday.

A month later, the *Chronicle* continued the debate about the quality of music in the Pump Room. One 'Frequenter of Concerts' wrote

I am sure W.E. Salmon does his best to provide us with as good music and artistes as lies within his power and funds; therefore it behoves us to help him rather than submit to any arrangement that turns away sixpences from the doors.

Another correspondent offered these sentiments

I agree with your correspondents respecting the inconvenience caused by the new regulations as to the seating, by which the season ticket holders are relegated to the cold and draughty part of the room, while visitors who subscribe to the waters have the most comfortable seats, in the best position and hear the music for nothing. It is manifestly an unfair arrangement.

Furthermore

> There are the Pump Room Concerts but these are only held
> three times in a week: Could not a small band be provided for
> the remaining afternoons, the expense of which might be met, as
> at other watering places, by voluntary contributions from those
> present. Probably some musician could be found to undertake it
> on such terms, and this place would not interfere in any way with
> the present concerts so admirably conducted by Salmon.

A Special Council meeting was called immediately before the
new season began. Eighteen years after the Baths and Pump Room
Committee first recommended a review, it agreed 'the distinguished
musical audiences that Bath possessed'[189] deserved a resident band all
year round. Some Councillors fought to retain Salmon 'in that position
and as Leader of the band, which he has so successfully and to the great
benefit of the city filled' for many years. Organised by Lady Carrington
of 33 St James Square, a petition signed by two hundred people was
personally handed to the Mayor by Salmon himself. It read

> We, the undersigned, are fully convinced that Salmon, the
> conductor for many seasons, has given complete satisfaction to
> his audiences, and we sincerely trust that he may be again re-
> appointed to the post he so ably occupied.
>   We, the undersigned beg to offer an entreaty to the
> Corporation of Bath on behalf of Mr. Salmon's services, talent
> and willingness to carry out any new feature the Corporation may
> (in their zeal for the city) suggest, we promise as householders
> to work individually with visitors on behalf of such refined
> amusement.[190]

Alderman Walker argued that the dismissal of Salmon was not a
'sacrifice of private rights to the public good' as audiences under Salmon
had not been 'flagging'; indeed they had been 'overflowing'. But in a
fait accompli the season's Pump Room Orchestra members had already
been selected by the new conductor – Herr van Praag. Alderman Walker
would *still* not surrender and went on to scrutinise the changes in the
orchestra personnel

> Out of the thirteen members of the band there were nine persons
> re-engaged . . . so there could not have been so much fault to be

found with the old band. Now there was a leader – a first violin. But had Mr. Salmon been so supported – it was his strong desire to have a first violin, so that he should not have had to do double duty – to play the violin and conduct also. With regard to the violoncello . . . certainly Pomeroy, who might be called a Bath man, was a very superior player on that instrument; and whether his son was equal to the double bass was another question. There was a cornet from the Italian Band [Bossi] and another cornet from among the old members, but the effect of having two cornets in the Pump Room would be very much to its prejudice instead of success – he would be sorry to be present with two cornets. There was an omission of the oboe, the old band possessing a very good one; and the effect was very good and gave great satisfaction. The result of all this was that he did not see, with the exception of the first violin, any marked change was to be made in the constitution of the band.

Undeterred, Walker then went on to stress the damage done to Salmon's reputation as a teacher in Bath

in the opinion of the proprietor of the school, [Salmon's dismissal] seriously interferes with the prestige when parents inquired, that a professor was employed who was Leader and conductor of the Pump Room Band at Bath.

Walker then challenged Herr van Praag's qualifications for the role on the basis that he had

never appeared in Bath except at the Quartette Concerts, as second violin, never having been Leader even there. In what public orchestra in this kingdom had Herr van Praag ever yet been Leader or conductor?

Walker need have looked no further than the Bath Orchestral Society for an affirmative response to this last question[191]. Alderman Walker's resolution to reinstate Mr. Salmon was seconded by Alderman Bright who also felt obliged to defend another displaced musician

There was Bartlett who had been to Eastbourne, and on returning found his place in the Pump Room Band filled up by another. Now Bartlett was a Bath man, and his family resided here; and though some years ago he was a tradesman in Southgate Street he had recently got his living as a flute player, and he looked for employment during the winter months in his native city.

Herr van Praag, who had patiently listened to the argument, now spoke explaining that he had 'understood Bartlett had left Bath, and [he] had engaged another – Broom, who was, however, also a ratepayer'.

This was Alderman Chaffin's cue to direct the debate to the less emotive area of investment. He stated that a

> body of gentlemen would support Herr van Praag with £100 or £500 – that if Salmon's friends would rally round him . . . and guarantee £500 in addition to the £100 voted by the Council, then they would be on equal terms, but not else.

The Chairman of the Baths and Pump Room Committee explained that he had

> conferred with a German physician, who had said we had the finest baths in Europe, but there was not a small town in Germany that had not a good band – why did we not look after that? Herr van Praag had been conductor to a London theatre band; he held credentials of a high order from the School of Music at the Hague; he was well-known in the city; he was honoured and respected by those who were competent to judge, and who were skilled musicians. He had been asked to associate himself with a band of amateurs distinguished for great assiduity, and for high determination; and he thought it would be greatly to their advantage if they had a higher order of music presented to them, and then the study of music would grow in an increasing degree in our city.

It was not to be Alderman Walker's day, but he was praised for the 'admirable and logically-constructed case he made . . . in favor of his motion for rescinding the contract with Herr van Praag'.[192] The Council had debated the matter in a 'reasoning, calm, and impartial spirit . . . '.[193] Herr van Praag's directorship of the Pump Room Orchestra was sealed.

Two weeks later the *Bath and Cheltenham Gazette*[194] gave a favourable report of the orchestra and its first concerts under Herr van Praag's baton in the Grand Pump Room

> Analysing the present band, we find the principal violinist or 'Leader,' is a new-comer, Mr. F. van Heddeghern, who once

occupied the same position at the Crystal Palace; with him is Mr. Fred Waite, well-known as a most competent player. The seconds and viola are old friends, Messrs. Owen, C. Watts and Wetten; Mr. S. van Gelder (late of Her Majesty's Opera) plays the 'cello, and Mr. E. Carrodas (Royal Italian Opera) the double bass. Mr. Broom's flute and piccolo render valuable service; the clarionet and euphonium are, as before, admirably played by Mr. Kopp and Signor Ulrico; Signor Bossi (late of the Italian Band) has been secured as first cornet, Mr. Alexander being second ditto; Mr. Thomas Head's percussion instruments, drums, cymbals and sundries complete the list. We may mention the conductor, Herr van Praag, studied at the Hague, and 'went through the mill' of professional routine in London as a member of the Royal Italian Opera and other orchestras.

The programme of 'popular' music was well selected, both as regards the compositions themselves, and for the opportunities given the various instrumentalists to display their ability as soloists –notably in the 'Ermani' and the 'Poet and Peasant' Overture. In other numbers of the programme was shown well-marked attention to nuances or shades of expression. A Festival March, tempo moderato, composed by the conductor – and well suited – for the occasion was produced; it is dedicated to his Worship the Mayor who with the Corporation was present. Herr van Praag also played a solo for the violin, accompanied on the pianoforte by Miss Ellaby. A crowded room was attracted, and the audience by constant attention and by frequent and sustained applause gave evidence of their enjoyment and satisfaction.

A capital rendering of several interesting pieces was given by the band; the playing and conduction of Auber's overture, 'Le Domino Noir' was specially good. We must object to the popping of corks in the 'Champagne' gallop; it is not music's mission to pop, and the composition would have sparkled quite as well without. Solos for the violoncello introduced Mr. S van Gelder, who showed in Goldterman's 'Andante,' the possession of good tone and expression, and displayed in the 'Drinking Song' of Dunkler, facility of execution generally, and in double-stopping in particular.

William Salmon's letter of appeal to the editor of the *Bath and Cheltenham Gazette* was printed nine days later.[195] Proudly undersigned Musical Conductor, it failed to mask his wounded feelings

SIR, – It was not my intention to have obtruded any remarks in print on this painful subject, although to me professionally a matter of deep importance. I feel, however, compelled to notice a letter I have received from Herr van Praag, containing an offer which I cannot but consider in the light of a studied insult supplementing a great injury; it is to play in his band, at a salary of two guineas per week, an instrument (the violoncello) which I have not attempted in public for the last 16 years. To accept this offer would, I fear, having been so long out of practice, seriously damage my reputation as an instrumentalist, and I must candidly admit a suspicion, that such an effect of my accepting, may possibly be anticipated.

In conclusion, I feel bound to remark I am much astonished at the unkind and incorrect statements which have been publicly made to my detriment, by gentlemen whose position in the city, and as amateurs in the musical world, should have ensured for me more careful and truthful treatment. That the Pump Room music has been conducted by me to the satisfaction of the great body of subscribers is testified, not only by crowded and increasing attendance, but also by the very numerous and kind letters I am daily receiving by post from ladies and gentlemen well-known as the principal supporters of music, and of all the concerts given in Bath, and therefore well qualified to judge of my doings in the post, and of my ability, if entrusted with the necessary support, to improve them in the future. I am, Sir, yours truly

W.E. SALMON,
Musical Conductor and Professor of the Violin
14 Great Stanhope Street, Bath

Salmon's entreaties fell on deaf ears; the new conductor was already attracting large audiences in the Pump Room.

Herr van Praag & Max Heymann

IN attendance at concerts under the new director was 'The Local
Lounger', the arbiter of social mores and scribe of the *Bath Gazette's*
'Notes By the Way'.

> On Saturday, when the room overflowed into the lobbies, only
> three windows were open! The more noticeable items of the
> programmes have been: – a Spanish dance, the Habenera, *'La
> Paloma,'* by Corbin (first time in England), welcome for its quaint
> prettiness, and encored; a musicianly valse by O Metra, *'L'Italie;'*
> ... The solos, appreciated and applauded, were for piccolo by Mr.
> Brown, whom we should like to hear on the flute, and for 'cello
> (with Miss Murray at the piano) by Mr. van Gelder, who appeared
> at one moment to be disconcerted by the continued entry of late
> arrivals, and no wonder; ordinary courtesy should suggest the
> propriety of their remaining outside till the conclusion of the
> piece. The same nuisance interfered with the enjoyment of one of
> the orchestral pieces, and we were glad to see the conductor, Herr
> van Praag protest against such rude treatment.[196]

The 'Lounger' further vents his frustration with 'the large and
fashionable audiences' who choose to leave before the national anthem
at the end of the concerts.

Two days after Christmas Day in 1884, Salmon's supporters
gathered in the Mayor's Room at the Guildhall to present a testimonial
to Salmon 'as a mark of their respect and esteem ... for his services to
the city of Bath, especially in the musical line, for many years past'. The
farewell speech referred to 'gentlemen in their midst – very gushing
gentlemen, who wished to have everything now, and to turn everything
upside down . . . [and regrettably] Salmon had fallen victim to the
competition of the day'. Heavy with innuendo, it was stated that any
'conductor of average merits', funded generously, could do justice to the
role. Salmon 'had struggled under great difficulties, having the band at
the theatre and Pump Room at a time when Bath was not prosperous as

at present'. It was hoped their appreciation might help to compensate 'for the pain that he must necessarily have felt in this matter'.[197]In thanks for a gift of fifty guineas and the sentiments offered, Salmon said he had difficulty in 'conveying his feelings' but expressed how especially indebted he was to Alderman Walker who 'had come at a time when this trouble had pressed very heavily upon him, and had enabled him to rally under the severe blow'.

Marking the end-of-year festivities, the Pump Room Orchestra performed the first of a new afternoon concert series in the Assembly Rooms, where the quality of the music was 'uninterrupted by the fountain and the echoes of the Pump Room'.[198] In the Octagon Room people could socialise over refreshments, while next door others gave their attention to the music. 'The meal without the music is worth the money and the music without the food is worth the fee'[199] quipped the *Gazette's* social columnist! This revamped band with its new director now earned, extravagantly claimed the *Gazette*, the attention of the International Press – 'the World, the Figaro and the Standard'.[200]

According to journalist and historian, the late Kenneth Gregory, William Salmon was so devastated that he left Bath in disgust. Earlier champion of his cause, Lady Carrington, now had a new campaign – the 'bad odour under the asphalt' newly laid on St James Square.[201]

A few streets away in a basement under The Corridor, a scientific instrument maker – the son of a Bath wood turner – was intently working in collaboration with a photographer. Both were venturing into pioneering work in moving pictures and the application of celluloid ribbon for commercial purposes. John Arthur Roebuck Rudge and William Friese-Greene were ignorant then of the impact the silent movie era would have on working opportunities for a massive proportion of musicians including many future Pump Room Orchestra members. 'Kinematography must be attributed to the labours of these two citizens of Bath where this wonderful invention undoubtedly received its birth.'[202]

Under Herr van Praag the Pump Room Orchestra thrived for eight years. Newly branded as the (fourteen piece) Bath City Band, it performed every winter afternoon in the Pump Room and on summer afternoons in Sydney Gardens. In the tradition established by Beau Nash, subscriptions still partly supported the band, but now were supplemented by grant funding from the Corporation's new initiative – 'The Society for Developing the Advantages of Bath'. Afternoon concerts were meticulously programmed with Thursdays' always classical – the audience politely requested to refrain from talking during the performance. An overture by Verdi, a Ukrainian dance by Muscat, a waltz by Waldteufel and selections by Cowen and Donizetti illustrate the type of repertoire played. In the orchestra then led by a Mr Skuse were two young musicians: Otto Heinrich, a German violinist, and Joseph Bossi, an Italian cornet and trumpet player. Ultimately the careers of both these men would end very differently.

Weekly cheques from the Corporation in 1889 were made out to 'Herr van Praag, Pump Room Band' for distribution to its members, whose earnings were two pounds a week for playing a minimum of five concerts. Violinist Herr J. W. Duys joined the band in 1890, simultaneously becoming leader of the Bath Choral and Orchestral Society, a position he held up to the First World War.[203]

When Herr van Praag left in 1892 Max Richard Heymann became the new Musical Director. A fine violinist he had played under the batons of Hans von Bülow, Karl Richter, Arthur Nikisch and at Crystal Palace, August Manns. A choir-boy in his native town, Johanngeorgenstad in Saxony, Germany, Heymann went on to study music at the Leipzig Conservatoire and violin under Felix Meyer, Concert Master to the Emperor of Germany. Joseph Bossi was now playing under his third Pump Room Orchestra conductor. In December 1895 Bossi was the solo trumpeter in the Bath Choral and Orchestral Society's *Messiah*. A full orchestra and two hundred strong choir at the Assembly Rooms was conducted by Henry Sims, (another Bath pianoforte and music seller) and led by Pump Room Band violinist Herr Duys.[204] The same year the Pavillion Music Hall on Sawclose reopened as the Lyric Theatre of Varieties. Charlie Chaplin, whose later silent movie career would owe much to the two inventors of cinematography from Bath, allegedly performed there as a child around the age of ten when 'touring the provinces'[205] with the Eight Lancashire Lads. (It is certainly feasible that Bath was on his itinerary.)

The Grand Pump Room was considered 'a fine room most successfully built for music'. Yet the Corporation decreed that it was unable to cater for both water drinkers and concert goers. So the solution was to build a new public facility – a palatial Concert Room linked by a wall to the Pump Room itself rebuilt a century earlier. Completed in 1897, the Concert Room's opulence would be reflected in lavishly designed concert programmes. Flanked with the words 'The City of Bath Pump Room Orchestra', a discreetly overarching banner served to remind the public that the orchestra was 'under the Control of the Corporation'. An afternoon concert of Beethoven's *Eroica Symphony* – as performed on November 19th, 1899, was typical of the 'substantial classical diet'[206] offered by the orchestra in its new home.

Robert Fenton Gower Brown was a young musician in the Pump Room Orchestra between 1902 and 1904 under Max Heymann's

Pump Room Orchestra Programme October 7 1899 (courtesy of the Bath Record Office, Bath & North East Somerset Council)

direction. His son, E F Brown, writing in his eightieth year[207], recalled his father playing both the violin and piano. The young musician's 'wanderlust' took him away from Bath to Buxton and Bridlington on what was to become a well trodden Spa orchestra trail. Between 1925 and 1933 Brown played in the viola section of the Hallé in Manchester, the city where he eventually settled. In 1906 Arthuro Riccardo Fernando Semprini, a French-horn player from Rimini, joined the orchestra. His middle son Alberto, born in Bath two years later, was to become a household name.

Two Ediths were billed on the programme for Max Heymann's annual benefit concert in 1906. One was the soprano Miss Edith Evans; the other, a solo pianist Madame Edith Meadows – 'Mrs Max Heymann' performing under her husband's baton. The Pump Room Orchestra in 1908 was made up of five violinists, a 'cellist, a violist, a double bass player, a bassoonist, a flautist, an oboist, two clarinettists, two horn players, two cornet players, a trombonist and a percussionist. Its nineteen members were each paid between two and three pounds a week. A thirty-two week seasonal subscription ticket was five shillings and an individual concert ticket was sixpence. Unable to generate a profit at these rates, a special committee was tasked with conducting a national spa orchestra survey. A simple questionnaire revealed Bath's orchestra to be less than half the size of Bournemouth's and Brighton's which played throughout the year. Even Llandudno's and Bridlington's were larger during their summer seasons. The committee's recommendation to enlarge the Pump Room Orchestra and that it play all year was welcomed by Max Heymann, but the Corporation resisted. The director advised a five shillings charge per concert instead of per seasonal ticket for two hundred concerts! 'If a tradesman gave away his wares in that fashion he would be considered a lunatic'.[208]

Among the Pump Room Orchestra's guest artists at the end of the decade and beginning of the next were the singer Hilda Blake, composer and conductor Edward German and violinist Dorothy Bridson who played a concerto composed by a gentleman in the audience. Dr Max Bruch 'expressed his entire satisfaction with her performance'.[209] The West African, Samuel Coleridge-Taylor, then Professor at the Guildhall School of Music, conducted the Pump Room Orchestra ten years after his composition *Hiawatha's Wedding Feast* was first performed in Bath[210].

Max Heymann's annual spring benefit concert in 1910 included Humperdinck's *Hansel and Gretel* overture and excerpts from Wagner's *Tristan and Isolde*. Appearing with a supplemented Pump Room Orchestra was the statuesque contralto Clara Butt. As a child in Bristol, Butt was told she 'had gold in her throat' and later became known as the

Voice of the Empire.[211] After the concert the Mayor, splendidly impressed, ventured to suggest that 'in the course of time [they] might be able to give Max Heymann his hearts desire, namely an increased orchestra'.

Two weeks later Heymann was too ill to attend the St George's Day concert, where 'two large Union Jacks were suspended from the balcony above the orchestra'.[212] His arrangements of music by British composers were highly commended. Presenting a table of other spa conductors' salaries, Heymann judiciously chose this time to appeal for an increase in pay. The Spa Committee conceded that, unlike his counterpart in Harrogate, Heymann worked in an office at home without any assistance and awarded him an extra hundred pounds a year. This he gratefully acknowledged would 'do him more good than any medicine'. Morning concerts and dances were planned events in the Pump Room during the wave of patriotism leading up to the proclamation of George V in May 1910.

But time was not on Heymann's side. Accompanied by his wife and child, he left Bath for his native Germany that summer to undergo treatment for a severe spinal complaint. He returned to Bath in a very depressed state.

FOUND SHOT IN HIS GARDEN – REVOLVER BY HIS SIDE
TERRIBLE END TO A LONG ILLNESS

was the shocking headline in the *Bath Chronicle* on the 8th September, 1910. Heymann's body had been found in the garden of his home 'Sunnymead' – the Victorian House at Beechen Cliff, with a bullet lodged in his right temple. An Inspector Payne reported that 'five unused cartridges were still in the weapon, which the deceased is believed to have had in his possession some time'.[213] On the study table was a note to his wife with the words 'Goodbye, take care of our darling'.[214] Characteristically fastidious, even in his darkest hour, Heymann had also written to the Coroner and the Chairman of the Baths Committee stating that 'ill-health would prevent him resuming his duties and that his life's work was finished'.[215]

Heymann was much loved in Bath where 'his good and conscientious efforts were appreciated . . . [and where] he had been the recipient of several gifts from the frequenters of the Pump Room and the subscribers to the concerts'.[216]

In a public 'Appreciation' a close friend acknowledged Max Heymann's onerous duties as Music Director.

A history of the Pump Room Orchestra during the period that

he was at its head was practically a history of his own life. He practically undertook the task of the higher musical education of the Bath public. The engagement of artists and entertainers was in his hands, and in this task . . . he displayed very great tact and discretion. He was a firm believer in the policy of securing the best talent and frequenters of the Pump Room concerts were often enabled to hear world-famous pianists whose performances could not have been enjoyed at other places of entertainment in the city for a reasonable (almost ridiculous) price. But he was equally ready where practicable to give opportunities and encouragement to local artistes.

Heymann's delivery of the large symphonic works of Bach, Haydn, Beethoven, Brahms, Tchaikovsky and Wagner 'with the comparative smallness of the Pump Room Orchestra rendered necessary much re-writing and rearrangement of parts, without which many of these works could not be performed in Bath at all'. It was a tragic end for a man only forty-eight years old whose doctor testified at the inquest that 'there was no reason why he should not get perfectly well'. The jury's unanimous verdict was that Heymann had shot himself 'when in a fit of insanity'. Heymann's scores and compositions were bought by the Corporation for one hundred pounds, and 'a small portion of his private music . . . and his upright Collard piano' were reserved for friends and admirers.[217]

Frank Tapp

THE first Pump Room Orchestra concert after Heymann's death was directed by the Deputy conductor, Dutchman Sichard Culp. Though poorly attended, a violin solo played by Ernest Read, who had led the second violins for some years, deserved praise. Soon after, at another Bath venue, the violist Lionel Tertis stood in at a recital given by the Bath Quartette Society. (Tertis later would greatly influence one particular string player in the Pump Room Orchestra.) In November, Heymann's widow, Madame Meadows, saw her gifted young pupil Master George Reeves perform Schubert's *Piano Concerto in A minor* with the Pump Room Orchestra. A larger audience attended Miss Tosta de Benici's ('the 'famous Swedish pianist')[218] rendition of Tchaikovsky's

Sichard Culp (Bath Herald 15 October 1910)

Concerto in B Flat minor. Gustav Holst came from Cheltenham, his hometown, to conduct the orchestra for the premiere of his *Somerset Rhapsody* in a programme that also included his composition *Songs from the West*.[219] A week later Madame Blanche Marchesi, ' the famous opera star . . . also a brilliant violinist and pianist',[220] made an appearance.

The issue of advertising for a new Musical Director was debated at Council meetings. Sichard Culp was considered by some to be doing a fine job and the violinist Charles Macdonald was now the deputy conductor. A week before Christmas, members of the Bath Quartette Society performed *Fantasia for String Trio in E minor* op 30 composed by a prodigal pianist who had returned to the city. It was enthusiastically reviewed in the *Bath Herald*. Still, some Council members were apprehensive – 'the composition certainly justifies the title and its commencement at once appeals to the listener as bizarre [though] graceful . . . it does not seem [Frank] Tapp has much to teach us here'.[221]

Attendance was disappointing at the Pump Room Christmas Concert, despite the promise of Culp's sister Juliette, another 'brilliant pianist',[222] according to the *Bath Herald*, who performed Saint Saens' *Piano Concerto No 2 in G minor*. A year marred with sadness ended with the Pump Room Orchestra's festive dinner at Fortts Restaurant on Milsom Street. Guests were then unaware that the new young Director of the Baths dining with them was on his way to becoming one of the most inspired and effective ambassadors of musical culture, both for the Pump Room and the city.

Frank Tapp (courtesy of Robert Matthew-Walker, Editor, *Musical Opinion*)

Seventy-five applications were received for the post of Music Director of the Pump Room Orchestra, over half before it was officially advertised, at a salary of two hundred and fifty pounds for a thirty-three week season. (The Council had increased Heymann's salary to three hundred and fifty pounds just months before his death.) Glowing testimonials from Professor Hadow of Oxford University, the author of 'Musical Form', and the composer Sir Charles Stanford from the Royal College of Music helped to secure Frank Tapp a place on the shortlist. Other contenders were the violinist Herr J Duys and the current acting conductor of the band, Sichard Culp, whose international experience as a leader included the Dannoch Wagner Opera in New York. A panel of Aldermen (a Music Sub-Committee) needed just seven minutes to interview Frank Tapp before agreeing to offer him the post on a January morning in 1911. (One might wonder whether this was because they had run out of questions or were wary of learning something new!)

Frank Tapp was born in Bath in 1884 the only son of a watchmaker. His accomplishments on the piano earned him, at the age of seventeen, a scholarship to the Royal College of Music. During his eight years there he studied composition under Sir Charles Villiers Stanford. Tapp was the pianist at the first performance of his own composition *Symphonic Variations for Piano and Orchestra on Tom Bowling* in June 1905 at the Queen's Hall in London. Herbert Lambert wrote of his school friend's broad musical taste, great mind and strong personality which, he believed, would enthuse and inspire the orchestra in Bath.[223] Tapp's 'catholicity of taste' was commended after his debut concert in the Pump Room where works by Mendelssohn, Mussorgsky, Daff and Wagner were played.

Of visiting soloists in the Pump Room concerts that followed, one was the pianist Marie Novello, the thirteen-year old adopted sister of Ivor Novello. Unable to speak German, she was at first rejected as a pupil in Vienna by Leschetizky, but after determinedly learning the language she became one of his final pupils. Tragically, Marie died at a young age from throat cancer. Louis Zimmerman, Professor of Violin at the Royal Academy of Music, performed Beethoven's *Violin Concerto* with the orchestra. Frank Tapp proudly maintained that guest vocalists to the Pump Room were 'chosen from among the best in the country . . . many have appeared as principals at Covent Garden Opera . . . and a large proportion are engaged for the Queen's Hall Promenade Concerts'.[224]

Tapp's remit for the Pump Room Orchestra in Bath was to 'plan a concert list for the whole season lasting eight months, consisting of varied types of programmes . . . '[225] A strict classical music enthusiast, he conducted all the Beethoven and Tchaikovsky symphonies and others by Dvorak, Brahms and Franck. Weekday afternoon concerts in the Concert Room were augmented in the Pump Room with public Wednesday morning rehearsals. There were two 'Special' performances on Saturdays with guest vocalists, in addition to popular weekday evening and special concerto concerts. 'Period' concerts with dances and suites from the eighteenth century were also offered. Performed twice in the Pump Room on November 13th 1913 was Tapp's *Symphony No 1 in E, 'The Tempest'*, his first large-scale work.

Joseph Bossi was now one of the orchestra's longest serving members; he had joined the orchestra a year before Tapp was born. A Memorandum of Agreement in 1913, signed in the director's flourishing hand, affirms that, as first trumpeter Bossi's weekly wage was three pounds. The Baths Committee stipulated the terms in this Agreement: dress code; disciplinary action if 'in a state of inebriety'; fines to be imposed if late for a performance and a week's notice if 'not competent to perform the music allotted to him'. Bossi had been a member of the orchestra for over thirty years. (His granddaughter Pam Hawker, at the age of eighty, recognised the identity of the witness on the Agreement as Alfred Wetton the 'well known Bath fishmonger'!)

Memorandum of Agreement made this   day of   *1913*

Between FRANK TAPP of the City of Bath, Musical Director of
the Bath Corporation Pump Room Concerts (hereinafter referred to as the
Musical Director) of the one part and   *Joseph Bossi*
of   of the other part.

The said FRANK TAPP agrees to engage the said   *Joseph Bossi*
to play the   *trumpet (1st)*   as a
member of the Pump Room Orchestra at a Salary of   *Three pounds*
£3 = 0 = 0 per week from the   *20th*   day of   *September*
to the   *9th*   day of   *May*   next, such Salary to be
paid on Friday in every week at the City Treasurer's Office, Guildhall, between
the hours of 10 a.m. and 3 p.m.

The said   *Joseph Bossi*   agrees to accept the
engagement on the terms named and to submit to the Rules and Regulations
set forth in the Schedule hereto.

In the event of the said   *Joseph Bossi*   not being
in the opinion of the Musical Director (whose decision thereon shall be conclusive)
competent to perform the music alloted to him, the said Musical Director shall be
at liberty with the sanction of the Chairman of the Roman Promenade Sub-
Committee of the Hot Mineral Baths and Pump Room Committee (hereinafter
referred to as the Baths Committee) of the Council of the said City of Bath to cancel
this agreement with the said   *Joseph Bossi*
after one week's notice.   As witness the hands of the said
parties.

Signed   *Frank Tapp*

Signed   *Joseph Bossi*

Witness   *Alfred Wetten*

Memorandum of Agreement: the re-engagement of Joseph Bossi, trumpeter, as a
member of the Pump Room Orchestra (courtesy of Pam Hawker)

No such Agreement was offered that year by the Baths Committee
to the German violinist Otto Heinrich. Three years earlier, in beautiful
penmanship, Otto had lovingly scribed the names of his large family
on the Census form, and declared his occupation as 'Musician (violin)

orchestral – City Band'. An official transcription of his surname as Hinricks was a sad indictment of the time. The First World War marked the end of his quarter of a century sojourn with the orchestra, and many happy and fulfilling years as a Bath musician, violinmaker and teacher. Otto, branded an 'alien' by the authorities, was 'threatened with internment and bleak times for his family of ten children'.[226]

Tapp conducted his symphony *The Tempest* in Bournemouth in November 1914 and both *The Times* and *Musical Times* commented on its seventy-minute length. But the latter enthused – 'Such are the fertility of ideas and the quality of the workmanship, that its appeal was fully sustained'.[227] When his composition *Symphonic Variations for Pianoforte and Orchestra* was performed at the final Pump Room

Otto Heinrich outside his house in Victoria Terrace, Bath 1910 (courtesy of Richard Barnard)

concert of the season in May 1915, Frank Tapp was said to have played the solo part 'with undeniable brilliance'.[228] Bath's Mayor expressed his appreciation for Tapp's efforts in seasons past, and that he was looking forward in anticipation to seasons to come.

Just two months later, with war darkening the nation, the Council became divided over whether or not it could afford both an outdoor summer band and a winter orchestra that had been performing in a half empty Concert Room. Tapp's orchestra was obliged by the Corporation to play in several of Bath's gardens in a trial 'to judge the suitability of al fresco concerts'. The sound of the orchestra in Victoria Park, advised the *Bath Chronicle,* should 'be brought well out to enable the occupants of carriages in the afternoons to enjoy the music without alighting [as the] patrons form a well-recognised class whom it would be unwise in the extreme to disappoint'. At a crisis meeting, a suggestion to 'scrap Tapp' was dismissed by those councillors who defended him as 'a man of genius', and who questioned the musical attributes of the proposer amongst much derisory laughter! Another suggestion, to have a septet, was rejected on the grounds that such an ensemble 'could be found in any ordinary hotel in the kingdom'. The notion of a twenty-seven piece band, however, 'capable of being used, if composed with some double-handled men, both indoors and out-doors' generated a frisson of excitement in the chamber. Such a new band would allow Bath to compete with other watering-places and spas: Harrogate, Scarborough and Buxton. It would require a conductor 'with an outstanding personality; a man who had a name, a man who would draw, and a man whose ability was unquestionable'. Attention at the meeting then reverted to Tapp, who was 'still a young man, and to scrap him now was neither honourable or right'.[229] Should the Council even be debating this issue 'when we are fighting for our existence as a nation?' asked the Mayor, and the proceedings ended in stalemate.

Debate it they did – a week later, when a report arguing for an 'all year round' orchestra, under one director was presented. The option of having solely one band in Bath had apparently been 'agitating the minds of the Council' for the past five years, but war forced the issue. Recently appointed as conductor of the summer band and the Bath Military Band, George Bainbridge Robinson 'offered' to direct an orchestra of twenty. A proposal that Frank Tapp be the deputy conductor 'added insult to injury' and he withdrew from the whole proceedings. 'They would not treat any other civic official as they were treating Mr. Tapp'[230] declared a distraught Alderman Baker. He then ventured into wearyingly familiar territory . . .

> *Alderman Baker:* The curse of it is that Tapp is a Bathonian (cries of dissent) . . . and that Tapp had no honour among his own people . . . and the day would come when they would be very sorry.
> *Alderman Biggs:* Why?
> *Alderman Baker:* Because he is a genius. Who is there here to judge a conductor? Who is your expert advisor? Have you any?
> *Several members:* The Public!

Testimonials in support of Tapp arrived in Bath from the esteemed composers Sirs Hubert Parry, Frederick Bridge and Charles Villiers Stanford. The latter lamented the Committee's decision to dispose of this 'loyal servant of Bath', at a time when his father's illness had imposed more responsibility on him and who had done 'splendid work' in the city. Henry Sims was among several Bath professors of music who petitioned on Tapp's behalf, rejecting Robinson's 'bid'. However, the consensus of these 'expert advisors' was buried under the collective weight of the opposition. The Musicians Union, the Bakers and Confectioners Union – 'seeing that he [G B Robinson] was prepared to

pay a living wage to his musicians and keep up the prestige of the city',
the Prudential Assurance Agents, the Bookbinders and Machine Rulers,
the Woodcutting Machinists, the Carpenters, the Engineers, and the
Operative Stonemasons Unions all favoured the change.[231] Against this
united backdrop, the National Union of Railwaymen's plea that Bath
support its local musicians, 'before engaging strangers', was dismissed
by one councillor as unrepresentative. An even more farcical scenario
presented itself with a 'test performance' staged in the Assembly
Rooms, with George Riseley, a Bristol conductor and, bizarrely, Frank
Tapp as two of three adjudicators appointed by the Music Committee.
The 'contestants' were Bainbridge Robinson, two brass players from
the Pump Room Orchestra, Joseph Russell and Joseph Bossi . . . and a
gentleman from Sheffield.

Bath was the only European spa accessible to the general public
during the war, maintained the Council, and as such, was receiving an
unprecedented number of visitors. Their needs, the Council continued
to argue, surely warranted a new scheme: an all year merged orchestra
led by a new conductor. Robinson was the man, a 'man of ability, a man
of personality, a man of no stereotyped methods'[232] – though a man the
Council was only prepared initially to offer a year's contract.

During his sojourn as director in the Pump Room, Tapp had been
proud of creating a 'delightfully homely . . . and indefinably intimate'[233]
atmosphere with the light classical and popular Saturday concerts
and their operatic selections. Under his baton the audience heard,
among other first performances, Elgar's *Enigma Variations* and Arnold
Schoenberg's *Five Orchestral Pieces*. The claim that Bath was 'unready for
Schoenberg'[234] may have swayed members of the Corporation in their
conviction that Tapp was too elitist. To be pensioned off at thirty-two
years of age in his native city must have been a humiliating experience
for a musician hailed a 'genius'.

'Restful Pictures, Good Music, Cosy Seating [and] Perfect
Ventilation' were advertised by the Vaudeville Picture Theatre on
Westgate Street. (Nearby was the West of England's first cinema built
in 1910, the Bath Electric Theatre, later re-named after Beau Nash.)
Providing the music for such films as *A Question of Trust* and the chilling
The Call of the Blood in 1921 was Frank Tapp's Vaudeville Orchestra. The
Vaudeville was only 'One minute from the Grand Pump Room' but a vast
distance separated the popular music of that era from Tapp's beloved
classics. His Vaudeville Orchestra played a mix of musical genres up
to three times a day for such films as *The Woman and the Puppet* and
The Woman in Room 13. At the end of that year, Frank Tapp's name was
absent from the Vaudeville billing for Charlie Chaplin's *A Dog's Life*!

Tapp went on to compose a significant amount of light music, including an *English Landmarks Suite* and the overture *Beachy Head*, (recorded in the 1940s among a collection of compositions reflecting newsreel mood music so popular at the time).

In his post Pump Room years, Tapp struggled for recognition by the BBC's Music Department, which advised him that his *Suite for Piano and Strings* 'needed a great deal of cutting down'. Also, his *Suite Symphonique* which he was 'convinced would broadcast splendidly'[235] was rejected by the BBC who judged it

> . . . a very laudable effort, showing fine musicianship and complete technical mastery of the medium employed. But [there is] a certain monotony in the general effect . . . somewhat pedantic in character.[236]

Internal sources revealed that Tapp criticised the BBC for the 'extraordinary treatment meted out [to him] and several other composers'.[237] In a memo to Percy Pitt, the conductor Aylmer Buesst wrote that Tapp's *Variations Fantastique (on Pop Goes the Weasle) for Piano and Orchestra* was musically a 'wonderful opportunity'. But that his *String Trio in E minor*

> . . . suffers from that defect which the composer shows in all his works – his inability to 'get out of himself' . . . with his tonality and with his mood. The resultant effect is one of almost dry pedantry and garrulousness which I am sure is at total variance with the composer's own temperament and feelings.[238]

Stolen from the back seat of Aylmer Buesst's car in London one June day in 1931, were several musical scores, including Frank Tapp's '*Symphonic Variations*'. Tapp, in his distress, suggested the BBC announce the theft on London Regional News and engage Scotland Yard 'for no re-copied score could ever seem the same to me as this one, on which I lavished nearly two years work'. [239]

In 1934, desperate for an accolade, Tapp was finally distinguished by the BBC. His piece *Metropolis* won second prize in the *Daily Telegraph's* Overture Competition. It was broadcast at a Promenade concert conducted by Sir Henry Wood in London's Queen's Hall.[240]

Tapp's earlier dissenters argued that as Music Director of the Pump Room Orchestra in Bath he was too autocratic. However his letters reveal him to have been passionately anti-elitist and anti-establishment.

The Orchestra during and after the Great War

GEORGE Bainbridge Robinson from Stockton-on-Tees was thirty-nine years old when in 1915 he was promoted to Director of the Pump Room Orchestra, while retaining the conductorship of the Summer Municipal band. The inclusive cost to ratepayers was three thousand pounds, with Robinson's annual salary being two hundred and seventy-eight pounds. An accomplished clarinettist, he had succeeded his father as conductor of the South Durham Military Band, a fact that probably impressed the Corporation in this time of war.

Ben Whitman, an American 'virtuoso, equipped with exceptional technical and intellectual gifts',[241] replaced Charles Macdonald as leader of the Pump Room Orchestra. Walter Lear had been Robinson's principal clarinettist in the Municipal Band. Rejected by the Army due to 'throat trouble', he became a second violinist in the orchestra. George Sinclair was the orchestra's solo clarinettist, a post he had in the summer band. Percussionist Thomas Head had 'held the longest record of service in the Pump Room Orchestra in which he had played for over 40 years'[242] under directors Salmon, van Praag, Heymann and Tapp. His replacement, appointed by Robinson, was from Leeds.

'Like his predecessor, Robinson did not hesitate to augment his eighteen piece orchestra with local and often amateur players.'[243] In *A Social History of English Music*, E D Mackerness wrote: 'the introduction of conscription in 1916 drew younger men away from the theatre pits and concert platform. Women musicians, however, came forward to take their place.' Three of Pump Room Orchestra cornet player Joseph Russell's sons served in the war and two of them were wounded. One was Reginald who had played the horn in the orchestra. Joseph was also a music teacher and both he and all nine of his children played several instruments. These were: cornet; trumpet; coronet; clarinet; horn; drums; contrabass; xylophone; glockenspiel; tubular bells; piano; harp; violin; tympani; 'cello and organ. Joseph's wife Lucy and two daughters, Olive and Eva, were singers. His eldest daughter Daisy was the 'harpist and pianista' in the Pump Room Orchestra. She married Walter Lear (who would later join the BBC Symphony Orchestra). As a boy, Ralph, the youngest of this uniquely musical family, entertained wounded soldiers during the war.

Concerts at the YMCA[244] in Bath gave the eight year old Alberto Semprini, who was proficient on the piano and 'cello, a platform. Alberto also played for the wounded soldiers who were convalescing in Bath hospitals. In 1917 Robinson's tenure as Music Director was extended for three years, or longer if the war should continue. The war, however, lost him one of his horn players. Arthuro Semprini, Alberto's father, enlisted in the Italian Army while his wife, Elizabeth remained in Bath and supported their three sons by teaching music from their home on Norfolk Crescent.

During the winter, under Robinson's baton, the orchestra performed six afternoon and two evening concerts in the Concert Room. While in the Pump Room a quintet of 'a piano, two violins, a violoncello and bass violin'[245] played for an hour every morning. In the summer the players were paid approximately two pounds and fifteen shillings for a twenty-four hour week. Each was expected to

> appear five minutes before the commencement of each concert in black coat and vest and dark trousers, dark tie and black boots at morning, afternoon and outdoor evening concerts and in evening dress with black-tie, dress shirt with stiff front and black boots at the evening concerts if held indoors.[246]

Provision and maintenance of all instruments 'in a state of thorough efficiency' was the responsibility of the Music Director, apart from the tubular bells and a piano, which were the Corporation's. Written consent of the Committee Chairman and Music Director was necessary before an orchestra member could accept any public or private engagement – tuition excluded.

After the war the Semprini family were re-united in Milan where Alberto's father, Arthuro, was appointed Librarian at La Scala Opera House. Demobbed musicians, some of whom had played under Robinson, returned home to Bath. Their employment prospects were poor and their cause was taken up by the Bath Trades & Labour Council.[247] Just before Christmas 1919 the engagement of Solomon 'the celebrated boy pianist' was recommended by Robinson for a special concert.

In this silent movie era, films shown at the Pump Room generated extra revenue for the Council and the orchestra. In early 1920, Bath viewers followed Sir Ernest Shackleton's team on its expedition to the Antarctic, to the accompaniment of the Pump Room Orchestra. A month later a Special Orchestra Week took a different theme each day: 'Music Inspired by Shakespeare', 'Music of the Orient', 'Slav Music' etc.

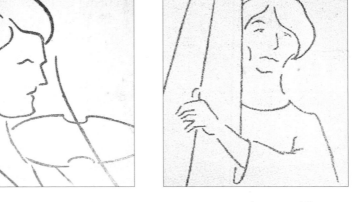

Miss Margaret Hatch by R W Oldham (*Bath Chronicle* 13 March 1920)	Miss Minnie Winter by R W Oldham (*Bath Chronicle* 28 February 1920)

In March that year R W Oldham, 'a Visitor' to the Pump Room,[248] lampooned orchestra members in quirky sketches. Those of string players Minnie Winter and Margaret Hatch are significant, as it was still unusual to see women in orchestras at that time. In the *Chronicle*'s social column Arm Chair Musings, 'The Bellman' paid tribute to Tom Fussell who had led the Pump Room Orchestra 'for some seasons' past, and who had later become deputy conductor at His Majesty's Theatre in London. Severe heart trouble forced Fussell to lay down his violin for the 'open air life on a farm'.[249]

George Bainbridge Robinson remained in post four years beyond the expiration of his first year contract. He helped to promote new music festivals, including a one day Welsh Festival with the 'Cymric Choristers', bravely introducing less well known compositions to Bath audiences. However, in the spring of 1920 the Baths and Pump Room Committee declared a deficit of seven thousand pounds, forcing the Council to admit 'their attempt to provide orchestra concerts was an absolute failure'.[250] Alderman Baker's warning five years earlier that the Council would come to regret the loss of Frank Tapp, was vindicated. Alderman Cooke, who had earlier failed in getting the Bristol conductor George Riseley appointed as Music Director, wistfully offered – 'last week Riseley was as virile as any man in the Council'! Baker newly posed the question how water, which costs nothing, cannot be made to pay! As the concerts were not cost effective, the Council 'unanimously decided to recommend the engagement of a septet of first class musicians . . . '[251] which could be augmented for special occasions.

Pump Room Orchestra musicians Margaret Hatch and Harald Mayall just married (*Bath Chronicle* 20th March 1920)

With drastic cuts pending, Robinson 'jumped before being pushed' and had already resigned from his post as Music Director. Wasting no time, he was to take up a new position as Musical Director to the Margate Corporation. Michael Doré performed both Brahms and Ernst violin concertos at his farewell benefit concert.

The *Bath Chronicle*'s 'Arm-Chair Muser' considered the idea of a septet 'a retrograde step', and wrote that 'the proof of the musical pudding will be in the assimilation'. That while acknowledging the charm of chamber music, he still felt Bath deserved a first-class orchestra. Torquay's decision to reduce *its* orchestra, which was in a similar plight, influenced the Council. It was estimated that a chamber ensemble in Bath would generate an annual saving of well over fifteen hundred pounds. The Pump Room's poor advertising and publicity were partly blamed for the deficit. In prestiigous Bath hotels many guests were content to listen in house to some of the 'best musicians', obviating the need to visit the Pump Room. While the unique selling point of the Grand Pump Room Hotel – (Telegrams to Pumpotel) was its claim to be 'The Only Hotel with a Lift and Stairway to the World Famous Corporation Baths' appealing to patrons with little interest in arduous exertion.

Under Bainbridge Robinson a Pump Room Orchestra romance led to the marriage of the violinist Margaret Hatch and 'cellist Harold Mayall (also deputy conductor). In Robinson's final Pump Room Festival a few days later, another lady violinist, Mary Wallace, joined the augmented Pump Room Orchestra. Edward German conducted the orchestra on the eve of the Festival in a programme of his own works. Guest soloists were pianists Arthur de Greef and Myra Hess, violinist Bronislaw Huberman, 'cellist Guilhermina Suggia, singers Edna

EDNA THORNTON

ALBERT COATES

MYRA HESS

ARTHUR DE GREEF

BRONISLAW HUBERMAN

PETER DAWSON

GUILHERMINA SUGGIA

EDWARD GERMAN

SYLVIA NELIS

International artists: Pump Room Festival April 1920 (*Bath Chronicle* 24th April 1920)

The Pump Room Orchestra with George Bainbridge Robinson – centre. Pianist Jan
Hurst – front left – looks away from the camera (*Bath Chronicle* 20th March 1920)

Thornton (contralto), Peter Dawson (baritone) and, in the final concert
which was conducted by Albert Coates, Sylvia Nelis (soprano). Suggia's,
Huberman's and Coates's fee was forty-two pounds each, twenty times
the weekly wage of most orchestra players.

    The proposal for a septet had been ratified at a Council meeting a
month before the Festival; many of the musicians in the orchestra facing
redundancy in Bath were to join Robinson at the East Coast resort.[252]
The new conductor in the Pump Room, declared the Mayor, would be 'a
first-class man who could also bring first-class artists to Bath'.[253]

Jan Hurst and the Spa Heyday

I N a BBC Radio Four programme, *Music By the Sea*, Fritz Spiegl related Bath's volatile musical life at the start of the 'twenties, to 'a kind of barometer of shifting musical and municipal values'.[254] Post war frugality had led to the abolition of the eighteen-piece Pump Room Orchestra –'a pretty severe trouncing' according to Mr Scholes of the *Observer*.

Jan Hurst had been a solo pianist under Bainbridge Robinson for two seasons, and in the summer months was Musical Director of the Victoria Pier concerts in Blackpool. 'A fine musician and master of

Jan Hurst the New Musical Director (*Bath Chronicle* 13th March 1920)

the pianoforte',[255] Hurst was appointed conductor of the Pump Room Musicians for the 1920 season. Taught to play the piano by his father, Hurst had studied at the Northern College of Music under Frederick Dawson and Egon Petri.[256] As a young pianist, Hurst was an accompanist in the Eastbourne and Scarborough orchestras and 'for a while [accompanied] the famous singer Clara Butt'.[257] During the Great War 'he enlisted in the Royal Army Service Corps and his talents were soon recognised. He was placed in charge of musical entertainments [with] at his disposal a large Service orchestra and choir.'[258]

In his new role as Director of the Pump Room Musicians, Hurst's salary was three hundred and fifty pounds for a thirty-four week autumn and winter season. Only two members of Robinson's orchestra, the violist Edwin Kierton and Joe Russell playing double bass, had been retained by Hurst. Joining them were the violinist and deputy conductor John Roberts, violinist S. Watkinson, 'cellist Lionel Taylor, and pianist Fred Dunworth. The Council relied on 'getting [each player] at six guineas a week – the minimum rate of the union being £6'.[259] Augmenting the group when required was the cornet and trumpet player Joe Bossi. During the summer Bossi played under Hurst when he conducted in Buxton and also took a band of his own to Cromer in Norfolk.

The Pump Room Septet. Back row l to r - Lionel Taylor, S. Watkinson, Edwin Kierton, Joseph Russell. Seated l to r – John Roberts, Jan Hurst (stylishly clad but bearing an almost raffish demeanour) and Fred Dunworth (*Bath Chronicle* 2nd October 1920)

Visitors to Bath during the autumn and winter season were treated to a variety of musical combinations: piano trios, string quartets, piano quintets and accompanied songs with guest vocalists. Despite the Corporation's fear that jazz, the popular music of the day, would creep into the programme, the new arrangement met with general approval.

Hurst's first festive season as conductor was marked by an afternoon *Thé Dansant*, a New Year's Eve Party and a New Year *Messiah* with the Pump Room Musicians and Pump Room Choir. Soloists were Hilda Stowar (soprano), May Keene (contralto), E H Head (tenor) and Glyn Eastman (baritone). Hurst, as Director, still performed on the piano with the Pump Room Musicians. In one concert featuring John Ireland's *Violin Sonata in A minor*, the composer was sitting in the Pump Room audience. Hurst asked Ireland if he would play the piano part, as he 'was not sure of it anyhow . . . '.[260]

'The Library of Vision' cinema at the Assembly Rooms, hoping to profit from a mushrooming industry, not only engaged an orchestra but also housed a 'Grand' American Aeolian Organ. Audiences could choose between the ABC Beau Nash and Vaudeville cinemas on Westgate Street, the Oldfield Park Picture House or, as in 1921 for example, they could catch showings of *The Will* and *The Manchester Man* in the hallowed atmosphere of the Pump Room.

Edward German conducted a 'specially augmented' Pump Room Orchestra in two concerts of his works in the Pump Room during April 1921. The previous year's glittering litany of guest artists returned in May for a Pump Room Festival devoted to modern British music; it included The Glastonbury Players' performance of Purcell's *Dido and Aeneas*. In critic Eric Blom's[261] generally favourable review, he remarked on a 'somewhat parochial feeling as soon as one entered the Pump Room'. Adversely affected by a rail strike, the Festival's disappointingly poor attendance belied the emergence of a new spa heyday in Bath. It was heralded by a councillor who had arrived in Bath from Buxton some years earlier.

John Hatton, the Bath Spa Committee chairman and Director of Baths, was described by Hurst as 'the finest manager anybody ever had'.[262] Hatton's fusion of cultural promotion and public relations was reminiscent of the visionary flair of Beau Nash, who he later reincarnated in his skilfully crafted public lectures. The motivational greeting card, sent to his staff every year in gratitude for their efforts, was 'one of the many reasons for the high regard the staff had of him'.[263]

When Hatton engaged Professor Thomas Dunhill from the Royal College of Music to talk on 'The Principles of Chamber Music', the lecture was illustrated with music played by the Pump Room Musicians. Hatton encouraged young people to visit the Pump Room by inviting under-sixteen year olds living within three miles to enter a piano competition.

'A pearl beyond price' was Kenneth Young's accolade to John Hatton in his endearingly affectionate tribute *Music's Great Days in the Spas and Watering-places*. Young questions whether any other spa orchestra at that time would have dared

John Hatton, Director of Baths at his desk overlooking the King's Bath (Courtesy of Tony Hatton)

to perform the work of the eccentric Glastonbury composer, Rutland Boughton! Under Hatton's management, Jan Hurst expanded the Pump Room Musicians into a small intimate orchestra offering a regular programme of afternoon tea concerts, popular evening concerts, *Thés Dansants*, trio and string quartet recitals. The latter were invariably performed by violinist John Roberts, viola player Edwin Kierton and newcomers, violinist Frank Platt and 'cellist Percy Auty.

As a double bass player, Joe Russell formed the transitory Russell Trio, restoring Morning Music to the Pump Room in May 1922. Arrangements by Jan Hurst were played. In the Pump Room Festival that year Pump Room Orchestra leader John Roberts performed John Ireland's Violin and Piano Sonata, with the composer again playing the piano. The orchestra's profile was further raised at the end of 1923 when it accompanied contralto Astra Desmond in concert. Briefly joining this highly regarded twelve-piece ensemble as a deputy in 1924 was a nineteen-year old violinist from Bristol. The Pump Room would later play a significant part in Sidney Jones's later career.

John Hatton communicated with the public through his *Weekly Notes* printed in the Pump Room programmes. They might offer a glimpse into Bath's Saxon past or share an extract of a letter from a visitor. One lady, for example, wrote of her pleasure in the music

> The String Quartette plays every morning in the Pump Room. The Pump Room Musicians play every day, and Jan Hurst arranges delightful programmes. Considering the small number of musicians the effects he gets are wonderful. The chamber concerts were a great treat to us, and so was a recital for two pianos by Jan Hurst and Fred Dunworth.

For those less inclined towards Morning Music, the Sun Terrace in 1925 was an alternative option. 'Facing due South and overlooking the Great Roman Bath . . . [it is] a delightful place to sit and read the morning papers, or enjoy a cup of coffee'.

Seventeen musicians were billed in the Pump Room Orchestra's 1925 autumn and winter season programme. Music Director Jan Hurst's outstanding accomplishment was in restoring the orchestra to its former glory, while continuing to deliver a full chamber music programme. Earning the attention of the BBC, Jan Hurst did his first broadcast in Bath. The *Bath Chronicle* wrote

> What Jan Hurst has done for the musical life of Bath cannot be overestimated. That he has brought the Pump Room concerts

up to a pitch as high as any in their long and splendid history cannot be gainsaid. Little wonder, then, that music lovers, appreciative of that fact, crowded his concerts on Saturday. Packed and intensely enthusiastic audiences both afternoon and evening were a tribute a like to his musicianly ability and his charming personality. That he will direct the City's winter music for many years is the earnest hope of everyone who has come under the spell of his baton.

Visitors taking tea on the Sun Terrace c. 1925 (courtesy of Robert Hyman/Bath Central Library

Composers Sir Charles Stanford and Edward German, who in a letter to John Hatton wrote of his 'many happy memories of Bath'[264], were familiar guests in the Pump Room. The orchestra also played under the prestigious batons of Sirs Edward Elgar and Thomas Beecham. Pianist Arthur Rubenstein performed recitals there in 1926 and 1929. After one particular concert, Beecham was reported to have 'congratulated Jan Hurst upon the direction of such an Orchestra'.[265] Formidable former suffragette Dame Ethel Smythe announced that it 'was a real pleasure for me to conduct as it was obvious that they had very carefully rehearsed my stuff'.[266] Other guest artists were violinist Daniel Melsa, who played the Brahms Concerto; three esteemed pianists, Alfred Cortot, Benno Moisewitsch and Solomon (Cutner; and the Lener Quartet (later known as 'the great quartet of the thirties'[267]), prior to its 'Extensive American Tour.'

Jan Hurst dovetailed directing the Pump Room Orchestra during the Bath season with summer engagements elsewhere. He left the Victoria Pier in Blackpool (a location not far from the source of his composition *Windermere Idyll*), after eight summer seasons in order to direct the orchestra at Bridlington's Floral Pavilion. Hurst also managed to promote his own benefit concerts in Buxton – an unfathomable workload.

In Bath during the 'twenties many Pump Room concerts were dignified by female soloists. Among them were violinists Leila Doubleday and Marie Hall, the pianist Edith Walton, the singer Dorothy D'Orsay, contraltos Astra Desmond and Margaret Balfour and the 'Distinguished English Soprano' Dora Labbette – whose affair with Thomas Beecham became public knowledge.[268] Beatrice Harrison, who gave the first radio broadcast of Elgar's 'cello concerto under his baton, wrote of her 'great admiration for Hurst's beautiful conducting of the Delius *Double Concerto*',[269] composed for her and her violinist sister May.

Tragic and unlucky incidents darkened all three Pump Room Orchestra performances of Frank's *D minor Symphony* during Hurst's tenure. An elderly lady dropped dead at the first; a cellist tripped and broke his leg on the way to the stage for the second and during the third, someone drowned in the Baths. 'Hurst never played it again.'[270] Although well liked in Bath, not all his musical selections were popular. In the interval of a concert where the young Arthur Bliss was conducting his own work, a peppery Victorian subscriber was encountered stomping up and down the corridor in a rage. Asked if he had enjoyed the concert, the gentleman replied 'Well if that's Bliss, give me Hell!'.[271] More palatable to some Bathonians was Hurst's own Intermezzo *Bells o' Somerset* played at summer concerts in the parks.[272] His predecessor Frank Tapp's composition, *Woodland Echoes*, was played by the Pump Room Orchestra in an afternoon concert in early 1928.

Billed as the Musical Event of the Season, the Pump Room Orchestra joined forces in February 1929 with the Bournemouth Municipal Orchestra. to perform a concert with sixty players at the Theatre Royal. In April that year, Columbia Gramophone sponsored a recital in which pianist Wilfred Wade played a solo piece by Chaminade. Toward the end of this season Jan Hurst played Mendelssohn's *Piano Concerto*, and with Wilfred Wade, Bach's *Concerto for Two Pianofortes in C major.*

Wilfred Wade, pianist
(courtesy of Shirley
George)

At the end of each Pump Room Orchestra season Hurst played Haydn's *'Farewell' Symphony* with all the stage effects; electric lights and chandeliers were extinguished. Each musician was provided with a candle on his stand by which to read the score. In the last movement as each finished his part, he extinguished his candle and stole softly from the platform leaving the conductor alone: solemnly, he extinguished his own candle, and departed. The season was over.[273]

Sadly, in 1929 Hurst's own sojourn in Bath was also over. He left, to his eternal regret, on an initial six-month contract as Musical Director to the Brighton Corporation. In this new role he would conduct the new Brighton Winter Season Orchestra with its twenty-seven performers and 'brighter' prospects. The *Bath Chronicle and Herald* echoed the city's reaction to this 'promotion'

> Bath has never had a more popular conductor of its music . . . and Hatton confesses that he will miss Hurst's ready help very much indeed. That Hurst is a clever musician and a great credit to Bath's musical history is agreed in all musical quarters . . . [274]

The Brighton Aquarium's dreadful acoustics and suffocating heat were castigated by Thomas Beecham as guest conductor during Jan Hurst 's sojourn in Brighton. However, Beecham's approval of the orchestra failed to save it from being axed by an 'ante-diluvian'[275] Town Council in April 1934. Popular with the Brighton public and praised by journalists for his elegant stick technique, Jan Hurst was forced to move on. In the interim it was back to Bath and his 'cathedral'– his beloved Pump Room. There he directed his own Octet with soprano Hilda Blake and his Jan Hurst Dance Band. But it was in Brighton, the inspiration for his composition *Brighton Sea Step*, where that summer he married the soprano Olive Tessier. Composed for the occasion, Hurst's own *Wedding March*, 'rich with the melodic effect which he so well knows how to produce . . . swelled through the aisles as the bridal procession retired'.[276] In typical chameleon fashion, Jan Hurst soon rebranded a new orchestra and 'like the homecoming of a lost relative',[277] was welcomed enthusiastically in Bridlington. There he filled the Floral Pavilion every night to overflowing, prompting ecstatic reviews in the local press. Following this

> from 1936 until the outbreak of the Second World War [Hurst] returned, with great distinction to Blackpool's South Pier which had formerly been known as the Victoria Pier.[278]

Edward Dunn & the Halcyon Days of the Pump Room Orchestra

THE post of Director of the Pump Room Music was advertised. Accompanying Hurst's departure were string players John Roberts, Frank Platt and Edwin Kierton while the 'cellist Lionel Taylor had already left. The *Bath Chronicle and Herald*, in the interim period, was optimistic that vacancies would be filled, as 'introduction of the talking film has meant that many musicians who are real artists are at present out of employment'.[279]

James Kershaw, violinist (courtesy of Shirley George)

Lawrence Lackland was one of the large battalion of musicians whose livelihoods had relied upon silent film. He joined the Pump Room Orchestra during this transition period along with another violinist, James Kershaw and horn player William B Waller. Lawrence's father, Frederick, had played violin and viola in the St Helens Orchestra under the young Thomas Beecham's baton in their home town.

With over a decade of playing the cornet and trumpet together, Joseph Russell moved on – to Brighton with Hurst, but Bossi remained. Alberto Semprini (the son of Bossi's earlier colleague, horn player Arthuro Semprini), graduated from the Conservatorio Verdi in

William B Waller, horn player (courtesy of Shirley George)

Milan with a Doctorate of Music in High Composition and went on occasionally to conduct at La Scala.

Art deco-esque posters publicised a special Festival at the start of the new season in 1929 celebrating two and a quarter centuries of Pump Room music.[280] John Hatton pronounced that

> Nowhere but Bath could hold such a celebration . . . but in the provision of music and dancing, and the varied entertainments which combine to make the Bath Pump Room a unique centre of interest there is no mere reliance on the past. This Festival is intended equally to show the continuity through all these two-and-a-quarter centuries and the present activities of the Pump Room Music and to demonstrate afresh the interest and real pleasure that can be given even by a small orchestra inspired by great traditions.[281]

The 'anniversary' concert season was further enhanced by 'Georgian' programmes in striking red, symbolising a new era for the Pump Room Orchestra, under a new Director's baton.

As a youth Edward Dunn had played clarinet in the Hallé Orchestra.[282] His debut season at the Pump Room culminated with Bath's first Festival of Contemporary Arts in the spring of 1930. Violinist Albert Sammons performed the Delius *Violin Concerto* to glowing reviews and John Ireland returned to the Pump Room to play his *Piano and Violin Sonata* with the Pump Room Orchestra's new leader and deputy conductor, Harry Lipman. 'Music in Bath' was the theme, interpreted in works of art, exhibitions of ancient instruments and recitals of modern poetry. Attracting widespread press attention, the Festival was commended for exposing 'cutting edge contemporary British art.'[283]

A showman as well as a 'brilliant' musician, Dunn introduced *Happy Nights* where the new timpanist Harold Smith entertained the audience with Stanley Holloway monologues and 'was wont to don a false nose and sing comic songs'. Costing sixpence to attend, these popular Monday evening concerts in the Concert Room attracted up to fifteen hundred people. The Sunday night Pump Room Orchestra concerts, also under

Harold Smith, timpanist
(courtesy of Shirley George)

(right) THE PUMP ROOM ORCHESTRA WITH EDWARD DUNN flanked by Councillors Hatton (centre right) and Hacker (centre left) (courtesy of the Bath Record Office, Bath & North East Somerset Council)

(below) A satirical look at Pump Room Orchestra musicians 'after hours'. (Courtesy of Pam Hawker)

Dunn's baton, became so successful that to accommodate the numbers they were moved to the Pavilion. Interestingly, Edward Dunn was also inclined to the didactic. His series of afternoon pre-concert 'Non-Technical' talks on the *'Construction and Musical Appreciation of the Symphony to be Performed'*, would have appealed to a more scholarly audience. One concert of Beethoven's overture *Coriolanus*, Coates's Fantasy *'The Three Bears'* and Grieg's *Peer Gynt* was 'preceded by a descriptive analysis together with practical illustrations by Dunn'.[284]

Dunn's sixteen piece orchestra had a new oboist, Harold Dixon; his son, also named Harold, wrote of his father's work

Harold Dixon, Oboe and Cor Anglais (Courtesy of Shirley George)

Lawrence Lackland (Courtesy of Shirley George)

The orchestra had an exhausting schedule. It performed symphony concerts on Monday and Tuesday evenings and Tuesday afternoons. It gave two more symphony concerts, with soloists on Wednesdays and there were concerts every day and in the mornings and afternoons. Three of the musicians formed the Pump Room Trio to play during coffee and tea time. Musicians had one day off a week and the principal oboist was paid six guineas a week.[285]

If the cartoons by C Candy[286] are a true reflection, Edward Dunn's Pump Room musicians had no problem unwinding offstage!

Lawrence Lackland made his debut in Bath as a soloist, playing the Max Bruch violin concerto no. 1 to enthusiastic acclaim. Trombonist John Rodgers, xylophonist (also timpanist and percussionist) Harold Smith, flautist (also piccolo) Ernest Woodward, 'cellist Brier Vestey and trumpeter Fred Davison all played solo pieces with the orchestra. Violinist Isolde Menges, who according to the *Daily Telegraph* had 'all the freshness and enthusiasm of buoyant youth', was a guest soloist at these concerts.

In Spring 1931 there was a Music Festival week; each day offered a different theme based on a composer such as Beethoven or Tchaikovsky. A concert of First Performance Works in Bath premiered Elgar's 'new' *Pomp and Circumstance March No. 5* and Gershwin's *Rhapsody in Blue*. American singer and future activist Paul Robeson sang with the orchestra. Well known by many for his rendition of *Old Man River* in the musical *Show Boat*, in Bath he was billed as 'The World's Greatest Negro Actor Vocalist'.

On route home from work in a florist's shop near Milsom Street, young Bathonian Irene Wilmott would see the same violinist from the Pump Room Orchestra. Later, at an Assembly Rooms ball the tall young man contrived to dance every turn with her. Irene and her friends also loved the Pump Room balls where, in their full-length gowns they would precariously walk around the Roman Baths during the interval, discreetly pursued by the orchestra musicians!

Henry Mayo Bateman's 1931 cartoon 'The Man who asked for a Double Scotch in the Grand Pump Room at Bath' shows a daytime

(*left*) Ernest Woodward, flute;   (*centre*) Fred C Davison, trumpet; (*right*) Brier Vestey, 'cello (all Courtesy of Shirley George)

(*left*) The Sun Terrace in the 1920s; (*centre*) Rachmaninoff's autograph; (*below left*) Solomon's signed photograph; (*below right*) Paul Robeson's signed photograph (all except Sun terrace courtesy of Bath Record Office, Bath & North East Somerset Council)

Pump Room with smartly dressed ladies and gentlemen clutching their glasses of spa water, affronted that alcohol should be requested in such a sanctified place. Up in the gallery music stands and empty chairs are evident.

> During the morning drinking hour, when the small orchestra plays in the Musicians' Gallery, the scene is very animated. The room has recently been entirely redecorated, every detail being carried out in strict accord with the period of the building. A perfect spring dance floor has also been laid down and the Grand Pump Room at Bath, famous shrine of healing by day, becomes at night a exquisite setting for the delightful Pump room dances.[287]

In his office overlooking the King's Bath, John Hatton worked tirelessly with his Spa Committee to foster amicable support from the public. One enterprising competition awarded a prize of a guinea to the person who could identify the most pieces played by the Pump Room Orchestra. Entrants in another challenge were asked, 'in order of general appeal' to name the thirteen instruments played by members of the orchestra. Later, in 1932, 'Ladies in the Audience' were invited to submit their own composition. The winner would conduct 'the fifteen gentlemen of the Pump Room Orchestra' and receive half a guinea. So popular was this idea men were invited to do the same, but for double the prize money. It was five years before equity prevailed. Admission to an 'Ordinary Orchestra Concert including Tea' was one shilling and threepence, and twice that for a Combined Concert and Dance. Under John Hatton's management the Pump Room delivered a whole package of entertainment at a range of prices accessible to many Bathonians and visitors alike.

In concert intervals, refreshments were served on the Sun Terrace overlooking the Great Bath. This was the area in the late 'twenties and early 'thirties presided over by the manageress whose airs earned her the nickname 'Royal Crescent'. Dorothy Smith collected autographs, press clippings and photos of over forty visiting musicians and celebrities. The signatories included Randolph Churchill, Paul Robeson, Isobel Baillie (soprano), Mohawk Chief Os-ke-non-ton – 'the celebrated barytone', Samuel Coleridge-Taylor, violinists Albert Sammons and Daniel Melsa and pianists Solomon and Sergei Rachmaninoff. (It was at the Bath Pavilion that Rachmaninoff performed, according to the late Kenneth Gregory). Jan Hurst's moniker was a musical sketch of 'Bells of Somerset', and Edward Dunn signed a photo of himself 'To Dorothy with kindest remembrances'.

John Reid was a 'cellist in the Pump Room Orchestra for one season. Vivien Griffiths, his daughter, informs us that the orchestra delivered a ' much more heavyweight repertoire than [she] had imagined, e.g. a Beethoven symphony cycle in 1930, a Brahms cycle in 1932, Schumann symphonies, violin concertos of Brahms, Lalo . . . '.

This is the world that local Bath girl Irene had spiralled into as Lawrence Lackland's fiancée. When she joined Lawrence during his 1931 summer engagement in Blackpool, it was for her the orchestra played *'Goodnight Irene'* at the end of each evening's concert. The couple married at St Saviour's Church in Bath on a May morning in 1932. Years later Irene would tell her grandchildren that never could she imagine that the violinist billed on posters displayed on the buses she rode in Bath would become her husband. A trip to Bristol, on one of Lawrence's rare evenings off, found them in the choir seats of a packed Colston Hall listening to a 'wonderful violinist' called

Lawrence Lackland and Irene Wilmott on their Wedding Day (Courtesy of Shirley George)

Fritz Kreisler. Their daughter Shirley would later hear her parents reminiscing over the Pump Room jazz band in which her violinist father played the saxophone 'and somebody by the name of Arthur Clark conducted . . . '. Clark also conducted the Pump Room Dance Orchestra, occasionally billed as the Dance Section of the (Pump Room) Orchestra, later sharing the role with Harold Smith – the entertaining timpanist from the *Happy Nights* concerts.

The Spa Committee agreed to a quartet 'or quintet' playing in the Pump Room during the summer months, and a trio playing Morning Music on the Terrace of the Roman Promenade, 'during the no-band weeks' in 1932. But with the Great Depression in the USA looming, travel from there was curtailed and the Committee elected to cease advertising in the *New York Herald Tribune*.

A string quartet offered daily Morning Music in the Pump Room in November 1932 and continued to do so sporadically for a couple of

(left) John Bennison, Clarinet; *(centre)* Harry Lipman, Leader and Deputy conductor; *(right)* William (Bill) Tweddle, Violin and Deputy Leader (all courtesy of Shirley George)

years. In the Pump Room Orchestra clarinettist John Bennison was joined by Leslie Golledge who also played the saxophone. Golledge was soon conducting the dance section of the orchestra and performing solo saxophone in the Sunday evening concerts. Harry Lipman was now deputy conductor as well as leader while William (Bill) Tweddle was the deputy leader. In March 1933 a quartet with Harry Lipman – first violin, James Kershaw – second violin, Brier Vestey – 'cello, and Lawrence Lackland playing the viola, performed Schubert's *Death and the Maiden* in the Pump Room.

One of the world's finest viola soloists at that time was promoting the virtues of a remarkable instrument; a sixteen and three quarter inch (long) version of the viola designed by him. At one concert in Bath, the iconic Lionel Tertis tapped the long-limbed violinist Lawrence Lackland on the shoulder and made a comment as he left the podium at the interval. Whatever was said shaped Lackland's future as a viola player in a career which culminated with him performing in the Covent Garden Orchestra and touring overseas with the London Symphony Orchestra and the Royal Philharmonic.

Other guests came to the Pump Room in various guises. Poet Laureate John Masefield read his own works while Marjorie Bowya, a 'Violinist-Entertainer with Playmakers' offered a 'Riot of Music, Colour and Fun'. Wireless comedian Stainless Stephen was the compère at the closing concert of the 1933 season; it featured a solo pianoforte performance by Wilfred Wade. That same year, the Lower Rooms where William Herschel had directed concerts two centuries earlier was demolished.

Bath's musical stature grew during the mid 'thirties with performances in the city by Fritz Kreisler, Heifetz, Mischa Elman,

Beecham's London Philharmonic Orchestra and Elizabeth Schumann. Demanding sixty-eight guineas plus ten pounds for her accompanist George Reeves, she refused the Corporation's offer to provide a locally based musician. 'Distinguished violinist'[288]Jelly D'Aranyi played with the Pump Room Orchestra and Daniel Melsa returned to perform both the Beethoven and Tchaikovsky violin concertos. The Lener Quartet billed as 'the World's Greatest String Ensemble' played Mozart, Schumann and Haydn quartets in the Pump Room. Jelly D'Aranyi returned with violinist Adila Fachiri to perform with an augmented Pump Room Orchestra under Edward Dunn's baton in the opening concert of the second Festival of Contemporary Arts in the spring of 1935. Both the daughters of Budapest's chief of police, they were also great nieces of the virtuoso violinist Joseph Joachim who 'performed frequently'[289] in Bath. Paintings and etchings were hung in the Pump Room and Concert Room and writers' manuscripts were displayed. In (Agatha) Christie-esque style, a robbery of the Festival's exhibits was foiled when the security guard's torch illuminated the culprits crouched on the terrace above the Roman Baths.

That season a series of Pump Room Orchestra morning concerts was broadcast by the BBC. Dunn, who was much in demand, was the chosen conductor for the newly formed eighty strong Bath Philharmonic Orchestra at the Pavilion. Gershwin's *Rhapsody in Blue* was on the programme of a charity midnight concert also conducted by Dunn, on behalf of the new Royal United Hospital. The venue for the concert was the largest cinema ever built in Bath. The Forum 'boasted a café, a dance hall and a fifty foot proscenium arch . . . a delightful interior with dome, chandeliers, and frieze in pure 1930s style'.[290]

'Which is the Oldest Orchestra in Great Britain?' asked the *Musical Times* in September 1935. Digressing from his work on Moral and Social Hygiene in the House of Commons, N Grattan-Doyle supplied the answer – 'The Pump Room Orchestra in Bath'.[291] After six years in the Pump Room Orchestra, oboist Harold Dixon left Bath for London and its larger platforms. Dixon was not alone with ambition and a yen for pastures new. John Hatton's son Tony recalls that

> Edward Dunn was a family friend as well as a conductor of the Pump Room Orchestra. He gave my brother and me a gift at Christmas and signed himself 'Uncle Eddie'. He was a portly and slightly flamboyant man and a good raconteur. I think he was quite popular with the lady concert-goers!
>
> I remember being told one evening by our parents that he was going to call later, and when we heard the garden gate opening my brother and I got out of bed to have a look. We saw

the red glow on his cigarette as he walked down the path. The next day we were told that he had come to inform my Father of his decision to resign and go to South Africa . . . [292]

Edward Dunn left Bath in 1935 to face new challenges as Director of Music to the Corporation of Durban in South Africa, escaping the horrors of war in Europe and impending professional limbo at home.

Dunn's International Arts League of Youth Festivals in South Africa 'attracted huge audiences during the post-war years'.[293] Four times married by his late seventies, Dunn was Head of Music at the Institute of Musical Art in Johannesburg. Over thirty-five years after Tony Hatton had been so intrigued by this charismatic colleague of his father, Hatton persuaded Dunn to give a talk to the students at the school in Southern Africa where he worked, and was amused to discover that Dunn's skill as a raconteur had not faded.

The death of 'Maestro Eddie Dunn' reached *Bath Chronicle* readers from South Africa on the 1st May 1973. One was Reginald Guy who, from his home in Melksham, wrote

as if a veil had been lifted and a flood of names and memories of past concerts and recitals and the appearances at the Pump Room and Pavilion of great artists as Solomon, Melsa, Bratza, Ania Dorfman, Kreisler, Rachmaninoff, Schnabel, Heifetz and the wonderful Chopin-playing Cortot, came back to me.

These were the halcyon days of the Pump Room Orchestra under Edward Dunn, with Harry Lipman (leader), Brier Vestey ('cellist), Bossi and Davis (trumpets), Lister (trombone), Woodward (flute) and Wilfred Wade, that fine pianist. I well remember him playing all the Beethoven piano concertos, but the driving force behind this highly professional orchestra, of course, was their director Edward Dunn.

His conducting of Wagner drew audiences that queued all around the concert hall corridors, spilling out into the Abbey Churchyard. He prefaced his Wagner concerts with a 15 minute talk on the various operas, his favourite being *Tristan*, and the performance he drew from this small orchestra in the Prelude to *Tristan* is one of my most unforgettable memories.

He was, like many brilliant musicians, a controversial figure in private life, but to me, a mere youngster of 18 years, and to many others, he was a fine musician, and brought to Bath and the surrounding towns an opportunity to hear worldwide renowned artists under his baton.[294]

The Bossi Legacy

THE *Musical Times* in December 1932[295] reported Joseph Bossi's Jubilee Concert in Bath where he was presented with

> a silver casket engraved 'To Joseph Bossi, A Tribute of appreciation on the completion of 50 years Membership of the Pump Room Orchestra from the Spa Committee and Director.

and in honour of the 'great delight given to at least two generations of music lovers in the city and the neighbourhood', a Special Fund was opened.

Joseph Bossi, Trumpet
(courtesy of Shirley George)

Italian born Bossi had performed under the batons of William Salmon, Van Praag, Frank Tapp, Jan Hurst and Edward Dunn. Originally from Guastalla in northern Italy where his brother was the town's Bishop, Joe came to England with 'the Italian Band'.[296] Once married and settled in Bath, to secure their Roman Catholicism, his children's education was divided between Italy and England. His son Reginald attended King Edward School between 1907 and 1920. Marjorie (Margaretta), Joe's daughter, became a professional singer in a career which took her to London and back to Italy. Reginald went on to run a watch and clockmaker business, Bossi's of Bath on Trim Bridge. In 1952 the *Horological Journal* published an article (a collaboration between Bossi and his fellow horologist Tony Robinson) on the specifications of the Pump Room's Tompion clock.

> Considering that the clock and its maker are both so famous, it seems strange that little has been written in description of the technical features of the movement of the Bath Tompion . . . I

Joseph Bossi with his son Reginald (top left) and his daughter Marjorie (top right).
Joe's baby granddaughter Pam is sitting on her mother Blanche's knee in this family
photo taken at Fairfield Rise in Bath. (courtesy of Pam Hawker)

was pleased to make a thorough inspection of the mechanism; and a further opportunity to collect information occurred when Bossi was wise and helpful enough to take very detailed notes on the movement, and has supplied me with a copy of these. It became apparent, as soon as the notes were compared with those published by Mr. R.E.M. Peach in the *Bath Chronicle* of November 9, 1893, and the other account in Britten's 'Old Clocks and Watches and Their Makers', that some quite astonishing discrepancies existed.[297]

One was the earlier claim that the 'ten-inch' large wheel containing

'over 2000 finely-cut teeth' was in fact '7 1/8 inches in diameter and has 486 teeth' . . . These figures Bossi fiercely insists are the correct ones . . . One of the most attractive features of the clock is the quiet but unostentatious dignity with which it seems to preside over the Pump Room.[298]

Reginald Bossi was contracted in 1962 to restore the famous Tompion Clock ten years after the *Horological Journal* article. Bossi's clocks were all inscribed with the insignia TEMPUS FUGIT (Time Flies). Trumpeter Joseph Bossi's time in the Pump Room Orchestra had lasted fifty years. Four generations later, brothers Joseph and Daniel demonstrate musical talent. Daniel reached Grade Eight on the trumpet, unaware that his great, great grandfather played the cornet and trumpet in the Pump Room from 1882.

Maurice Miles, the Last Conductor of the Pump Room Orchestra

THE strikingly handsome Frank Gomez – clarinettist, conductor and composer, was contracted as Director of the Pump Room Orchestra for one year following Dunn's departure. It is very likely his father was the clarinettist, Frank Gomez, the 'father of the orchestra' in Belfast and member of the original Promenade orchestra in the Queens Hall.[299] The younger Frank Gomez' 'brisk, efficient way with the lighter classics'[300] helped to put the Spa Orchestra at Whitby, which he conducted for fifteen years, 'on the musical map'.[301] *Climbing the Abbey Steps at Whitby*, Gomez's pizzicato novelty (becoming progressively slower as the one hundred and ninety nine steps are triumphed) was popular with local audiences.

The orchestra conducted by Gomez during the 1935/36, season was now down to fifteen players. Afternoon Tea Concerts and occasional Morning Music sessions continued, with Sunday and Monday evening concerts returning to the Pump Room from the Pavilion. Gomez replaced Wilfred Wade with Maurice Arnold – one of the 'splendid players in his band'[302]at Whitby. The BBC paid the Pump Room Orchestra fifteen guineas for a forty-five minute outside broadcast from the Pavilion. At the end of the season both pianists, Lawrence Lackland, and several other orchestra members went to Whitby for the summer. Like birds on the wing, musicians migrated from out of season winter spa orchestras such as Bath, to play at Blackpool, Buxton, Brighton, Bridlington, Harrogate, Scarborough and Whitby. Listeners, used to tuning in to the Empire beam for broadcasts from the greenhouse conditions of Whitby's Spa (Floral) Pavilion, could now hear the concerts on the BBC World Service.

The Pump Room Orchestra performed next door in the Bath Abbey with the Abbey Choir at its Christmas Festival in 1935. Gomez and E W Maynard the Abbey organist were, according to the Rector, Sydney Adolphus Boyd,[303] 'entitled to high praise for their skill in conducting'. The Pump Room and Victoria Art Gallery were the Spa Committee's chosen venues for the 1936 Bath Spring Festival with its ambitious Arts of the Three Centuries theme. Frank Gomez arranged the concert programmes; pianist Harriet Cohen and viola player Lionel Tertis were guest performers. There was drama, literature, architecture and a massive art exhibition where paintings purported to be by John Nash, Rodin, Rowlandson, Degas, Matisse, Picasso and Turner were for sale. One patron enthused, 'these festivals are not only very enjoyable, but have real educational value. If I lived a little nearer to Bath I should be in and out of the Pump Room every day'.[304] But against this dazzling cultural backdrop economic concerns prevailed.

The City Council's proposal to discontinue the Pump Room Orchestra, whose ill-attended evening concerts apparently resulted in a four thousand pound deficit that year, forced the Spa Committee to issue a reassuring press release. Some councillors clearly resented any expectation to attend these concerts themselves, in addition to their 'other work'.[305] The late Kenneth Gregory was dismissive of 'the vast majority of the City Fathers who never came to anything. It wouldn't matter what music the orchestra was playing. They were bored to distraction!'[306] The 'Save the Orchestra' movement lauded the popularity of the Morning Quartet sessions and the full orchestra broadcasts on Thursdays 'evidenced by the crowded gatherings!'[307] Frank Gomez' request 'to have a quintet of high standard instead of an orchestra'[308] was addressed at a public meeting. Council figures were scrutinised by one of the attendees, the marketing minded stationmaster of Bath's Great Western Railway, John Allen, who estimated that

> based upon the average Spa Committee takings over 31 weeks, plus season ticket receipts, plus the receipts of 35 broadcasts, and plus the takings at the Tuesday evening dances, and at the mornings at the Pump Room, the balance on the wrong side is just £1000, and if the total suggested advertising value of the morning broadcast each week (£1000) is taken into account, no loss at all can be attributed to the orchestra.[309]

The orchestra was saved. Perhaps to avoid future embarrassment, the Council sought the advice of the BBC in judging the applicants' merits (including those of Frank Gomez) for the post of Director of Music.

Maurice Miles, an ex choral scholar at Wells Cathedral, was selected as the new Music Director. He was soon to marry Eileen Spencer Wood, whose grandfather Thomas Henry Guppy was a librarian at Manchester's John Rylands library for nearly half a century.[310] Miles began the 1936/37 season reassuring the Patrons of the Pump Room

Maurice Miles conducting the Pump Room Orchestra (courtesy of Bath Record Office, Bath & North East Somerset)

Concerts that 'great care has been exercised in the choice of musicians to form the Pump Room Orchestra'. Several of the musicians were from the summer Spa Orchestra in Buxton where Miles was a conductor. Eight strings, five winds, three brass, a timpanist and pianist were led by newcomer violinist Norman Rouse. Other new faces in the Pump Room Orchestra were violinists James Wright and Melville Cooper, John A. Reid – violoncello, flautist Geoffrey Brook, Frank Patrick on the clarinet, E Poston on bassoon, and trumpeter J. G Reed. Lawrence Lackland, already known to Maurice Miles from summers in Buxton, hung on to his position as did trombonist Haydn Lister, timpanist Bernard Medcalf, oboist H. Wilfred Allen and clarinettist John Bennison.

The new orchestra's first concert at the Pavilion included an Offenbach Overture, a March by Souza and Puccini excerpts. Miles divided his time between the Pavilion and the Pump Room during the season from October to May. It was in Bath that Miles's first daughter Ann was born. Wilfred Wade was reunited with the orchestra as its pianist and accompanist. As a boy, Wade's son Noel recalls his father playing Morning Music during the summer months in the Pump Room with violinist Norman Rouse and 'cellist Brier Vestey (who was not in Miles's full orchestra).

Recitals and appearances of visiting guest soloists dovetailed with regular Pump Room Orchestra concerts. In October 1936, on 'A Flying Visit', Beecham brought his 'Full London Philharmonic

Maurice Miles, his wife Eileen and Ann as a baby, with his parents in law and grandparents in law (courtesy of Ann Somerset Miles)

Orchestra, the Finest Orchestra in the Kingdom'. The Lener String Quartet continued to perform in Bath. 'Cellist John Reid, and Lawrence Lackland (as a violist), were soloists in the 1936 Pavilion concerts. (Both of their daughters, Vivien Griffiths and Shirley George respectively, discovered their common legacy when they met as members of an amateur orchestra in North London years later). After just one season John Reid left the Pump Room Orchestra to join the (coincidentally named) Reid String Quartet in Edinburgh. (Visiting Bath with her son in recent years, Reid's daughter Vivien was amazed to discover there was still music in the Pump Room). Tea dances, supper dances and even children's parties continued to animate the Pump Room between symphony, light classical, popular, choral concerts and the occasional lecture.

Miles's eighteen piece Pump Room Orchestra was still considered by some to be a drain on the city's finances. Coffee concerts were introduced in the Concert Room, but patrons' complaints at not being able to hear themselves above the 'din' of music by Mozart and Beethoven characterised letters to councillors. The orchestra played on a raised platform at the north end of the Room; its acoustics were said to double the sound. Kenneth Gregory once commented 'if you wished to be heard in conversation you needed to aim diagonally at the large glass portholes in the doors in order for the sound of your voice to rebound off'. The *Ballet Rambert* dancers were 'assisted' by the Pump Room Orchestra in a 1937 Easter concert at the Pavilion. Further performances of this well received troupe gave full acknowledgement to the orchestra. To the joy of Bathonians, more recitals were given by Kreisler in the city.

A gold leaf crown, in honour of Elizabeth, wife and Queen consort of King George VI, adorns the cover of the May 1937 Pump Room Programme. Included in this programme was a personal letter

> We have not been to Bath since last Christmas but we have listened many times over the air and it is extraordinarily good this season. Maurice Miles, the conductor is doing good work and I think that even you would approve, although you have said some pretty biting things about small orchestras in England!

Preceding a broadcast of Miles's Orchestra was the famous spoonerism – 'You will now hear a concert by the Bathroom Orchestra from Pump'. The gaffe was allegedly made by BBC announcer Stuart Hibberd, but has since been attributed to an unnamed colleague in his memoirs.[311]

(*Previous page*) The Pump Room Orchestra 1935/36 season. Seated left to right: Wilfrid Wade (pianist and accompanist); Norman Rouse (leader); Maurice Miles (conductor); James Wright (sub-leader); Haydn Lister (trombone). Centre: Lawrence Lackland (viola); E Poston (bassoon); Bernard Medcalf (tympani); John A Reid (cello); Clifford Walker (violin); J G Reed (1st trumpet); Charles Sharman (2nd trumpet); John Sullivan jun (bass). Back row: Eric Holt (violin); Wilfred Allen (oboe); Geoffrey Brook (flute); Frank Patrick (2nd clarinet); John (Jack) Bennison (1st clarinet); Melville Cooper (violin). The photo was taken outside the Sun Terrace (courtesy of Vivien Griffiths);

(*Above*) Maurice Miles conducting the eighteen piece Pump Room Orchestra in the Concert Room. (courtesy of Shirley George)

By 1937 Lawrence Lackland had left his violin behind and was playing the viola in the orchestra. During his solo performance of Handel's *Concerto for Viola and String Orchestra*, a certain F.H. Fortey in the audience was inspired to compose a poem which he presented in calligraphic writing to the violist. Equally impressed was a critic at this February 1938 concert at the Pavilion, who praised Lackland for playing 'this attractive work admirably, and the peculiarly mellow tone associated with the compass of his instrument proved extremely pleasing . . . ' The same critic applauded Maurice Miles for endeavouring, with such a small string section, to perform Tchaikovsky's *Symphony Pathètique* 'in its entirety . . . Wednesday's interpretation was a pronounced artistic success. The orchestra received a well-merited ovation.'

BATH SPA ORCHESTRA.

TRIBUTE TO LAWRENCE LACKLAND
Soloist in Handel's Concerto for Viola and Orchestra.
(Improvised at the Symphony Concert, by F.H. Fortey)
Bath.

Though thou lack land none say thou dost lack skill,—
Playing the viola with such deep feeling
That Handel's lovely music ever will
Be with us as his soul thou art revealing!

Now rippling notes; now grave as life's own measure;
A silvery stream; or mighty ocean grand:
I would poetic art could tell the pleasure
The bow doth give in thy enchanter's hand!

Yet not hand only but with heart devotion
Do artistes such as thou make music live
And he who plays not—hears not—with emotion
Can never know the bliss that sweet tones give!

Lawrence Lackland Esqr
with the Writer's Compliments
Bath. Feb. 2d 1938.

Tribute to Lawrence Lackland (courtesy of Shirley George)

That year, a certain Comtesse de Vilme-Hautmont of Australia wrote 'Just Passing By' in the Pump Room Visitors Book – clearly with no inclination, in the manner of her Georgian predecessors, to forge new acquaintances.

The pale blue and grey design of the programme cover for The Bath Spring Music Festival of 1938 was based on Pinchbeck's fan exquisitely painted two centuries earlier. It showed the first 'band of musick' playing up in the gallery in the Pump Room. An exhibition of eighteenth century wind instruments advanced the theme. Three concerts performed by an augmented forty-piece Pump Room Orchestra were broadcast by the BBC. The conducting of the last concert of the Festival was divided between Eric Coates, Montague Phillips and Haydn Wood. Coates conducted his own works, the *Saxo-Rhapsody for Alto Saxophone and Orchestra* (Deryk Fawcett as soloist) and the *Three Bears Phantasy*.[312]

Perennial rumblings of cutbacks continued while Maurice Miles was occupied with doubling his musicians to form the Pump Room Festival Orchestra. Norman Rouse was to lead and Sir Henry Wood to conduct on the first night. Guest conductors followed on subsequent evenings. 'Cellist Beatrice Harrison was a soloist under Miles's baton and the orchestra was billed on equal terms with Sir Thomas Beecham's London Philharmonic Orchestra. While Festival concerts took place in the Pavilion – scathingly dismissed by Beecham as a bus garage,[313] morning harpsichord trio recitals could be enjoyed in the Pump Room. This early Bath Music Festival acknowledged the excellence of the Pump Room musicians, with Maurice Miles and his Orchestra commended by music critics in the national press. Other artists in the Festival included violinist Albert Sammons, the Fleet Street Choir and 'Henry Hall and his Band' who already boasted a recording with Columbia Records. Sir Henry Wood praised the Festival and Bath's musical life in general, and remarked that if he were undergoing a 'cure', Bath would be the place that he would come.

Flushed with pride, the Spa Committee re-engaged Maurice Miles and the eighteen orchestra members for the 1938/39 season, agreeing to increase leader Norman Rouse's weekly salary by ten shillings a week. The profile of this orchestra had spread far and wide with requests from Jan Hurst and Edward Dunn to conduct for just one performance. Dunn's generous Durban salary funded regular visits to Bath. Demonic associations with the Franck Symphony, emanating from Hurst's time, were finally dispelled. 'We played the Franck Symphony on the 13th April, 1938 . . . and in spite of the ominous date nothing untoward happened to either the orchestra or the audience . . . ' retired flautist Geoffrey Brook wrote many years later to the *Radio Times*.

Sir Henry Wood and Sir Adrian Boult both pledged to appear in the 1939 Bath Spring Festival and Albert Sammons promised a violin concerto. Buoyed along on a wave of optimism and fuelled with new ideas from John Hatton's tour of the continental spas two years earlier, the Corporation was determined to return the city to its glory days. But these were uncertain times. Spa Committee minutes recorded occasional references to the building of air raid shelters and potential benefits of the 'Bath cure' to servicemen in the likelihood of war. In March 1939, the Spa Committee

> carefully reviewed the situation arising out of a lack of support accorded to the splendid Orchestra provided during the winter months and recommended that the orchestra be not re-engaged for the next winter season.

Regardless, the 1939 Spring Festival at the Pavilion went ahead with modest publicity. Sirs Wood and Boult fulfilled their obligations. Albert Sammons' Elgar *Violin Concerto*, accompanied by a forty-two piece augmented Pump Room Orchestra (with fourteen musicians from London), was broadcast.

New York's *Time* magazine extravagantly reported in its April 1939 issue, that

> Last week word leaked out that the famous Pump Room Orchestra [now conducted by handsome Maurice Miles] was to be disbanded. Reason: for its size, Bath's orchestra had set a new record in box-office flops. This year's expected deficit: $25,000.

Forebodingly, Tchaikovsky's *Fifth Symphony* and pieces by Mozart and Dvorak were sandwiched between a Wagner Overture and his *Ride of the Valkyries*, in the Thirtieth and Final Symphony Concert of the Season in May 1939. Four months later Britain declared war on Germany.

Henry Venn Lansdown, *The Mid Eighteenth Century Pump Room* (courtesy of the
Victoria Art Gallery, Bath & North East Somerset Council)

English School, *Bandmaster at the Pump Room* (courtesy of the Victoria Art Gallery,
Bath & North East Somerset Council)

John Nixon, *Interior of the Pump Room*, 1792 (courtesy of the Victoria Art Gallery, Bath & North East Somerset Council)

Pump Room Orchestra programme cover. The design was based on a Georgian theme in celebration of two and a quarter centuries of music (courtesy of Tony Hatton/ Robert Hyman)

'The Man Who Asked for a Double Scotch in the Grand Pump Room in Bath' by H. M. Bateman (Copyright H. M. Bateman Designs)

Ray Miller's 100th birthday visit to the Pump Room with trio members (l to r) Derek Stuart-Clark, Robert Hyman and Keith Tempest (courtesy of Sam Farr)

Relaxing to music played by the trio of Shena Power, Alistair Hinton and Sidney Jones
c. 1980 (courtesy of David Paskett)

Sid perched on a stool behind a lyre music stand (courtesy of the Bath Record Office, Bath & North East Somerset Council)

Mike Evans, Alistair Hinton and Shena Power c. 1985 (courtesy of the Bath Record Office, Bath & North East Somerset Council)

Georgian Serenade Album Cover 1975 (courtesy of Gregory Kynaston)

The Pump Room Trio, Bath Album Cover 1981 (courtesy of David Paskett)

Trio at the Pump Room in Bath by Michael Aubrey (further prints courtesy of Michael Aubrey www.michaelaubrey.co.uk)

Jane Austen Festival *Leaving the Pump Room* (courtesy of Lynn Hyman Butler www.lynnhbutler.com)

The Pump Room Trio Today: co-violinists Lorna Osbon and Robert Hyman, pianist
Derek Stuart-Clark and cellist Keith Tempest – (courtesy of the Roman Baths, Bath &
North East Somerset Council)

The Chicago Pump Room

INSPIRED by his visit to Bath, hotelier Ernie Byfield opened his own Pump Room on 1st October 1938 at the Ambassador East Hotel on Chicago's Gold Coast. The launch was perfectly timed to coincide with actress Gertrude Lawrence's ninety-day run in *Susan and God* at the Harris Theatre. Following each performance Lawrence entertained her friends in Chicago's new Pump Room. The exclusive Booth One soon became 'the place to see and be seen'[314].

In those years preceding the aviation boom, the preferred mode of transport from Los Angeles to New York was by train via Chicago. Limousines were sent by Ernie to the station to transport Hollywood stars and other celebrities to the Pump Room and his hotel. Often Bette Davis 'could be found curled up on the piano bench'.[315] Allegedly patronised by members of the Mafia and Chicago locals, one regular was 'ol blue eyes' Frank Sinatra, whose crooning tones were frequently heard over the sound system.

At that time the Room attracted such stars as Clark Gable, Greer Garson, Dick Powell and Betty Hutton. Later came Marilyn Monroe, Elizabeth Taylor and Judy Garland, whose daughter Lisa Minelli would spend much of her childhood in the restaurant.

In 1943 *Life* magazine hailed the Pump Room 'the most exotic dining place in

Entrance to Chicago's Pump Room (courtesy of Paul J Lauritsen)

Hollywood actors mingle with socialites in Chicago's Pump Room (courtesy of Paul J Lauritsen)

the U.S. The ultimate in cuisine and culinary showmanship.' A year later Humphrey Bogart and Lauren Bacall reportedly got 'bombed on their honeymoon' in Booth One.

The War and the Bath Blitz

THE War forced the Council to disband the Pump Room Orchestra, and any surplus funds went towards the cost of an air-raid shelter below the Pump Room. In early 1940 the musical void in the Pump Room was partially filled by an 'Instrumental Trio' playing for an hour in the morning. Impressed by his courtesy,[316] a visitor to Bath had invited Maurice Miles to conduct in South America. The Bath Branch of the National Council of Women, in order to boost morale, organised an Eighteenth Century Tea Party on February 29th, 1940. It resurrected such luminaries as the Linley sisters, the Countess of Huntingdon and Jane Austen. A string quartet, partially fashioned from the disbanded orchestra, along with former Pump Room 'cellist Brier Vestey, played Purcell dances and chamber pieces by Handel and Mozart. Lawrence Lackland played Bach's *Air on a G String*. The Tea Party ended with a sketch from *Pride and Prejudice*.

In the scramble for work in the Pump Room and Pavilion, like phantoms from the ashes, Jan Hurst and Frank Gomez each promoted their Octets to the Entertainments Manager. Depletion of available professional musicians due to engagement in active service, as night fire watchmen or home guards was inevitable. Consequently, both Hurst and Gomez managed to obtain occasional hourly slots in the Pump Room with their 'quartets derived from the Octets'. But Gomez had the edge; anticipating the popularity of dance music, he secured bookings for his Frank Gomez Dance Orchestra and also for musical comedies. One Pavilion concert re-united Hurst with his 'twenties orchestra colleague 'cellist Brier Vestey. An accommodation office was set up in the Pump Room to cope with the demand for beds after the Saturday night wartime dances in Bath. Ration books were dispensed from there and in the Concert Room beds were lined up for those donating blood.[317] Admission to the Pump Room for wounded members of the armed forces was free of charge.

While most seasonal seaside orchestras disbanded during the war, music continued on the north Somerset coast. Taking his young family with him, violist Lawrence Lackland found work in the summer

The Gomez Octet next to the Great Bath with the suave figure of Frank Gomez
standing in the centre (courtesy of Bath Central Library)

of 1940 in Weston-super-Mare under Mozart Allan's baton. Mozart Allan playing the 'cello, joined pianist Wilfred Wade and violinist Norman Rouse in a trio to play Morning Music in the Pump Room. Allan had been in the original Scarborough Spa Orchestra and later became 'one of the finest players of the Scottish Orchestra'.[318] Wade, Rouse and Allan then contested against Jan Hurst and Frank Gomez in the race for octet or orchestra bookings at the Pump Room and Pavilion. (Noel Wade, Wilfred's son remembers his parents entertaining ex Pump Room Orchestra flautist, Geoffrey Brook 'while he was on leave during war service'.) Whether driven by funding limitations or the need to impose restrictive practices, the Council in September 1940 decided not to re-engage the Hurst, Gomez or Mozart Allan Octets. However, Allan contrived one last booking for his orchestra in October playing at both the Pump Room and Pavilion. Maurice Miles had joined the Army upon his return from South America, and was based at Catterick Garrison and Barnard Castle.[319]

Under the indefatigable Arthur Clark, the Pump Room Dance Orchestra joined the big bands as major providers of war time dances in the Pump Room, Concert Room and Pavilion. The Mantovani, Joe

Loss, Henry Hall, Jack Payne Orchestras, as well as the Reg Ball and Billy Thorburn Bands magnetised Bath at night into a dancing city. The British soldiers' perennial whinge at the 'Overpaid, Oversexed and Over here' uniformed American forces (GIs) could well apply to wartime Bath. Over four thousand signatures in the Pump Room's Overseas Visitors Book between 1940 and 1944 confirm they were here, but the Kentucky and Oregon home addresses are a moving reminder of just how far from home they really were. 'Full of uniforms and bonny Bath girls' [320] was RAF airman John Madigan's memory of Saturday nights in the Concert Room and Pump Room. One of those girls was Peggy whose father George Sinclair had been a solo clarinettist in the Pump Room Orchestra when she was a little girl. When her husband was home from the Navy they would go dancing in the Pump Room. Peggy shared these happy memories years later with her daughter Madeleine.[321] Another 'bonny Bath girl' was Ivy who still comes to the Pump Room every week with her husband of over fifty years. One very hot night an inebriated sailor, dancing around the fountain, suddenly lurched and fell head first through the open, blacked out French windows and landed in the Sacred Springs below.

An opportune time for female musicians in Europe, the De Vito Ladies Orchestra made many appearances in Bath. The earlier Bath Philharmonic had disbanded, but A Ernest Monk's new Bath Philharmonic String Orchestra performed in the Pump Room that year. Frank Tapp was the pianist in one of their concerts playing his own pieces *Be Quick*, *Sailor Town* and *Birthright*. In a further concert, his *Five Cameos*[322] was on the programme. Of this composition, the conductor A Ernest Monk wrote to Sir Adrian Boult, 'it is beautifully and skilfully written and has some very great moments'.[323]

The incorrigible Jan Hurst formed an orchestra which played in the Parade Gardens, and occasionally performed his own compositions such as *March*, while his Dance Orchestra at the Pavilion met the popular appeal of the time. One of the regimental orchestras visiting Bath was led by Harry Lipman. Dances at the Pump Room were still popular, but by 1941 the war effort demanded the suspension of Morning Music. A 'Pavilion Orchestra' concert, under the direction of Norman Rouse, ended the year. Rouse had led Maurice Miles's Pump Room Orchestra, but later was to occupy the fourth place in the first violin section of Beecham's new Royal Philharmonic Orchestra founded after the war.

Subscription tickets at one guinea were advertised for 'the right to drink the Mineral Waters, with use of the Roman Promenade, Smoking Room, Drawing Room, etc. (daily and weekly papers), and admitting to the Roman Baths'. The Council quibbled laboriously over whether to restore Morning Music in the Pump Room, but the German Baedeker Raids put an end to their dilemma.

When Bath was bombed in April 1942 three hundred people died and two thousand buildings were damaged. The Assembly Rooms was almost entirely burnt out except for the card room, club room, restaurant and kitchen. The Theatre Royal escaped the bombing but not the Bath Oliver biscuit factory. Many hundreds of homeless Bathonians sought refuge in the Pump Room, sharing the basement with *Bath Chronicle* staff who were bombed out of their own premises. Over a three month period about sixteen thousand meals and many more cups of tea were provided. The Roman statues overlooking the Great Bath supported makeshift washing lines fixed up by catering staff.

Washing hung to dry over the Great Bath (courtesy of the *Bath Chronicle*)

Lawrence Lackland was working in a woodworks factory and taking his turn at night as a fire watchman. His home on Kipling Avenue was damaged in the Blitz, forcing a move with his young family to his mother (a gifted pianist) in St Helens. Its local newspaper wrote, 'Lackland's departure from Bath was a matter of great regret in professional music circles, for he was regarded as the only professional viola player in the city'. Bath's loss was Liverpool's gain. The New Year of 1943 marked the Pump Room's restoration to its usual function with music and, at a time of strict rationing, free coffee! In the spring Lackland returned to Bath on a tour with the Liverpool Philharmonic Orchestra under Malcolm Sargent, an event the *Chronicle* marked with a headline, 'Viola Player's Return'.

Frank Tapp worked on his compositions with characteristic vigour throughout the war. From his north London base, the Mansfield Hotel, he wrote to his colleague A Ernest Monk in Bath

> The Symphony is going full steam ahead like the Russians, and I
> hope when it is produced, it will hit the public as hard as J Stalin &

Co are hitting A Hitler & Co . . . a good deal of it is very emotional but controlled emotion, and that is why I think it should be a success with the man in the street, as well as with the blue, pink and red Highbrows.[324]

Maurice Miles and Lawrence Lackland were among the swell of musicians who entertained armed forces personnel with ENSA, the Entertainments National Service Association. The BBC decided Miles's popularity in South America would 'help us in Latin American broadcasts [and that] transcriptions by Miles will claim more than usual audiences there'.[325] However Trooper Miles of the Royal Army Corps, from his Barnard Castle base, respectfully urged the BBC to give him more home broadcasts. Injuring his back shovelling snow, Miles was invalided out of the army and the rest of his conducting life was plagued by the problem.[326]

In 1945 Sir Thomas Beecham arranged pieces of Handel's music into a suite for a ballet called *The Great Elopement*. Set in eighteenth century Bath, the pieces allude to that period: '*Beau Nash*', '*the Linleys*', '*the Pump Room*', etc. The suite known as *Love in Bath*,[327] was first performed in America, where Beecham spent much of the war.

Jan Hurst ended the war conducting the thirty piece National Philharmonic Orchestra's arrangement of Edward German's *Merrie England* at the Prince's Theatre on Shaftesbury Avenue. The war was finally over and Princess Elizabeth's visit to the Pump Room in October 1945 marked a new wave of optimism in Bath.

PRINCESS ELIZABETH takes the waters in the Pump Room. 1945 (courtesy of the *Bath Chronicle*)

A Post War Pump Room Trio

Post war penury restrained Council spending; Messrs C. Milsom and Sons' offer of 'a radiogram, records and operator' for the Pump Room when 'electricity restrictions were lifted'[328] was laboriously debated. Optimistically, A Ernest Monk added brass and woodwind players to his string orchestra to form the forty-five strong Bath Philharmonic Orchestra. 'A large and appreciative audience' attended the BPOs concert in the Pump Room on the first of April 1946,[329] which featured pieces by Frank Tapp. The first performance of Tapp's *Pastorale* was in Bath Abbey under the baton of Monk, who reserved for Tapp 'an undisguised admiration'.[330] These two collaborators corresponded on musical and other matters up until Tapp's death. In one letter Tapp vented his irritation with the BBC for again 'politely' returning the score of a string suite he had written. 'I wonder how many people realise that the creation of a big orchestral work is a biological experience; I am quite sure the B.B.C do not understand this fact.'[331]

In 1946 'after thirty-seven years of devoted and invaluable service to the Spa Committee and the City of Bath,' John Hatton retired. From over three hundred applicants for the post, James Boddington, the Spa Manager from Buxton was appointed, at a salary of one thousand pounds per annum. Talks had started on a new Spring Arts Festival to be called the Bath Assembly, and Boddington attended the Edinburgh Festival in the search for fresh ideas. One that he applied in Bath was a Festival Club, to be held in a newly refurbished Pump Room. (Surplus plates from this refurbishment were offered to the Pump Room in Chicago). John Morava, the graceful conductor of Llandudno's summer Pier Orchestra, brought his quintet to play coffee and tea concerts in the Pump Room. Joining the horde of demobbed musicians hoping for engagements through London's informal music agency on Archer Street was pianist Reg Brain. His lucky break came with the offer of work not far from his Bristol home in Bath's Pump Room.

A fire in the Concert Room did not deter Elizabeth Schumann fulfilling an engagement there for a one hundred and fifty guinea fee, nor dissuade the BBC Symphony Orchestra from booking the venue for the following year. The Corporation agreed that the Bath Chamber Music Group would deliver a winter season of Saturday afternoon concerts, but Council minutes lamented the lack of entertainment for young people in a city rebuilding itself after the war. Saturday night dancing returned to the Pump Room with Arthur Clark's 'Pump Room Dance Orchestra'. However, future use of the brand 'Pump Room Orchestra', the Council cautiously resolved, could only be used at its discretion. At a St Patrick's Night Dance, Bathonian John Madigan with his wife (both amateur pianists) played on the Pump Room 'Grand' to keep the dancing going through the interval.

Miles's contract with the BBC ceased in the spring of 1947. Released from the constraining politics of the BBC, Miles's appointment as first conductor of the newly formed Yorkshire Symphony Orchestra that year offered a fresh start. Bath councillors might well have reconsidered their reaction to the eighteen instruments in Miles's pre-war Pump Room Orchestra, if treated to the full sound of the seventy-four piece orchestra in Leeds. The *Musical Times* acknowledged the orchestra's early success. 'To Miles must go the major credit for the Y.S.O's fine record of achievement . . . '

Around this time Miles went to London to direct the first performance of *Homage to Bach,* a new work by one of his Bath predecessors. Miles 'was so favourably impressed that he decided to broadcast all three movements'. [332]

TWO CONDUCTORS MEET
Frank Tapp, who was the conductor of the Bath Pump Room Orchestra, in succession to the late Max Heymann, from 1911 to 1915, met, for the first time, Maurice Miles – the last holder of the appointment before the musicians were disbanded – in interesting circumstances a week ago at the B.B.C studio in London.[333]

After its initial rejection by the BBC's music panel, Miles's connections ensured the work was broadcast in Latin America at some point during 1948/49.

The Bath Assembly, 'the brainchild of the impresario Ian Hunter',[334] and forerunner to the Bath International Music Festival, was launched in 1948. As its patron, the seventeen year old Princess Margaret was obliged to taste the waters in the Pump Room, a precedent set by her older sister three years earlier. Poor sales for coffee and tea in the Pump Room finally compelled the Spa Committee to revive the tradition of daily Morning Music played by a trio but limited to one and a quarter hour sessions.

A quartet was engaged to play for Saturday afternoon tea dances and occasionally a trio played on Sunday afternoons. City of Bath enthusiast, poet John Betjeman was on the panel of the BBC radio programme 'The Brains Trust', which was broadcast from the Pump Room. Aubrey Evans from Chicago's Pump Room, in its tenth anniversary year, offered to link up with Bath 'with a view to attracting American visitors to the City'.

In a saga of conflict with the Italian authorities spanning two decades, the brilliant boy musician who left Bath just after the Great War, came home. Accompanying the forty-one year old Alberto Semprini was a young Spanish dancer, Maria de la Concepcion

PRINCESS MARGARET takes the waters in the Pump Room. 1948 (courtesy of the *Bath Chronicle*)

Consuelo Garcia Cardoso, whom he was to marry three years later. [335]

The Spa Committee began 1949 optimistic that

> The introduction of a trio playing light music, mornings and Sunday afternoons has undoubtedly been a success and created a brighter atmosphere.

With few broadcasting bookings for his orchestra, from his Brighton home Jan Hurst made anxious enquiries to the BBC's Light Music Supervisor, Douglas Lawrence, seeking reassurance that he was not 'in disgrace'. When on a gruelling tour, Hurst wrote from his hotel to Kenneth Baynes, the *Music While You Work* organiser;

> We have been on this racket for months now with little or no rest, a show every day, sometimes two a day, long journeys on Sunday, Swansea this week, Nottingham next week, a nine and a half hour journey . . . [336]

Postwar shortages in Bath were partially alleviated by food parcels donated by the mayor of Durban, prompting the *Chronicle* to gratefully acknowledge the link between our two cities by reason of the fact that Edward Dunn, once Bath's Director of Music, is now the conductor of Durban's renowned municipal orchestra.[337]

Later that year a decision was made to close the Pump Room on Sunday afternoons. However further investment in publicity increased the number of visitors and the Council spoke of replacing the Rogers Concert Grand in the Pump Room with a 'suitable second hand piano'. Advice from the Musicians Union not to economise, and to 'expend the permissible sixpence [in the pound] rate on entertainment' was rejected by the Spa Committee. The same committee also felt obliged to hide the trio behind a curtain (much like that of the 'heard but not seen' tradition of the Titanic chamber musicians) when it played the national anthem at the ceremony granting Winston Churchill the Freedom of the City in 1950.

> Suddenly the curtain was pulled aside and there stood Churchill. He looked for a moment and then said 'you've found a cosy little place for yourselves' before depositing his hat on the piano and allowing the curtains to close.[338]

Pianist Reg Brain, 'cellist Ted Jones and his violinist brother Sidney each took turns wearing Churchill's hat while performing. (The year would mark a watershed with the commencement of over sixty years of continuous musical performance by a trio in the Pump Room.)

That same year Ernie Byfield, founder of the American Pump Room, died. Telegrams and telephone calls flooded the Ambassador East Hotel in Chicago. His legacy was immortalized by Judy Garland in the musical *Chicago* by the words, 'we'll eat at The Pump Room/ Ambassador East to say the least'.

In October, the BBC Light Music Organiser, Kenneth Baynes received another anguished letter from Jan Hurst[339]

> What have I done? I have not got one date in my book for you and have not had one since September 11th. I do hope I am not in disgrace? Have you heard that next summer I am to go to Scarborough as Conductor of the Famous Spa Orchestra which job Kneale Kelly has held for so many years. I am looking forward to it very much.

Hurst, like a salmon returning to its breeding ground, made his way to Scarborough to rescue the declining Spa Orchestra. In its very first season in 1912 he had played a Mendelssohn Piano Concerto under Alick Maclean's baton. (The Scarborough Spa Orchestra still performs evening concerts and offers Morning Music today in anticipation of its centenary year in 2012). In 1954, the long serving Pump Room Orchestra pianist Wilfred Wade, L.R.A.M., A.R.C.O., A.R.C.M, returned to his hometown of Whitby, but sadly died a year later at the early age of fifty-five.

After his short stint with the Liverpool Philharmonic, Lawrence Lackland and his family moved south. Lawrence's daughter Shirley recalls his arduous but exciting years at Covent Garden Opera House and subsequently as a freelance player undertaking tours abroad with leading London orchestras. When Lackland worked with the Royal Philharmonic, the elderly Sir Thomas Beecham would shake his hand in deference to Lawrence's father, Frederick, whom he knew from the early years in St Helens.

The New Music Festival and a Trio in Transition

JAMES Boddington's military background had ill-equipped him for the role of running the Bath Assembly 'foisted upon him by his political masters'.[340] Others on the Spa Committee who helped coordinate and manage the Festival were ensnared in heated debates on its future. Perhaps to dispel accusations of being too 'highbrow', Music of the West Country was the chosen theme for the 1951 Bath Assembly. The Hallé Orchestra under Sir John Barbirolli played a *Rhapsody for Two Pianos and Double String Orchestra*, by Frank Tapp. But soon after this concert the Spa Director, learning that the Hallé's funds might prohibit further visits to Bath, declared 'Tragedy is close!'[341] That year Frank Tapp wrote an article for the *Critic* arts magazine, 'Should Bath Revive the Pump Room Orchestra?' Such a revival would depend upon providing, he argued, 'an immense variety of music . . . to make it sufficiently interesting for public consumption'. Perhaps alluding to his own experience, Tapp feared that any permanent conductor in Bath would be 'in danger of becoming a mere human machine'.

Sadly, Frank Tapp died in 1953 at his home in Golders Green shortly after relocating from a large, cold flat 'just opposite the Royal Crescent' in Bath. The performance of his *Intermezzo* at the Palace Theatre in Bath in September that year was a fitting memoriam; Semprini was the pianist, born in 1908 the year of its composition.

Towards the end of his career, Jan Hurst was caught up in a struggle for diminishing engagements and wrote to the BBC

> I have not had a broadcast from London now for over twelve months and I am so distressed to feel that I might be dropped for ever.[342]

Hurst's final broadcast prompted the following comment in an annual BBC review

> How refreshing to see one of our conductors leaving the music to
> take itself along and using the right and particularly left hand for
> effect only . . . [343]

In this era of light music a BBC radio broadcast was the gold
standard. Regrettably, the Corporation's internal culture of confidentiality
in the 'fifties did little to relieve Hurst's inner turmoil as he drifted
towards retirement.

In 1953 Sidney Jones left his role as director and leader of the
twelve piece Cheltenham Spa Orchestra, to become the regular leader of
the Pump Room Trio. Just a year later, the Spa Committee terminated
the Pump Room Trio's arrangement 'relative to the provision of morning
music . . . '[344]. But fortunately the year ended with the trio being offered
revised terms of engagement. (Reg's daughter Mary remembers the
anxiety caused by the constant uncertainty over the lack of a contract.)

Honoured by Rastafarians the world over, Emperor Haile Selassie
of Ethiopia returned to Bath where he had lived as an exile for five years.
The Pump Room Trio played for this 'Lion of Judah' when, resplendent
in his robes, he received the Freedom of the City. On his departure the
Emperor bequeathed Fairfield House, his earlier refuge, and his walking
cane (engraved HS) to Bath.

Maurice Miles's period with the Yorkshire Symphony Orchestra
ended the same year having already been 'subject to political
intervention'.[345] While one door closed the one he had been hankering
after opened! Miles was invited to conduct twenty Prom concerts with
the LSO, the LPO and the RPO at the Royal Albert Hall. He was also
appointed Professor of Conducting at the Royal Academy of Music
around this time. (Miles's eldest daughter Ann, who was born in
Bath, was to study the teaching of theatre, speech and drama at the
same establishment.) More BBC broadcasts followed and then the
conductorship of the Belfast Symphony Orchestra.

Accusations of 'selling the family silver' could have been made
when the Pump Room's stylish eighteenth century gilt settee fetched a
hundred and five guineas at a Christies' auction. At the same time the
Council deemed it necessary to increase the cost of Morning Coffee with
Music in the Pump Room by tuppence. In the meantime the glamorous
reputation of Chicago's Pump Room had spread to Toronto where a
new hotel and Pump Room opened. Courtesy of the (Bath) Council,
various Bath literature, a copy of John Natte's print of the Pump Room,
a reproduction of Beau Nash's statue and an eighteenth century cane
'believed to have been used by Beau Nash' were dispatched to Toronto.
Visitors to the Roman Baths and Pump Room in Bath over the past ten

years had more than doubled. Revenue from the Pump Room's Morning Coffee with Music sessions was over thirty thousand pounds a year, with the trio costing the Bath Corporation less than a thousand. On behalf of the trio, the Musicians Union negotiated with the Spa Committee a one pound musician's fee for a ninety minute session in the Pump Room.

In the late 'fifties and early 'sixties, a stream of royal and aristocratic visitors came to the Pump Room – Princess Alexandra, the Duke of Beaufort and the elderly Marina, Duchess of Kent. The Royal Visitors Book is embellished with their signatures, not least the childish hands of Charles and Anne in 1957. A year later, it was in Chicago's Pump Room where their mother, Queen Elizabeth II, lunched after opening the city's St Lawrence Seaway. During the 1960 presidential campaign John F and Robert Kennedy huddled in a discreet corner with their touring party. There, three years later, Robert Wagner celebrated his marriage to Natalie Wood born the year the American room opened.

Yehudi Menuhin had become the Artistic Director of the Bath Assembly in 1959 and Paul Robeson returned to sing in the 1960 Festival. Leslie Golledge re-emerged to direct a Pump Room Dance Orchestra, formed especially for the Festival and Christmas celebrations that year. The Pump Room was again alive with dancers tastefully endowed in their obligatory evening dress. Golledge had played the saxophone and clarinet in the early 'thirties Pump Room Orchestra but it was assumed he had left for Durban with Edward Dunn.[346]

Ted Jones left the trio in 1960. A member since the late 'forties, the last seven years he sat opposite his brother. Thea Morelle, a 'cellist with the Bristol Chamber Orchestra, took his place. Her husband was theatre, dance band and Bristol café society percussionist Ken Morgan, whose violinist father had conducted an ensemble at the Picture House on Whiteladies Road in Bristol. Pursuing her ambition to be an opera singer, Thea practised her arias in the Parade Gardens where the trio played on summer afternoons. Her fun-loving personality did not fail to make an impression on Sidney Jones who spoke vividly of her years later! Colour photography and writing poetry

Pump Room Trio 'cellist Thea Morelle with violinist Sidney Jones (*Bath Chronicle* 18th August 1962)

were among Thea's hobbies, and in an interview she declared vodka was her favourite tipple.

Sidney Jones' Quartet was booked for Old Time Dances on a Friday evening in the Pump Room from March 1961, but Councillor Giles's own band succeeded with a more attractive bid the following year. Saturday night dances with the Pump Room Dance Orchestra continued under Leslie Golledge. This was the beginning of the Swinging Sixties which licensed the popular night-time swim in the Great Bath featured in the Bath Festival. *The Roman Orgy* though, 'continued to rankle with Menuhin nearly forty years later' [347]

> . . . I must say I was not particularly pleased about the 'Roman Orgy'. I thought this was a music festival. If we'd gone deeply into the subject and found out what kind of music the Romans were listening to, and followed up the archaeology and the history, that would have interested me enormously. I love frivolity. I love gaiety, I love abandonment, I love improvisation. But to see a lot of rich people get together and find some excuse for getting drunk – that attitude was at odds with my own feeling about it.

Thea Morelle tragically died from breast cancer in 1967 at a young age. Ray Miller, who had occasionally deputised in the Pump Room Trio, became the next 'cellist. Thus began a new phase in Ray's career, a year before his seventieth birthday.

Jan Hurst, one of the last of the generation of conductors 'whose life work was with the resort orchestras',[348] died in 1967 aged 81. After the death of his wife Olive, he had retired with his grand piano to a flat on Weston-super-Mare's sea front. Hurst had conducted at Bath, Blackpool, Bridlington, Brighton and Scarborough and had done regular broadcasts for the BBC. Immensely popular with the public and highly respected in the profession, of his illustrious career he modestly proffered, 'I made a living – I didn't make a fortune but I was careful'.

Philip Jones, a gifted young trumpeter from Wellsway in Bath, had been awarded a scholarship to the Royal College of Music during the last year of the war. His maternal grandfather, Leonard Copestake, was a percussionist in the Pump Room Orchestra under Jan Hurst along with Philip's trombonist father, John Jones. Between 1927 and 1931, Philip's father had also played the trombone under Hurst's successor Edward Dunn. Over his career Philip Jones was principal trumpeter with six London orchestras, raising the profile of brass instrumentalists worldwide. The Philip Jones Brass Ensemble opened the Bath Festival outside the Pump Room, in front of a packed Abbey Churchyard on a May evening in 1969.

An Old Fashioned Pump Room

IN 1972 'the pearl beyond price,'[349] and 'one of Bath's finest ambassadors'[350]John Hatton, Director of Music during Bath Spa's musical heyday before the war, died at the age of 90. A close friend paid tribute to his work

> . . . for the City of Bath which he loved so well . . . Those who saw him about his official duties in the Georgian elegance of the Pump Room suite could not fail to be impressed by his personal charm, courtesy and dignity . . .

In the 'seventies the MOD played a vital role in Bath, with its huge workforce keeping the economy afloat. The Tri-service's occupation of prestigious properties and hotels was an immense resource to the city. The trio played at an MOD scheme's twenty fifth anniversary concert.[351] The year 1972 broke previous records for visitors to the Pump Room and Baths – over twenty five thousand during March alone, many from the United States. A jibe contained in an article 'Shoestring Sabbatical' by James Ayres now seems disingenuous.

> It is sometimes said with derision that Bath is a place where young people cannot live and old people won't die. In fact there is only one place in Bath where the statement has any truth and that is the Pump Room. To drink morning coffee or to take tea on a Sunday afternoon in this room is a hilarious experience. The potted palms of a now rather dusty Edwardian day are still to be found, and there is also a splendid string trio sawing away at boringly polite music.

Ayres was the curator of the John Judkyn Memorial at Freshford Manor and co-founder of Bath's American Museum. The 'splendid string trio' was of course the piano trio of Reg Brain, Ray Miller and Sid Jones.

In the 'seventies it was usual for friends to rendezvous at the Pump Room on Saturday mornings, proprietarily occupying the benches and large oval tables. These regulars knew the veteran Council waitresses by name. They also recognised, at a certain time of year, a petite American lady who made an annual pilgrimage to Bath by ocean liner. Daily occupying the same table, she would crochet while listening to the trio. Staff shortages were the catalyst for Pump Room catering manager Gerald Redgers, in May 1972, to declare that 'the days of sedate morning coffee are gone'. Redgers's veiled warning that the Pump Room would become a cafeteria led Edward Goring in his Day by Day feature in the *Chronicle* to write, 'as long as they don't pension off the string trio and switch to piped music . . . '.[352] Goring's allusion to a 'string trio' exposed his own unfamiliarity with music at the Pump Room. But neither floods nor high water could break Bath's proud pre-war tradition of summer music in the Parade Gardens. The three men in a boat crossing the flood waters to the bandstand in torrential rain one stormy afternoon were the three musicians of the Pump Room Trio!

Every Saturday for sixty years Pump Room patrons would have passed near Granny Davies selling flowers under the Colonnade. Through both world wars and the bombing of Bath she carried on trading. Two years of excavations on the corner of York and Stall Streets,

Granny Davies selling flowers under The Colonnade (courtesy of the *Bath Chronicle*)

revealing a large heated room, may well have hastened her retirement in the winter of 1972.

In 1974 the two and a half century tradition of the Subscription Book in the Pump Room was discontinued. Another institution came to an end with the retirement of pianist Reg Brain. Twenty-seven of his fifty-five year long career as a pianist had been spent in the Pump Room.

A revolving door of musicians taking up positions, both temporary and longer term, in the Pump Room characterised the 'seventies and 'eighties. Reg's immediate successor, a Mr Smith, to Ray Miller's irritation, took a few nips of sustenance while on stage and unsurprisingly lasted less than a year. Royal College of Music trained pianist and composer Alistair Hinton initially filled the role for a few months during 1975 and 1976. Alistair later stated 'Had [Smith] been sober and sensible, I might never have been invited to join Sid's Pump Room Trio . . . '.

Sadly, Lawrence Lackland died in 1976 leaving the lovely Irene nostalgic for those years in Bath up until her death at the age of ninety-four. Pianist Philip Taylor joined the trio in 1977, playing with Sid Jones and Ray Miller. A year later a sixteen percent pay rise was awarded the trio. Sid was paid five pounds and sixty pence a week, fifty pence more than the other two musicians.

Reg Brain

Born in 1907, as a child Reg helped with packaging and cleaning in his father's thriving bespoke tailoring business in Bristol. During his free time he taught himself the piano. Unfortunately the eventual failure of the business was his father's undoing. Reg, at only twelve years old, the eldest of four boys, was now homeless. He was forced to sleep in the garden shed of a friend, whose mother gave him Sunday lunch in return for piano lessons. Reg owed his survival to the popular appeal of the silent films where, still a child, he found regular employment. The cinema introduced Reg to the music of American jazz pianist Fats Waller

Reg Brain (front right with saxophone) and his wartime jazz band (courtesy of Mary Syms)

and Billy Mayerl who inspired his fascination for syncopation, before he developed a love for the classical repertoire. It was his flair for this technique that so impressed one local aspiring lady. Love Harris became his pupil although she could not afford to pay him.

In 1932 Reg married Minnie Lovering, a machinist who made suits for Austin Reed; a year later their baby girl was born. Reg was now working as a cinema projectionist at Fishponds' Old Van Dyke Cinema as well as a pianist. But along with many other musicians who played the live score to silent films, Reg was rendered redundant by the advent of the 'Talkies'. (Years later he accompanied a silent film featured in a BBC TV feature called 'Movie Magic').

Reg Brain in the Parade Gardens (Courtesy of Mary Syms)

The glamorous accompanist at the local ballet school attended by his daughter Mary was none other than Miss (Love) Harris. She would say to Mary 'Your father gave me a new life'. Mary was also tutored by Reg and became a keen amateur pianist. With a wall dividing father and daughter at home, they would play duets. Childhood memories are of Reg spending hours practising left hand exercises until he had perfected them.

In the air force during the Second World War, Reg founded the Lichfield RAF station orchestra and dance band – *The Silver Wings*. Empty orchestra seats at rehearsals often signalled, much to Reg's distress, the tragic death of a young talented musician. The self-taught pianist, who had never had a lesson, was given instruction by the organist at Lichfield Cathedral. Reg's love of jazz was indulged by playing the saxophone, accordion and clarinet in the air force band. When the war ended Reg was mentioned in Despatches and given a gold oak leaf for 'services to morale' and a silver-etched baton to commemorate his wartime conducting.

After the war, Reg walked daily the two miles to Hanham where he caught the Bath bus to the Pump Room – a return journey he did for twenty-seven years. Never known to have a day off, Reg attributed his good health to the four miles of walking every day. Bristol based violinist Dennis Cole, who deputised in the Pump Room, said Reg was 'such a natural pianist. He could play anything and was a super accompanist. He never imposed on anyone and not once asked for a lift.'

Reg Brain playing his beloved Hammond Organ (courtesy of Mary Syms)

Alongside his work in the Pump Room, other regular gigs included tea dances at the Berkeley Café and playing at the Mile Three and Ashton Court country clubs where singers Frank Ifield, Elaine Delmar and Petula Clark were among the visiting stars. Reg accompanied many of them but declined Miss Clark's invitation to accompany her further, but he did agree to play his beloved Hammond organ every year for the Clevedon Light Opera Club.

From left to right Robert Syms, Reg's grandson, Ray Miller and Julie Miller at Reg's Funeral (Courtesy of Mary Syms)

Reg was so much in demand as a dance musician that, to the delight of the neighbours, Victor Silvester's limousine drew up outside his Fishponds council house one day. Reg was invited to be one of the two pianists in Victor Silvester's famous Dance Orchestra at the National Ballroom Dancing Championships, which took place at the Victoria Rooms in Bristol. Later Reg swore 'it was the easiest money I had ever earned'. A less glamorous gig was a circus performance at the Hippodrome. The noxious smell coming from the caged lions under the stage forced members of the orchestra to exit one by one leaving Reg playing alone! Reg's brilliant jazz inspired improvisational flourishes on the piano, led a particularly irascible Sid to down his violin and leave the stage, one Pump Room session. Reg filled in with a little Chopin. During the applause he looked up to see Semprini, who nodded at him in respectful acknowledgement. A year after his retirement Reg returned to the Pump Room telling his family, 'My moment has come'. His playing was finally immortalized on vinyl with the *Georgian Serenade* recording of the trio.

Reg Brain died in 1992 at the age of eighty-five. Reg's wife Minnie, who never went to the Pump Room, died the day after his funeral. Reg left his Brinsmead grand piano to his granddaughter Annabelle but did not live long enough to see his grandson Robert Syms become a Member of Parliament in 1997. Reg's daughter Mary still plays the piano and two of his small great grandchildren are now inadvertently drawn to the keyboard.

Ray Miller

Ray Miller, whose 'cello playing had enhanced the trio's profile for over fifteen years, retired in 1979.

Anecdotes of Ray's childhood reveal glimpses of provincial life and the discipline that prevailed during the years leading up to the First World War. His father, a very good amateur violinist, had overlooked Ray's sister's desperate wish to be a pianist in favour of the boy in the family. As a child Ray was made to sit on a dining table before a mirror to ensure that his bow arm was straight. His strict German teacher threatened to throw him out on to the street, along with his 'cello, if he did not practise. One day, while travelling on a bus through Bristol with his teacher, Ray pointed out the cinema that he aspired to play in. 'No, no,' his teacher retorted, 'a concert hall for you!' During the First World War, the cruel internment of this teacher saw an end to Ray's lessons. Arguably it was the 'cello which saved the seventeen year old Ray's life when in the Artillery. The colonel in his regiment had formed an orchestra, The Sons of Guns that played to the troops. Ray's membership protected him from the front line, though he did see some action. Riding a mule and wearing a bracelet inscribed with the name of the orchestra, Ray led the brigade.

After the First World War Ray's childhood ambition of playing in cinemas in Bristol was at last realised. He also played at other venues in the city including the Cadena Café on Wine Street. Like Sid Jones, Ray went on to perform on ocean cruise liners to Europe and New York, but this is where the similarity ends. Smuggling small items back and forth across the Atlantic, Ray recklessly cut himself with the Sheffield Steel cutlery which he had hidden in his clothes, intended for a cousin in the States. More care however was applied to his job, inspecting cracks in aircraft engines at Rolls Royce's munitions factory during the Second World War.

Ray's tendency toward perfectionism earned him work with the BBC Welsh Symphony Orchestra after the war. Living in Cardiff for a short time, Ray would be bussed with the orchestra into the Valleys to play in the Eisteddfods. During that period he rejected a job offer from the BBC Scottish Symphony Orchestra to avoid the inevitable separation from his young family. The BBC Orchestra schedules were particularly demanding, and some musicians were expected to double up on other instruments. Ray played several, including the drums and xylophone. His proficiency on the latter was demonstrated in a live radio broadcast. Ray's commitment to the BBC took its toll on his family life and denied him the time to play golf, a sport he excelled in. Of the many soloists' idiosyncrasies Ray observed while playing in orchestras over the years, he was particularly averse to Nigel Kennedy's trademark practice of pacing up and down the stage! Ray was one of the musicians in the BBC West of England Light Orchestra (WELO) wearing French berets for BBC West's *Concert Hour*; the footage used for a TV comedy show. From 1955 Ray was the principal 'cellist with this orchestra. His playing was described as 'very musical and intelligent' in an audition report for the position.[353] Years later, Norman Fulton as Head of West Regional Music, endorsed this opinion when issues over age and retirement generated several memos within the BBC. A thorn in the side of Joyce Rainbow, the Head of Programme Contracts, Ray refused to go quietly when the BBC rebranded the West of England Light Orchestra the West of England Players, weeding out the most senior members. The Musicians Union failed in their appeal to the BBC not to retire Ray seven months before his compulsory state pension. But Bristol's loss was Bath's gain when he became the Pump Room Trio's regular 'cellist, a position he held until his voluntary retirement at the age of eighty!

At the age of seventy-four Ray married again – to Julie Riley, a violinist he met at a local amateur musicians concert. For a time they lived in Bath in the row of houses known as The Vineyards from where, daily, Ray walked downhill to work in the Pump Room. Carrying his 'cello, Ray's route via The Circus provided him railings that he could hang on to in icy weather. Later residing near the Cross Baths, the Abbey clock's Sunday three o'clock chime became the signal for Ray to put on his jacket and wander over to the Pump Room for a three fifteen start.

Ray played on a Jansen 'cello in the Pump Room. His dream of acquiring a Strad one day, to some extent was fulfilled. A couple from Sheffield offered him an Italian 'cello which had suffered years of disuse due to a family bereavement. It was not a particularly pretty instrument, but it was a Eureka moment for Ray as he first drew his bow across its strings. 'This is it!' he exclaimed. Only special occasions in the Pump Room were honoured with this 'cello.

CENTENARIAN TAKES A BOW WITH TRIO headed a *Chronicle* report in 1998. Ray Miller's hundredth birthday visit to the Pump Room, where he had played the 'cello for fifteen years, was a pleasant surprise even to

Ray Miller behind the flowers on the stage with Reg and Sid (courtesy of Julie Walker)

the current trio, unaware that he was still alive. The centenarian quipped that his colleagues used to hide him behind the flowers because of his age. Another long serving member of the Pump Room Band, who also lived to be a hundred, was Robert Peck, two centuries earlier.

Ray died just before his hundred and first birthday. Ironically, his musical gift was passed down through the grandchildren of the sister whose gender had thwarted her aspiration to become a pianist. They play flute, piano and 'cello.

Unsettling Times

IN its municipal wisdom, the Council advertised the post vacated by Ray in the local Job Centre, where fortuitously a young 'cellist had registered for work. So began seven and half years in the trio for Shena Power whose irreverent jollity lightened Sid's last years in the Pump Room.

The King's Bath was excavated in 1979/80 revealing the Roman Sacred Spring. Professor Barry Cunliffe, Oxford University's Professor of European Archaeology, hailed it 'one of the major projects of the decade'. Noise and disruption during the trio's playing were inevitable as the Pump Room was underpinned with steel girders. Contrastingly, it is a sense of tranquillity that was skilfully evoked in a painting of the Pump Room by David Paskett, with its 'old British Rail-like silver trays, curly water jugs, crockery and cutlery and quaint warmth'.

Ted Jones, Sid's elder brother and 'cellist in the Pump Room from 1947 to 1960, died in 1980. Early in his career Ted had apparently reached the exacting standards required to deputise with the BBC. In the mid 'sixties he was principal 'cellist in the Bristol Choral Society's concerts, where he was joined by his brother Sid and Bob Bennett – a Bristol violinist who became a director of primary school concerts. Pump Room deputy violinist Dennis Cole remembers Ted as 'a lovely chap', and the 'cello he played as being a very fine instrument.

Alistair was unexpectedly called back by Sid to play in the trio following a tragic event. Missing pianist (Hugh) Philip Taylor, who had played in the trio for more than three years, was found dead on the railway line near Corston late in April 1980. Job insecurity and low pay had compounded personal issues. Philip was 35 years old.

Reading *The Times* one morning in the Pump Room, soon after his engagement as pianist, Alistair was shocked to read of the trio's impending redundancy. With contracts due to expire in early 1981, this was an ominous start to the new decade. Axing the trio would save the Council ten thousand pounds per annum, but so appalled were the press and public that the Spa Committee was forced to reject the proposal. One particularly shocked visitor from Dallas argued

The Pump Room Trio c. 1980 (l to r) Alistair Hinton, Sidney Jones and Shena Power
(courtesy of the Bath Record Office, Bath & North East Somerset Council)

They are superb. They give some character and class to the place.
It is the atmosphere people long for. It is unique and a real treat.
It would be terrible to take them off![354]

The trio survived that storm, but still continued having to battle
with real gales when playing in the Parade Gardens on summer
afternoons. Sheet music had to be battened down by pegs, and music
stands ballasted in the wind and rain, while megaphones barking at
people to return their deckchairs drowned the sweet tones of the trio.
Potential damage to valuable instruments was another serious concern.
Impervious to the elements, the dogged Miss Shipp and a seagull were
often the only audience in the Gardens, while the Pump Room was
bustling and without music! Common sense prevailed; in 1981 the Spa
Committee reluctantly agreed that the trio should provide Music in the
Parade Gardens during fine weather only.

The compromise would not benefit Sid, as he decided to retire
that year. But not before the Pump Room featured in Brian Johnston's
1500th edition of the BBC Radio Four programme *Down Your Way*.

Sidney Jones

S IDNEY and his younger brother Ronald were taught to play the violin by their flautist father in the belief that it would offer them 'a greater chance of successful careers . . . rather than the piano which they preferred'.[355] Sid's career as a relief pianist at the Livermore Palace cinema in Baldwin Street, Bristol, began in the 'twenties but ended with the first Al Johnson trade show. Reflecting on the silent film era, Sid recalled playing almost non-stop for two hours and forty minutes during *Way Down East*.

> When Lillian Gish was escaping from the villain, the ice began to crack and grind. So I stopped while the special effects men behind the screen turned a barrel with stones in it – it sounded like the breaking ice.

Forced to sea by the arrival of the 'Talkies', he worked as a cruise ship violinist for Cunard and Canadian Pacific on the Mediterranean and Atlantic. Already in his possession was a Weishold – his favourite bow, a gift from his father. In 1933 Sid spent seventy-five pounds of his earnings on a violin he believed to be a 1737 Testore. Back ashore in 1935, he did gigs at the Prince's Theatre in Bristol (later blitzed in the war) with The Carl Rosa Opera, The D'Oyly Carte Opera Company and with major pantomimes. He worked with many big name conductors, but considered the Scot, Sir Harry Lauder the most difficult of all the maestros.[356]

Married to Marjorie a milliner in 1940, Sid spent the war years working in a factory near Bristol. In 1953, a transition period between the Cheltenham Spa Orchestra and the Pump Room Trio saw him playing in Cheltenham Town Hall in the morning and the Pump Room in Bath in the afternoon. As leader of the trio, Sid arranged much of the lighter music himself and dispersed the fees for outside gigs to the other players, Reg and Ray. He alone could trace a particular piece from the library, if requested, setting out the music the day before each session. Once asked to play Tchaikovsky's *1812 Overture*, Sid retorted 'we haven't got a canon'. If a session was particularly flat, he initiated a trick of playing 'Happy Birthday' to induce some applause. Sid usually sat 'on a high stool well into the curve of the piano, but if television cameras were present he would often stand'.[357]

Saving every penny 'to pay off his mortgage', he daily recorded and checked all his expenses in a little black book. Once seen polishing his violin with a piece of beech-nut, Sid maintained that it never once needed a repair. He also said that he would never pick it up unless it was earning him money. Sid's only indulgences were a holiday to Torquay and a new Ford Capri each year. As a young man, Sid had been caught speeding in his navy Capri. When the officer asked his occupation, he crossly retorted that he was 'on the fiddle'. The cars mercifully escaped his wife Marjorie's penchant for powder pink, their entire Keynsham bungalow awash in the hue. The couple both considered it indecorous for a wife to enter her husband's place of work, but on her few visits to the Pump Room, Marjorie was dressed for the occasion. She is remembered affectionately for her rather smudged red lipstick clashing with her pink hand knits and tea-cosy style hats.

Of his years in the Pump Room Sid mused,

> People come and people go. You see them, talk to them, you know what they like you to play. But you never know their names or where they go. Some you see year after year and then, suddenly, you don't see them again.

Which is exactly what occurred when one couple came every day for a week and sat at one of the front tables. The trio assumed they were newly married until a domestic debacle stopped the music. The wife had arrived, and teacups began flying! Sheet music also went flying, from Sid's music stand one session in a rare display of irritation; this time in the direction of the pianist. Sid Jones prided himself on never having been out of work and would have considered participation in any employment or pay negotiations as beneath him. He was proud to have performed approximately fourteen and a half thousand times in his twenty-eight years in the Pump Room.

Sidney Jones died in 1996 at the age of ninety, four years after losing his wife Marjorie.

A New Era

S ID Jones, the last of the old guard, was succeeded by violinist Mike
Evans, who with Alistair and Shena formed a new generation Pump
Room Trio. Mike was an early member of Stackridge, the West Country
rock band distinguished by playing the first note at Glastonbury's debut
Festival. (The band's track *The Man in the Bowler Hat* was produced
by George Martin and considered by some his best work outside the
Beatles). Mike's 'superb fiddling and occasional deadpan vocals were
always a key ingredient of the classic 1970-1973 line-up'.[358] Signed
up with Elton John's Rocket Record Company, by 1976 the band had
imploded, only to reunite years later.

Awarded a first class degree in music, one of Mike's trademarks in
the Pump Room was to strum his violin like a guitar. A bit of a showman,
sessions often ended with the *Can Can* to the delight of patrons. One of
those patrons, a young Scot, would come to the Pump Room wearing
a hand knitted sweater, a wedding gift from his fiancée, adorned with a
woollen image of this trio. The Scot's love of old buildings and museums
had been cultivated by visits there with his parents. Another visitor from
London was highly impressed by the trio.

> Their phrasing is immaculate, their tempi are delicately judged,
> their ensemble is perfect and their attack is wonderfully crisp . . . [359]

Alistair's tortuous daily journey from Weston-super-Mare and
dash to the station to catch the train home after the sessions, earned
him the nickname 'Toulouse le Train'. Shena's mornings were more
leisurely; a swim followed by a coffee at Poppins set her up for work
each morning. But it was the themed musical events, organised by Pip
Phillips in the Council, with Bristol actor Paul Cresswell joining them,
which Shena and Mike remember most fondly. Mike attributes Pip with
shielding 'the Trio's interests from Bath City Council's excessive zeal to
change things'. Victorian, Viennese, Parisian, Italian, Georgian literary
pastiches and candlelit romantic evenings illuminated the Pump Room
during the early 'eighties. Shena sang with a barbershop choir, and guest

artists were invited to appear with the trio; her friendly banter with the audience boosted sales of their recordings.

Peering indignantly through the louvred screen by the kitchen – ('Oooh . . . I'm not serving 'er!'), were the Council waitresses, one of the more comical images that Shena cherishes from those years. Deputy pianist Edna Blackwell recalls the assiduous head waitress who fiercely presided over the tables, insisting they remain unoccupied until the prescribed time for service. David Cox, the head chef during those years, blamed the lack of profit generated in the Pump Room on municipal marketing inertia and 'the old devils who would sit for hours over one cup of coffee at the large tables'.

Modest salad bar beginnings to the award-winning Hole in the Wall restaurant under George Perry-Smith in Bath, progressing to historic buildings and London museums, was Michael and Penelope Milburn's pathway to the Pump Room. 'Milburn's' was contracted by the Council in 1982 to make the Pump Room restaurant commercially viable. It advertised the trio's album on the new menus and chose more contemporary crockery. Coffee, black with cream or iced was under fifty pence. A scone, fruit or cheese with butter was twenty pence. Meanwhile excavations in and around the Pump Room continued throughout 1982 and '83, revealing the precinct and steps of the Temple of Sulis Minerva.

Daily doses of Prokofiev were delivered by the Pump Room Trio in acknowledgement of Anatoly Karpov's visits to the Pump Room in 1983. This failed to lead the Russian to victory as he competed in the BBC Master's Chess Tournament in Bath. Karpov was beaten by Britain's first Grandmaster, Anthony John Miles.

Maurice Miles, the last Pump Room Orchestra director, in one of his many letters to his grand-daughter Caroline, wrote in August 1983

> I had to retire from the RAM as I am 75 and all the professors retire then. I think 30 years is quite long enough and a new person is essential for progress of ideas. As to retirement – I shan't realise it fully until September. I shall miss the fellowship of my colleagues and the work with the young students. But I shan't have to get up early on Mondays![360]

Redolent of the ominous letter awaiting band leader Francis Fleming one Pump Room morning two centuries earlier, was a missive that reached Mike Evans in February 1984. It stated that his annual contract would not be renewed. Ironically the Della Costa violin Mike had just acquired, with support from the Worshipful Company of

Musicians, had been made just three years before Fleming was given *his* notice. Its previous owner, then 'a very promising young player', was Richard Ireland whose father Patrick was the violist in the Allegri String Quartet.

Mike was reported in the *Chronicle* as saying 'This decision has been taken by people with no musical judgement . . . '. 'Discord in Pump Room' (*Sunday Telegraph*); 'Leader Fiddles while Council Fumes' (*Daily Telegraph*) were the headlines in the national press. The 'crescendo of support' for Mike came in petitions organised by musical colleagues and members of the public, the staunch Miss Ivy Shipp, to name one. Letters of complaint were received by the Council and the press, including one from Ray Miller who wholeheartedly endorsed Mike's musical abilities. Ray, digressing, insisted that dark lounge suits should be worn rather than 'dance band white coats [and that Evans should] stand up to play to patrons in the traditional manner'.

Mike's reinstatement within days caused the Spa Committee some embarrassment. Takings went up by a third in the Pump Room and Mike's autograph was in demand, leading to the headline 'Idol of the Pump Room' in the *Daily Mail*. Failing to remove the violinist, the Department of Leisure and Tourism's next potential victims were the Pump Room's ninety Chippendale chairs. Their horse-hair stuffed seats were enjoyed by many posteriors over the decades. Public opinion rescued their substitution with the modern stacking variety, and the same chairs are carefully maintained by an in-house carpenter to this day.

After the upheaval in 1984, talks between the Council and the Musicians Union on procedures and contracts took place. It was recommended that in the future a 'musical expert' be appointed who would be the final arbiter in any dispute. But it was another year before the Council ratified the agreement.

In *Fat Man on a Roman Road* published in 1985, Tom Vernon chronicled his three-week bicycle ride from Exeter to Edinburgh. Revisiting the Pump Room, he was heartened by its 'brighter' atmosphere and saw 'highly professional musicians' – regulars Alistair and Shena, playing with violin deputy Peter Schreker. In the chapter, *Beyond the Bun*, Tom describes the Pump Room scene:

> There was a tremendous tinnitus of tea-spoons and coffee cups as a perpetual percussion to the Gilbert and Sullivan . . . I came to the conclusion that the skeletal air was not the trio's fault, but the natural consequence of eliminating Gilbert entirely, and reducing the work of Sullivan, a full orchestra, opera chorus and

soloists to a piano, 'cello and violin . . . There was something immensely British and endearing about it: there was none of this continental showing-off about them – they got on with the Gilbert and Sullivan, and no mucking about. [The trio] were less mature than I had expected: the young beard and glasses at the piano and the slinky blond lady cellist . . . Afterwards I invited them to coffee: the lady cellist had taken off her conventional lady-cellist's dress, and somehow insinuated herself into black velvet trousers and a tee-shirt so that she looked even more feline than before, and introduced herself as Shena . . .

Two ladies relaxing in a spa pool in New Zealand discovered they shared a common interest: the city of Bath in England with its famous Pump Room and lovely music. After one of the ladies had described the 'sweet, blonde 'cellist' of the Pump Room Trio, she was astonished when her companion offered her a hand to shake saying, 'Meet her mother!'.

Described by comedian Ken Dodd as 'the last of the old fashioned agents', Bath Leisure consultant John Cunningham retired after representing the Pump Room Trio for many years. In the 'sixties he had organised events at the Victorian Grand Pump Room Hotel on Stall Street. In the 'seventies he had revived the sedan chair as transport in Bath, and organised theatre balls in the Assembly Rooms.

The trio has received hundreds of appreciative letters over the years, some with specific requests for a piece to be played for a birthday or anniversary. 'Dear Delightful Trio' was not an unusual salutation, though one disaffected correspondent enquired,

> Where were the light entrancing airs and amusing little melodies which should accompany a light tea in such attractive surroundings? Please remember that you are not occupying your privileged position to instruct and improve, but to lighten our hearts and give pleasure to an idle hour.

As occupiers of 'privileged position[s]' the professional musicians of the trio were still paid below the lowest Musicians Union rate for performers. Negotiations on improving their salaries reached stalemate when the Department of Leisure and Tourism suggested that a pay rise be linked to local government pay awards. This was dismissed as a 'ludicrous parallel' by the Musicians Union. In 1985 the Council's Policy Committee agreed to an annual one thousand pound pay increase.

Retired RAF officer George Perrett and his wife Patricia enjoyed their weekly coffee sojourn in the Pump Room. In December that year they told a journalist, who was writing a feature for *Woman and Home*, 'This is the last bastion of gracious living. I wouldn't miss it for the world.' Equally impressed was one voluble tourist overheard exclaiming – 'This is one hilluva keffateria!'.

Maurice Miles, the last and 'most distinguished'[361] director of the Pump Room Orchestra before the war, died aged 77. His daughter Ann Somerset Miles wrote that 'he was always in the shadow of the previous generation of conductors: Boult, Sargent, Raybould etc'. He had conducted the Yorkshire Symphony Orchestra, where Ann acknowledged he 'innovated all sorts of activities including the apprentice conductor scheme'.[362] For thirty years he had been Professor of Conducting at the Royal Academy of Music. One of his most gifted students at the RAM was Simon Rattle. Lorna Osbon, a violinist in today's Pump Room Trio, played the Elgar and Walton violin concertos under Miles's baton while at the R.A.M., and remembers the venerable tutor's kindness. Ann Somerset Miles wrote

> He specialised in the interpretation of English works at a time when they were not popular: Elgar, Delius, Butterworth, Vaughan Williams, Arnold Bax etc

During one of the summer school courses he ran at Gypsy Hill, Professor Miles was pleasantly surprised to learn that a lady in the violin section was the daughter of Lawrence Lackland.

In 1986 the Pump Room was treated to eighty thousand pounds worth of redecoration. During the refurbishment the trio played next door in the Four Seasons Restaurant – (which took its name from the four goddesses sculpted in relief on the domed ceiling of the Concert Room). The Pump Room walls were newly painted in shades of grey and blue and the columns white; the only gilding retained was on the ceiling rose. The chandelier bought in Madrid, thought at the time of purchase to be an antique, twinkled in the silverware. A new carpet 'marked the official delineation between Milburn's and Bath City Council – what happened on the carpet was Milburn's responsibility, what happened off it was Bath City Council's!'.[363] The trio returned to new music stands, a stage re-clad in maple and windows still awaiting the three hundred metres of green and blush pink drapery from the Gainsborough Silk Company.

The Pumper

ALMOST as long as there has been music in the Pump Room there
has been a pumper, an enviable role endowed with honorary status.
It was secured with a tenure perceived as a 'sinecure that guaranteed
a good profit'.[364] Charles Stone paid £230 annual rent in 1713 for the
privilege of disseminating the water inside the Pump Room.[365] Clients
would select one of different sized glasses displayed on the 'bar' and it
was filled with 'hot and sparkling water from the pump'[366]. Quantities
ingested varied, depending on their prescription or their faith in
the powers of the water. Many drank excessively. In May 1741 Ralph
Thicknesse died performing his violin concerto at a breakfast concert,
his friend Dr Oliver by his side. His eccentric brother Philip claimed
his death was due to 'drinking plentifully . . . of the Bath waters' with
his bread rolls.[367] Eighteenth century records from Bath Mineral Water
Hospital indicate that patients appeared to benefit from the 'cure'. It
is possible that one pumper's daughter had a hand in any potential
placebo effect. Molly Lawrence was

> not only good-looking but coolly efficient with it, she was equally
> praised for her skill in handing out, besides glasses of water, the
> pills, boluses, drops, draughts, potions and powders variously
> prescribed to her customers.[368]

One beguiled visitor wrote that when she 'gives us Water, but with
each touch / alas The wicked girl electrifies the glass'.

Christopher Anstey's Simkin Blunderhead[369] humorously distin-
guishes between the benefits of the Pump Room music and the water

> Ods Bobs! How delighted I was unawares
> With the Fiddles I heard in the Room above Stairs,
> For Music is wholesome the Doctors all think
> For Ladies that bathe, and for Ladies that drink . . .
> . . . They say it is right that for every Glass
> A Tune you should take, that the Water may pass;

So while little Tabby was washing her Rump,
The Ladies kept drinking it out of a Pump.

To some extent the Pumper assumed the regulatory authority earlier provided by Beau Nash. John Davies was a Pumper and member of the Corporation. Pumper (and former hosier and hatter) Thomas Carey's approval was necessary for

A Subscription Book to be placed in the Pump Room during the time the musick is performed for the purposes of receiving subscriptions towards a fund for paying for the musick . . .

The theft of a brass cock from the Pump Room was reported in the *Chronicle* in late October 1771. The two guinea reward was matched by the Pumper, James Banbury 'for information leading to conviction of those guilty of various indecencies there'.

From 1776 the Pumper was indentured to the Mayor with a three-year lease from the Corporation. The position was still unsalaried and the rent extracted would rise substantially. When the tenure expired it was usual for the outgoing pumper to place a request in the *Chronicle* for any outstanding dues. Mr Tagg, a pastry cook, was elected Pumper in 1784. Such was his status that when Mrs Tagg later died in London it was announced in the *Bath Chronicle*.

Up until 1792 the Pumpers were normally men; Mrs Harrington was an exception. Respectable widows of professional Bath residents were now more commonly elected to the post, the profits supposedly ensuring security in their later life.[370] Martha Wingrove was a mother of four children and widow of William Wingrove, a partner in the respected family firm of brewers.

With the opening of the new Grand Pump Room in 1795 it was feared that 'when the waters began to operate' the new facilities would be inadequate for those who were prescribed up to a gallon of water a day. Elizabeth Foreman was 'chosen Pumper of the [new Grand] Pump Rooms, for one year, with the use and sale of the Hot Waters at the Kings and Queens Baths, Hot Bath and Cross Bath. Rent £840'[371].

When George Hoskins died at the end of the century the newspaper paid tribute to his having been 'a pumper for many years at the Great Pump Room'. Normally supported by two assistants, or under-pumpers, the Pumper was responsible for repairs in the Pump Room, and in his or her quarters above the Abbey Churchyard entrance, expected to accommodate guests. The Pumper's Kitchen was below the stage where the current trio now play. 'Only the Pump Room music and care of the famous Tompion clock escaped [the Pumper's] jurisdiction.'[372]

Elizabeth Foreman must have coped with the demands of the post as her contract was extended. Mrs Sarah Dart, the widow of Rev. Philip Dart, succeeded her on the same terms and was also obliged to pay £840 in rent. Male members of Mrs Ann Phillott's family were granted the lease 'in trust for her'[373] in 1802 but a year later Charlotte Pritchard took on the role.

In 1807 an appeal was made to Bath Corporation by a widow living in dire poverty in Richmond. Twenty pounds per annum was 'allowed Mrs Elizabeth Wood [widow of John Wood the Younger] she being 80 years of age and in a very distressed condition'.[374] The family's disastrous fortunes would probably account for sisters Sarah and Catherine Wood being elected as joint Pumpers in 1810, although the latter was later accused by the Abbey Curate of hiding the Pump Room Subscription Book.[375] She was consequently 'directed to put the book in a prominent place, that all may have access to it'.[376] A year later the Chamberlain reported that 'the sum of 600 guineas was due for the rent of the Pump Room, Miss Wood declaring her inability to pay the same'. Mr J H Spry guaranteed the rent on her behalf but Miss Wood's rent arrears coloured the tenancy of her successor, the widow Mary Needes. By 1816 the rent,

Mrs. Marshall, Pump Rooms, Bath by John Nixon (courtesy of the Victoria Art Gallery, Bath & North East Somerset Council/Bridgeman Art Library)

which had escalated dramatically during the last century, was reduced as the pumps were generating significantly less profit.

John Nixon's caricature of Mrs Marshall, the official Pumper in 1819, belies the dignity of the role which was continuously under the scrutiny of the Corporation. In 1820 it charitably paid one hundred pounds to Mrs Barnes 'in consideration of her ill success at the Pumps'; eleven years later the Pumper, Mrs Alymer, was granted the house 'contiguous' to the Pump Room, rent free.[377]

Commercial exploitation was widespread and fraudulent practices inevitable. In November 1769 the *Chronicle* reported 'that Bath Waters are clandestinely carried to other parts of the country by stage coachmen. Who ever is detected in future will be prosecuted.' Pumpers 'took pains to license particular dealers and to seal every bottle with the city arms and their own name'.[378] In early May 1836 the Baths Committee moved that 'an enquiry be made as to the state of the Pumper at the large Pump Room and as to his adequacy to perform his duties'. A year later Edward Lyons was disciplined for receiving from a gentleman 'seven shillings for drinking the water during the time the Pump Room was closed as a gratuity to himself'.

For Charles Dickens, the spa water with its forty-three minerals evoked 'the taste of flat irons'. His character Mr Pickwick met other water-drinkers in the Pump Room every morning to consume the beverage at

> a large bar with a marble vase, out of which the pumper gets the water; and there are a number of yellow-looking tumblers, out of which the company get it . . .

During this regime

> Mr Pickwick declared, in the most solemn and emphatic terms, that he felt a great deal better: whereat his friends were very much delighted, though they had not been previously aware that there was anything the matter with him.

In wishing to 'draw attention to Bath in the United States' the Baths and Pump Room Committee entered into negotiations in April 1875 with an 'individual able and willing to develop a large trade in bottled Bath water'.[379] The Council so relied upon the spa water to attract visitors to Bath that the Music Committee insisted 'special care be taken the water drinkers be not inconvenienced [by the music]'.[380]

In its *Bath News* column, the weekly *Bath and Cheltenham Gazette* not only published the numbers of visitors to the Baths and Pump Room, but also the number of glasses of spa water consumed. In 1884 figures provided by the superintendent J B Yates ranged between three and five hundred a week. Cater, Stoffell & Fortt Ltd in the early nineteen thirties, claiming to be the 'Sole Concessionaires under The Bath Corporation' was licensed to sell bottled 'Sulis, the same water from the same Spring that supplies the Pump Room (Aerated)'. For a period of time after the Second World War spa water was dispensed free of charge. In July 1949 the Spa (Baths and Pump Room) Sub-Committee recommended that the supervision of 'serving of mineral water from the Pump Room fountain . . . should in future be that of the Catering Manageress'.

In 1961 Sainsbury's coveted the sole rights to the mineral water from the City's hot springs 'for bottling and subsequent sale by retail to the public as "table water"'.[381] But it was a local hairdresser, Patrick Michallat-Cox, who succeeded in acquiring the worldwide rights to the water for his *Aquae Sulis* spa beauty products.

'One taste was enough' for controversial 'seventies broadcaster and journalist Bernard Levin whose future intent to 'stick to G and T's' was aired. The hot spa water fountain was restored in 1985, but the Pump Room's tipple was dismissed by one lugubrious gentleman from Buxton as a 'rip off', used as he was to free spa water in his town.

As a six year old with a love of castles and knights, Martin Salter never forgot his school trip to the Pump Room in Bath. Many years later he was working in the Pump Room kitchen when a disaster with an apple chutney recipe brought him front of house. He would eventually come to inhabit the Pumper's role, wearing Georgian costume with a powdered face and donning a wig for special guests. Over a period of ten years Martin, previously a shy man, metamorphosed behind the persona as he served spa water to visitors from all over the world. In gratitude for his hospitality and congeniality, many of them corresponded with him, some enclosing photos from their visit. Catherine Garver from California spoke to him of her connection with Chicago's Ambassador East Hotel, the location of the American Pump Room. 'You are a wonderful ambassador for the Pump Room and I felt your presence and countenance portrayed the elegance and pomp of the period of its founding', wrote Catherine on returning to the US.

Another letter from one gentleman read,

> As I have MS and am always looking for the miracle cure – I thought that it might be a good idea to try the spa water. This was after an enjoyable lunch with my girlfriend. The results were amazing!!! I'm afraid that the powers of the water are yet to kick in – but the kindness, helpfulness and thoughtfulness of the gent

who served me was instant (it kept me smiling all day).

Reider Fritid, the Norwegian newspaper, featured Martin in his role as Pumper on the front page of a February 1998 issue. Carefully researched for authenticity by the Bath Museum of Costume's curator Penelope Ruddick in 2000, Martin was fitted with

> a linen shirt and neck cloth, dark blue woollen cloth waistcoat and matching knee breeches, knitted cotton stockings and black leather buckled shoes. Because the Pumper worked indoors sometimes in a warm and steamy atmosphere, gone is the wig and make-up and elaborate velvet brocade.[382]

Two quarts of spa water a day was the recommended dose in the 1730s, but in 2001 Martin was sponsored to drink seventeen glasses in a challenge to raise funds for BBC's *Children in Need*.

Pumper Martin Salter's new costume
(courtesy of Martin Salter)

During his ten years 'in office' Martin served many actors and musicians including Lesley Joseph, Gene Wilder, Nigel Havers, Una Stubbs, Rula Lenska, Tracey Ullman, The Crickets and Roland Gift, the lead singer of Fine Young Cannibals. Active in promotional media events for the Council, Martin was filmed in *Watercolour Challenge* with Hannah Gordon and with David Dickinson in a cameo for BBC's *Bargain Hunt*. Martin also appeared in BBC TVs *A Week in Bath* with actress Janie Dee who was performing in the Peter Hall series at the Theatre Royal. In 2003 – Domingo's, Pavarotti's and Carreras's vocal chords were flushed with 'spa' water presented by Martin prior to the *Three Tenors Concert*.

Claiming its medicinal properties had been taken

seriously when he was a student, an eminent retired London surgeon ordered a glass. When served, the doctor roared with laughter at an implication made in a joke about the water's curative effects and his future manhood! Martin was nominated an 'unsung hero' in the city in 2005 for his charity and ambassadorial work. Ironically Martin left the Pump Room for health reasons. Now, in customary Georgian attire, he greets visitors to the Jane Austen Centre and is occasionally engaged in the Mayor's Office, dressed as Beau Nash.

Roman Baths and Pump Room manager Stephen Clews remarks that these days 'it is fashionable to be sceptical about the curative properties of spa water, although spas in Europe remain popular'. Spa water is free to B&NES residents and to the disabled, but tourists appear the more eager to try it. The water is now served by a member of Searcy's restaurant staff in 'undoubtedly the most impressive surviving Pump Room in Britain; a working pump room still furnished as it was in the eighteenth century'.[383]

Recordings

DAVID Lord, conductor, pianist, composer and one time student of Maurice Miles, trained at the Royal Academy of Music. His compositions have been played by the London Symphony Orchestra and also performed in the Bath International Music Festival. Lord's first abode in Bath was on Camden Crescent. From there he would walk down to the Pump Room where he had coffee 'in a very civilised place and where tourists were less conspicuous than now'.

Following the shock of his first BBC royalty cheque (for a short piece of signature music he had composed for the Schools' programme), Lord bought the Nagra tape recorder of his dreams from a man who shared his passion for recording. Brian Preston took his young family in the early 'seventies to the Pump Room and loved its 'very relaxed' atmosphere. Lord was fascinated by the trio's style of playing, unchanged for so many years, and was driven by an urge to preserve the 'whole phenomenon of the Pump Room music'. Crescent Records was born.

Joining Sid Jones and Ray Miller, Reg Brain emerged from retirement for the project. The recording, which took place over two evenings, was done using two AKG mikes and coincident techniques. The piano came off the stage for acoustical reasons. Lord remembers 'cellist Ray Miller's beautiful sound and Reg's 'spellbinding' solo improvisations during

Sid, Reg and Ray at the Pump Room Fountain – featured on the back of the trio's first album cover, Georgian Serenade (courtesy of Gregory Kynaston)

their breaks, while Preston recalls Reg's 'wonderful touch'. Photographer Gregory Kynaston (brother to organist Nicholas Kynaston) took the photo for the album cover through the internal oval window on the north side of the east wall, from the 'ghost room' high up above the restaurant. Kynaston recalled using a slow shutter speed to capture the waitresses flitting about serving lunch and the magnificent light of the Pump Room.

Georgian Serenade, the Pump Room Trio's first album, was released in 1975 officially launching the *Crescent Records* label. Two thousand albums sold in the first year. A *Gramophone* review hoped the 'highly competent' trio would record 'some successors to this entertaining debut', while *Records and Recording* conceded that the trio were 'generally well trained musicians'.

Requests during Pump Room sessions for Ivor Novello selections, Sullivan's *Pirates of Penzance* and Josef Strauss's *The Dragon Fly*, all from the album, pleased Sid Jones 'It's nice to know that our sort of music is still popular'. (Arthur Sullivan, who had conducted *The Martyr of Antioch* a century earlier as President of the Bath Philharmonic Society, would perhaps have shared this sentiment).

Joseph Andrews starring Ann Margret was filmed a year after the LP *Georgian Serenade* was recorded in Bath. In a scene depicting the Pump Room Band of 1742 one of the musicians playing on the balcony of the Concert Room was David Lord. Brian Preston, the sound man, described the 'wonderful' collaboration with Lord, who was 'no fool with equipment' and that Lord's global connections in the music world as well as his editing skills enhanced the partnership. Hatched in the Pump Room this partnership produced further albums under the *Crescent Records* label. Word soon reached a young musician who needed some tapes copied. Knocking on Lord's door on Camden Crescent one day was Peter Gabriel, not long after he had broken away from the band Genesis. This brief encounter led Lord to the 'highest point in the non-classical world of rock', touring with Gabriel as his live sound engineer.

In 1981 *Crescent Records* recorded the Pump Room Trio of Alistair Hinton, Mike Evans and Shena Power. The album and cassette, simply called *The Pump Room Trio, Bath,* were launched in a special concert with folk musicians Dave Griffiths and David Paskett. Currently President of the Royal Watercolour Society, the latter is a highly acclaimed artist. Inspired by the eighteenth century Pinchbeck fan, David Paskett's painting adorns the cover of this second Pump Room Trio album.[384] Shena's backing vocals were used on two tracks in the album *Sticky George* released that year by The Korgis band. It was produced by David Lord who was also the keyboard player, sound engineer and strings arranger.

Spa Music, the Bath Pump Room Trio, the third and last album, was launched in 1985 at the official re-opening of the newly presented Pump Room. Collaboration with Bruno Schreker, then 'cellist with the Allegri String Quartet, relieved Lord of the 'whole weight of responsibility' for the production. Alistair had 'expressed grave reservations' over the marketing value of producing a second album and cassette at a time when CDs were beginning to emerge. The Council had financed the recordings, but their 'wearisome and dispiriting dilatoriness and lack of bigger-picture interest'[385] around that time, forced Alistair to contact media and music agencies himself to flag up some reviews.

The Chairman of the City of London Phonograph and Gramophone Society was flattering

> All members of this Society drag a foot in the past or they wouldn't be in it, and this record evokes pleasant memories of days of innocence; only the sounds of crockery and conversation are missing . . .

The Vintage Light Music Society acknowledged the new album was 'well played and recorded' but that its contents 'underestimated the tourists'. Comparing it to *Georgian Serenade,* the Society maintained the earlier release was 'stimulating enough to make it interesting and enduring over the years'. Another review favoured Spa Music's *By the Sleepy Lagoon,* and complimented the trio's rendition of *Tik-Tak Polka* – 'the sparks fly' and Boccherini's *Minuet in A* 'with all its delicacy'.

David Lord's Crescent Studio was then on Walcot Street, where Peter Gabriel would work on 'various bits and bobs'. Lord had co-produced Gabriel's fourth album (called *Security* in the USA). He also co-produced *Measure for Measure,* an album released in 1986 by Icehouse, an Australian rock synthpop band. Shena Power did the backing vocals for this and the band's next album, *Man of Colours,* which sold over seven hundred thousand copies. It topped the Australian charts for eleven weeks from October 1987 and 'marked the zenith of Icehouse's commercial success, both locally and internationally'.[386]

Intense pressure of the rock music business, and the struggle to save his studio from Council bulldozers, eventually forced David Lord to retreat. Gold and silver discs, coupled with his awards in all musical genres are testament to the modest brilliance of a man who began his recording career preserving the elegant sounds of the Pump Room Trio.

The Regulars

IN a 2009 Royal Institute of British Architects 'construction for seduction' poll, the Roman Baths and Pump Room was voted the most romantic building in Britain. (Over a century earlier the RIBA was embroiled in rivalry over the Concert Room designs). Pat Dunlop, the Roman Baths and Pump Room Commercial Marketing Manager, attributes this acclaim to

> the Romans and Celts who [when they] came here regarded the spring as the dwelling place of the goddess Sulis-Minerva – goddess of wisdom and healing – so it has been a special place for 2000 years.[387]

Marriage proposals are often made in the Pump Room and wedding vows are sometimes exchanged next to the Great Bath.

The Pump Room Trio played at Chris and Ann (née Leyton) Parsons' wedding reception in 1962. The bride entered the Pump Room through an archway of Naval Guards with drawn swords.

Malcolm and Ivy Brown visit weekly 'for the beautiful setting, and the music, but not the food'. From their usual table near the fountain, they relish the drinkers' reactions to the sulphurous smell and unusual taste of the spa water, also drunk by Malcolm for his health. Affectionately known as 'the Sleepy Lagoon couple' by the trio, he affects to wipe his brow in mock relief when the chords of Ivy's favourite piece of music invariably strike up. She swoons to the strains of the theme tune from BBC Radio Four's *Desert Island Discs*. Ivy recalls that when she was a young girl, Rudyard Kipling had tasted the spa water in the Pump Room. A teenager before the war, she reminisces over the 'wonderful' Sunday evening Pavilion concerts conducted by Maurice Miles. She also remains nostalgic for the Saturday evening dances in the Pump Room and adjacent Concert Room, which were so abruptly curtailed by the Bath Blitz. Home from her WRAF station that fateful April weekend, Ivy's house in Southdown was damaged in the bombing. Tragically, the family next door were all killed.

The couple were at the Pump Room when Alberto Semprini played the piano during one of the trio's sessions. Semprini was famous for his light music radio programme, *Semprini Serenade*, which ran for twenty-five years – 'Old ones, new ones, loved ones, neglected ones'. On his retirement he took part in a television interview in the Pump Room. Recently home from a holiday in Austria, Malcolm and Ivy approached the stage one morning and bestowed the trio with a violin-shaped box of chocolates from Beethoven's

Ray Miller with Semprini in the Pump Room (courtesy of Julie Walker)

hometown. Satisfied nods and pleasantries were exchanged with a nearby couple as they returned to their table.

For over four decades, three times a week, Godfrey and Frances Abbott have enjoyed music in the Pump Room. Beginning with *Georgian Serenade*, they have loyally purchased all the recordings. Godfrey chuckles at the memory of the 'fearsome ladies' – the waitresses in the Pump Room when it was run by the Council. A more alluring image, the Abbotts recall from these early years, was that of the actress and former Bond girl Jane Seymour taking coffee in the Pump Room.

Local singer and actress Kate Yeoman is emphatic that a visit to the Pump Room to hear the music is a wonderful tonic. Resident in Bath since the age of four, she has performed as a soprano in light opera productions, has presented a community radio show, been filmed in *Casualty* and is now studying the guitar with an urge to move on to the mandolin. Kate still hopes 'for a part in comedy'. Meanwhile she and her friends continue to enjoy the ambience of the Pump Room.

Marie Ennis, following the Jane Austen trail, first came to Bath in 1974 from another Georgian City – Dublin. Her father, a lover of classical music, would often play the piano at home. As a child she would hear the music of Tchaikovsky and Mozart and the voices of Italian tenors, such as Beniamino Gigli, emanating from his wind-up gramophone. Marie remembers going with her school music appreciation class to the Phoenix Hall, at that time home of RTE (Raidió Teilifís Éireann) Symphony and Irish (Republic) Broadcasting. Her interest in classical music was further inspired by hearing the orchestra rehearsing Benjamin Britten's *Young Person's Guide to the Orchestra*. Philip points out that the orchestra had an international membership including many Italians, one of whom was the leader. There was no concert hall to speak of in Dublin when Marie was younger, but every week she applied for free tickets to the Phoenix Hall. She also attended concerts at the Gaiety Theatre and would listen to the Irish Tenor John McCormack on the radio.

On her first trip to Bath, she was on her way to Blue Anchor Bay in West Somerset and stopped to have lunch in the Pump Room. On a separate occasion she had dinner in the evening on the Terrace. She met her husband Philip - an engineer for the BBC, in Ireland and they moved to High Wickham, Buckinghamshire. Philip's mother was an excellent pianist and used to play John Field's Nocturnes. Dublin-born Field was a virtuoso pianist and the first composer of this form. Chopin apparently took inspiration for his own composing and playing of nocturnes from hearing Field play at a concert in Warsaw. Philip, who had read *Persuasion*, also wished to see Bath, and the couple made several visits for the Music Festival, some during Yehudi Menuhin's time. On most trips they also heard the Pump Room Trio play, although once they found that the Pump Room was being redecorated! Philip retired in 1997 and they decided to move to Bath the following year. Finding property was terribly expensive in the centre, they bought a detached house on a new estate just south of Bath in Peasedown St John.

Marie is a regular concert goer, often attending recitals in Bath, Bristol - (including many at St. George's Brandon Hill) and London. The couple regularly frequent the Pump Room when the trio are playing, and their keen knowledgeable attention is particularly appreciated.

Having been sent by the Admiralty to South Africa in 1939, Gordon Spurrell attended a concert in Durban. He read in the programme that the Music Director, Edward Dunn, only a few years earlier had occupied the equivalent position with the Pump Room Orchestra in Bath. 'This made a lasting impression on me, and when I moved to Bath in the early fifties, I visited the Pump Room to find a trio playing.'

But it was the tea dances and other social events that engaged Gordon in those years when he first visited. He and his wife Anne remember the last 'Country Dance' after a swim in the Roman Baths during the 1961 'Roman Orgy', an event disapproving Festival organisers later renamed 'Roman Rendezvous'. Anne recalls the higher water level then, and how the only route out of the Baths was to swim through the eye shaped gap at risk of knocking into the underwater seat.

Gordon established his business, *Multi-serve*, a shoe repair shop in The Corridor. His workday ritual began with a short amble along Union Passage to the Pump Room where he would have coffee. Joined by several local businessmen, the *ad hoc* consortium would appropriate a large table. Restaurant policy decreed that other customers should join their table, so they met people from all sorts of backgrounds, as far afield as Canada and Australia. The whole ritual was sorely missed when the large tables were replaced with smaller ones.[388] Now retired, the couple come only once or twice a week to the Pump Room and find they miss the many regulars of the past. Among them were Patrick Michallat-Cox, well-known hairdresser and wig maker, Alan who sang for the Admiralty Voice Choir and John Willis. There were also the three Georges: George the curator of the Abbey Church House, George the plumber from Oldfield Park who moved to Midsomer Norton and 'G & S' George.

On holiday at the Belmont Hotel in Sidmouth one year, the Spurrells mentioned Bath to the resident pianist, who proudly declared that he had been 'invited to play at the Pump Room on more than one occasion'. The couple's own grand piano was accommodated in an extension to their Lansdown house, which had been built by a local doctor. The doctor's son was Jonathan Lynn, the TV sitcom co-writer of *Yes Minister*. It was in the Pump Room that the Spurrells made the acquaintance of Shirley Allan, discovering that they shared a mutual friendship from their early years in Plymouth – Charles, the best man at Gordon's and Anne's wedding.

Shirley Allan, a retired head teacher, has brought guests to the Pump Room from as far away as New Zealand and Australia. Her father, the eldest of ten children, was a coal miner with aspirations to be a mining engineer. Lack of opportunities in the pits of South Wales forced a move to Pennsylvania in the USA, and it was in Nanticoke where Shirley was born and where hard earned wages funded trips home. By seven years of age she had crossed the Atlantic three times, once on the Mauritania. William James, her father, was a diehard Labour supporter, but admitted his discomfiture with blacks, Catholics and Jews and that he had joined the Ku Klux Klan. Told he would never walk again after a terrible mining accident, James took his family to Detroit where there was work at the Ford car factory. During the 1930s Depression he managed a grocery store, but there he was held up by gangsters. Shirley's mother had had enough. The family returned to Plymouth and Shirley later married a Catholic of whom her father approved! These days she occasionally meets her friend, ex mayor Will 'Bill' Johns – who also hales from Plymouth, in the 'wonderful' Pump Room. In Shirley's words – 'there is no place quite like it'.

At the age of eleven Patrick Michallat-Cox worked after school in a barbershop in his hometown in County Offaly. (Currently an admirer of Barack Obama, Patrick was intrigued to learn that the President's Irish roots originate there). Patrick opened his own hairdressing salon in 1958 on Bath's Savile Row and then two more in The Corridor. Daily coffee in the Pump Room, where the waitresses refilled your coffee cup and carried loose change in their frilly apron pockets, became *de rigueur*. In the 'sixties, inspired by Jackie Kennedy's coiffeured elegance, Patrick expanded into wig making and had offices all over Europe. A Chinese embargo on the supply of real hair led to the demise of a successful business when the artificial alternative turned pink if exposed to the sun! To this trendy young hairdresser, trio musicians Sid, Reg and Ray – sporting little hair between them, looked quite ancient!

A younger, more hirsute trio played at Patrick and his wife Madeleine's silver wedding celebration at their home several years later. By this time, Patrick had acquired the sole worldwide selling rights to the Bath spring water. Collected from cellars under the Pump Room it was used in a range of spa products. The first delivery to the Pump Room of the Aquae Sulis range was carried by a Roman chariot driven by galloping horses. Hugely successful in the Pump Room shop and marketed across Europe, the range appeared to bring ill luck to the company's founder. Traumatised after a work accident at a crucial stage in the brand's development, it was well over a year before Patrick could face venturing into Bath and the Pump Room. But return he did with vigour, testified by a press photograph of him lifting a chair above his head in the Pump Room. Patrick attributed being Irish to him leading a group uprising against the threatened removal of the Chippendale chairs, and the reduction of gilding on the columns and elsewhere. A fear, which prevailed among his 'gang', was that the architectural integrity of the Pump Room was effectively being undermined.

The threat to Mike Evans's position in 1984 was perceived by the same group as the first stage in the elimination of the trio.

> I thought the Pump Room would close down entirely for coffee
> and music because there was such a rumpus over Mike.[389]

However, the trio survived and was to play again at Patrick's and Madeleine's wedding anniversary – their fortieth. In 2009 Patrick celebrated his eightieth birthday with family and friends on the Terrace, not far from his beloved Pump Room.

Peggy McNutt from Alabama first visited the Pump Room at the suggestion of her landlady when a postgraduate student at Bath

University in 1979. Eleven years later, she returned with her partner Warren White to live in Warminster, when not spending winters in Arizona. Peggy has brought many friends and acquaintances from England and the US to the Pump Room. One from her home state, Julie Priest, sat with tears in her eyes saying, 'this is heaven on earth', and still talks about it many years later. Warren, a former goldsmith designer, is now a painter and has given sketches of the musicians to the trio as a token 'for all the years of wonderful music'.

Brian and Angela Skinner were thrilled to discover the 'lovely buttery stonework of a much more expansive city' than anticipated from their impressions of Bath gleaned from Patrick O'Brian's *Jack Aubrey* series and Georgette Heyer's romantic histories. Besotted with the city, they elected to rent accommodation on Great Pulteney Street and River Street, before eventually buying their own piece of Georgian Bath. Ironically, on researching his family history, Brian found he already had roots in the city. In the late nineteenth century his great, great uncle, a science teacher, had moved to Bath from Nottingham occupying, with his young bride, a flat in Cleveland Buildings.

Angela had been evacuated from Guernsey during the Second World War, and went on to study piano and voice at the Royal College of Music, where Brian's brother now teaches percussion. (Brian recalls his brother Michael Skinner, principal percussionist with Sadler's Wells and later the Royal Opera House, having to dress in Nazi uniform during session work with Frank Zappa). The Skinners 'come to the Pump Room because it is very civilised – where you can do crossword puzzles, read the newspaper, daydream that you're in another place or another time'.

In 1976, to celebrate the bicentennial year of America's Declaration of Independence, a small group from the West Country travelled to Bristol, Rhode Island to see the Bristol Tapestry. The museum's host, Canadian-born Janet Billson, was invited back to Bristol (England) by a member of the group. The gentleman took her to the Pump Room in Bath where a romance was sown. After two years, both married with young children, Janet decided, 'it could not work across the pond'. Annual visits to the Pump Room though 'gave me solace' and have continued for over thirty-two years. Enriched by getting to know members of the trio the trips became

a gift to myself. But the biggest present, without the trio realising it, was the playing of the *Dumky Trio*. I went straight to a CD shop afterwards to buy it and have played it almost every day of my life since.

Janet's two-week sojourns in Bath enabled her to complete several books. In 2003/04 she was a visiting scholar with the University of Bath's 'Wellbeing in Developing Countries' research group

> I would write in the morning, print it off [at the end of the day], and take it the next day to the Pump Room for the morning music. I used to sit and edit what I had written while I listened to the music, before I really knew any of you. Then I would write in the afternoon at the flat, print it off, and go back to the Pump Room for afternoon tea and piano. What a life!

It was certainly a very different life from that of her English great grandfather. Benjamin Robert Billson, born in 1847, became a foreman at the Royal Victoria Docks in London's East End. Turning down a young man who applied for a job, Benjamin was later attacked by the man and his mates and died after hitting his head on a curb. His wife, Emily (née Mathewson), unable to support thirteen children on a widow's pension, moved in 1907 to Wallaceburg, Ontario. Their son George E. Billson (Janet's grandfather) was sixteen at the time. After the Great Depression, he was to become an architect and his work became well known throughout Toronto and Hamilton. However, his first venture was to open Billson's Tea Rooms in Hamilton.

Nearly three quarters of a century later, when Janet was on safari in Tanzania, another room – the Pump Room – emerged like a mirage in the desert. Across a campfire, one of Janet's fellow travellers who turned out to be from Bath, divulged that for years she had secretly been enamoured with the Pump Room Trio 'cellist, her former teacher! Janet now lives in Woolwich, Maine across the river from Bath, Maine . . . with its Georgian architecture.

Martin Tomes used to cycle on a tandem with a school friend from Swanage to Chepstow, taking the ferry across the River Severn from Beachley to Aust. (This was the same crossing in the early eighteenth century that Daniel Defoe was reluctant to risk due to its swift current, and where in May 1966 Bob Dylan posed for a photo for Martin Scorsese's film *No Direction Home*). The cyclists would stay in a caravan parked in the garden of a friend's brother. On their return journey they would go via Chipping Sodbury in order to enjoy the long down hill run to Bath. This was how Martin first became familiar with the city.

In later years he married Susan who used to bring their son Jason at the age of eight to the Pump Room as he liked music. These visits must have influenced him because he achieved grade eight on the piano. Susan remembers the journey from Swanage well, as they used to chug along in an old Riley Elf. Jason keeps his interest in music alive, playing regularly with a group of friends in Oxford where he is a freelance lecturer.

Susan's love of Bath was heightened by having read Kilvert's diaries with its observations of the city - 'it adds to the pleasure', enthuses Susan. 'We used to come every day of our holidays'. Recently they came to the Pump Room for Susan's sixtieth birthday for coffee and lunch. 'Where else could we go to sit down and listen to a trio playing in this environment with such ambience' posed Martin. 'It is the music that we come for', Susan insists, 'it would still be nice, but not as special without it - it's a bonus!' It is her favourite place and they will find any excuse to go. 'No trip is complete without the music!'

Leonard Pearcey and Peter Child, devotees of morning coffee at the Pump Room, which is 'imbued with a marvellous atmosphere' and where 'the music is excellent', have been resident in Bath for nine years. A broadcaster and former Music Director at the Guildhall School of Music and Drama, Leonard is now Director of the Music at Leisure weekends, which has featured musicians such as John Lill and the Alberni String Quartet. As a retrospective tribute to the tercentenary anniversary of the Pump Room, Leonard and Peter presented musical scores from the Martin Loveday Palm Court Trio library to the trio in 2008. Martin Loveday had been leader of the BBC Concert Orchestra, whose broadcasts Leonard introduced for many years. Active with Peter in the children's Egg Theatre fundraising project in Bath, this gesture is testament to their disposition to the city they both love.

Recent Times

In 1987 the Pump Room acquired a Steinway piano. It was a gift from Gertrud Rosenberger to the city of Bath for sheltering her and her husband Walter, a former Berlin judge, after fleeing Nazi Germany. One musician, according to the *Chronicle*, likened it to 'a vintage Daimler after four years with a Ford Fiesta'. Its horsepower needed restraining, however, after Michael Milburn wrote to Alistair 'at the risk of wounding [his] musical pride' pleading with him to play *pianissimo* during his afternoon solo sessions in the Pump Room. 'Pump Room Trio Goes Dutch' wrote the *Chronicle* when in that year Mike, Alistair and Shena attended the tercentennial anniversary of Dutch composer Willem de Fesch, in Bath's twin town of Alkmaar. Another twinning event in the Dutch city that same year featured a 'West Country' themed trade exhibition. A 'Pump Room Trio' played while guests enjoyed cream teas served by British Army catering personnel. Back in Bath the Council converted the grandiose, late Victorian Concert Room into the Roman Baths visitor reception hall. This marked the demise of the Four Seasons restaurant, with meals now served only in the Pump Room.

Successful auction bids led to a *soupçon* of the Pump Room in Mike Evans's Somerset living room. The Leutke piano that preceded the Pump Room's (earlier) Steinway, and the piano's original stool – a birthday present from Alistair and Shena, both stand on a piece of the Wilton deep rose carpet from the Pump Room. Another refurbishment casualty was the green silk brocade curtains which now grace Mike's windows.

After seven and a half years in the trio, Shena left in May in order to diversify her career, pithily telling the press she was leaving for some 'fresh air on the streets of Bath'. On her last day Mike and Alistair bid their farewell to her in a music hall ditty – 'Beware of shoulder pains | railway trains | Dollin and Daines[390] | Collapsing bars | ill-fitting bras . . . | Take good care of yourself'. The session, characteristically, ended with the Can-Can.

The post of 'cellist with the Pump Room Trio was advertised in the *Daily Telegraph*; applications came in from all over Europe and even

Australia. A capacity audience of over a hundred were in the Pump Room to hear Keith Tempest the new 'cellist at his debut performance. He played John Foulds' *Keltic Lament* and Lehar's *Gold and Silver Waltz*.

Keith had completed his 'cello studies in Manchester at the Royal Northern College of Music in 1980. He went on to work with the Bournemouth Symphony Orchestra, the Welsh National Opera and was principal 'cellist of the Severn Sound Radio Orchestra. Venturing into chamber music, Keith performed recitals with pianist Mary Gilmartin and the harp trio Esprit. He has performed as concerto soloist with many amateur orchestras in the South West, including the first performance of the 'cello concerto by Robert Ely.[391] More recently he was principal 'cellist of the Bristol (formerly Emerald) Ensemble. As today's longest post-war serving 'cellist, Keith looks forward to performing for another twenty-three years in the Pump Room. A job he is still 'excited about' and grateful to the City of Bath 'who pay and support us'.

> We are entrusted to get on with what we do, without an overseer. There is an element of being open and of being varied and having a sixth sense of what to play.

Unhappy with refurbishments in March 1988, one regular Pump Room visitor wrote to the *Chronicle*

> I sadly witnessed the final desecration of the beautiful Pump Room; and no one had the courtesy to offer Beau Nash a blindfold to protect his sensibilities from such madness. Gone is the elegant ambience of the white-clothed tables around whose ample circumference many old friends regularly met and where new friendships were often formed, and in their place went small, drab, reproduction rubbish that reflected a sombre mood which not even the trio at their best could hope to lift. It all left a cheap and tasteless atmosphere that hovered a little above that of an expensively decorated transport café with live music. Those herded around the clutter of uncovered tables will no doubt satisfy the financial equations of the Philistines but, please, a blindfold for Beau Nash. Did I see a tear? Perhaps not.[392]

VIOLINIST BOWS OUT ON A FLAT NOTE was a newspaper headline four years after Mike Evans's reinstatement as the trio's violinist. With underlying tensions persisting, suddenly, with 'no send off . . . nothing; he resigned one day and left the next'.[393] At this time Alistair Hinton took a break from the trio, to produce the world premier recording of Kaikhosru

Lorna Osbon, Alistair Hinton and Keith Tempest: The Pump Room Trio c. 1988
(courtesy of Matthew Bale)

Sorabji's *Symphony for Organ Solo* and to fulfil other musical obligations. He also founded The Sorabji Archive of which he is still the curator.

A dozen musicians made it to the final auditions for the vacant post of violinist in the Pump Room Trio. The successful candidate was Lorna Osbon. Lorna had studied at the Royal Academy of Music where she was awarded various prestigious prizes and scholarships, and gave a highly acclaimed performance of Elgar's *Violin Concerto*. Her teachers included Emanuel Hurwitz, Frederick Grinke and Ernst Kovacic – professor at the Vienna Conservatoire. Lorna's husband Matthew Bale had just begun a new role as Musical Director of Bath Choral Society, and she was to lead its first *Messiah* under his baton.

One disappointed finalist, Matthew Taylor, sought refuge in a cup of coffee at Poppins café, then frequented by Pump Room restaurant staff. The sight of his violin case by one member of Poppins' staff sparked off a conversation and a great friendship was forged. Both men were then unaware their paths would later cross again via a more circuitous route. Ken Ritchie, a self-taught viola player, would become a waiter in the Pump Room. Initially he was under a 'fabulously good restaurant manager, Clare Humphries, who inspired people to work in the most positive way'.

On the morning of the 20th May 1988, the new Steinway piano in the Pump Room rippled with the melodies of Irving Berlin. The trio devoted the session exclusively to the composer on his hundredth birthday.

That summer, the Lawn Tennis Association booked the trio to play at their centenary dinner in the exclusive Members' Enclosure at Wimbledon. (Stefan Edberg and Steffi Graff were to be that year's Singles Champions) Tight security restricted access into the hallowed All England Club, but once through, the trio were asked to play over thirty national anthems. Argentina's was remembered as particularly long. During this marathon, the hired Model D Steinway started to sink into the grass, soggy with two weeks of pre-tournament rain. There was no escape, not even in the 'ladies' where a rather patriotic Dutch woman cornered Lorna and berated her, upset that no one had stood during her country's national anthem.

Lorna's first year in the Pump Room was curtailed by a (temporary) shoulder problem, forcing her to resign her post. Consequently, violinist Matthew Taylor received an unexpected phone call one February day in 1989. Having already been a close contender with Lorna for the original position, he was invited back for a trial and started with the trio in early June that year.

Matthew Taylor, violinist in the Pump Room Trio 1989 - 1993 (courtesy of Ken Ritchie)

After graduating from the Royal Northern College of Music, where he studied under Yossi Zivoni, Matthew then joined Yfrah Neaman's Solo Studies class at the Guildhall School of Music. After eighteen months with the BBC Symphony Orchestra, Matthew embarked on a final period of study with the virtuoso Maurice Hasson. In the Pump Room Matthew renewed his earlier acquaintance with Ken Ritchie, who was by then assistant manager of the restaurant. Ken recalls one piece of advice from the general manager around this time

> Ken, you must always be polite to customers but if you find one that wants to give you an argument, the customer is always right and you must give them what they want. So if they want an argument give 'em one!

Another recollection was when the yapping of a small dog drove the then rather irascible restaurant manager into a frenzy of searching under tables; the two-legged mimic was presumably aware that dogs were not allowed in the Pump Room!

Hamilton Caswell, a well-known former Bristol stringed instrument dealer, knew Matthew from his days with the Cornwall Youth Orchestra. Years later he wrote

> I went to see him lead the Pump Room Trio. Matthew is tall, lean and distinguished in appearance, so I expected him to look most imposing when standing and leading the trio (in the Continental tradition of trios and quartets in Paris, Vienna, Venice etc.), but was a little disappointed to find him playing sitting down. Excellent playing of course, but perhaps a missed opportunity to woo the audience even more.

It was this trio of Matthew Taylor, Alistair Hinton and Keith Tempest that Robert Hyman came upon when walking through the Pump Room with his family one day, soon after moving to Bath from London. That chance discovery led to Robert deputising for Matthew from 1990.

In June 1991 Alistair left the Pump Room Trio, declaring his intention to devote more time to composing and working on the Sorabji Archive. Also frustrated with the lack of 'professionally managed and co-ordinated PR/marketing thrust' behind the trio, Alistair was convinced it should be 'a kind of ambassadorial entity to represent the city . . . not a fixture taken for granted'. It was around this time that American pianist Donna Amato played one of Alistair's compositions, *Variations and Fugue on a Theme by Grieg,* (earlier performed to critical acclaim at London's Purcell Room). Alistair's legacy to the trio was the acquisition of self-employed sole trader status for its members, after over a century of Council control. The transfer in status had necessitated two applications to the Secretary of State. These were based on the trio members' ownership of their own library, and their right to select which music to play in each session and the order of its delivery. Alistair's farewell send off was recalled by Ken Ritchie as being a very sad occasion.

Over four hundred applications were received for the vacant post of pianist with the Pump Room Trio. Of four eventual finalists, Derek Stuart-Clark, who had deputized for Alistair, was selected. Derek had trained at the Royal Academy of Music where he gained many prizes; as a postgraduate he concentrated on singing and accompanying. Returning to Bristol, Derek built up an extensive teaching practice and his all round musical skills have earned him commissions as a composer.

Of the Pump Room Trio job, Derek acknowledges its demands,

> yet the trio is more important than any of its members. I see us as custodians in the ever-lengthening life of music in the Pump Room. We took the reins from our predecessors and will hand them to our successors. That's my privilege.

David Poole, an amateur violinist who dabbled in violins and bows, took a keen interest in Matthew Taylor, often coming up to the stage to chat when he visited the Pump Room with his wife Marcia. He eventually sold Matthew one of his bows. Matthew also acquired the violin Sid Jones had been so proud of. It transpired, however, that its provenance was not that of a Testore, and to this day has not been determined. The violin was eventually sold to Daniel Bristow, a violin dealer in Tetbury.

Matthew Taylor resigned from the trio in the summer of 1993. The gulf left by him was resolved by an unprecedented job share arrangement with the reinstatement of Lorna Osbon and the engagement of Robert Hyman.

Lorna's work with specialist contemporary ensembles, such as Lontano and Music Projects/London has involved regular TV and radio broadcasts, recordings for Decca and Virgin Classics and performances at major international festivals, including leading one of the first Western ensembles to perform at the Warsaw Autumn Festival. She has worked closely with composers such as Arvo Pärt, Iannis Xenakis and Witold Lutosławski. Lorna has led the London Gala Orchestra, the Bath Phil and has worked with the LPO and City of London Sinfonia. In the Pump

Room she has performed with the trio for Her Majesty Queen Elizabeth II. Solo engagements include performances of the unaccompanied Bach Sonatas and Partitas in Bath Abbey. Hugh Canning wrote in the *Sunday Times* that her performance of the Lutosławski *Partita* was 'thrillingly realised'. Lorna directs the Lorien Ensemble together with her husband Matthew Bale.

Robert studied violin with Ivan Galamian and Margaret Pardee at the Juilliard School of Music in New York. There he studied chamber music with members of the Juilliard String Quartet and was awarded a Master of Music degree in 1981. (He had also co-founded the Juilliard Tennis Club). Two seasons with the Bergen Symphony Orchestra in Norway were followed by freelance work with the Royal Philharmonic, the Royal Liverpool Philharmonic, the Bournemouth Symphony and the Bournemouth Sinfonietta. After moving to Bath, Robert founded the Ceres String Quartet and did a recording in Madrid with Agustin Maruri for guitar and string quartet. He is also a member of Goya, a West Country based chamber ensemble that has performed in the Bath Fringe Festival.

The job share arrangement between both violinists has possibly been a key to the current Pump Room Trio's stability. It allows Lorna and Robert each to continue their other musical pursuits and provides diversity for the group. Lorna describes the Pump Room as an 'oasis of private memories,' with the visits from the regulars especially rewarding. For Lorna the intimacy of playing in the trio and maintaining a high standard means that each session is a fresh challenge, the sense of newness never waning. Performing on a stage above the ancient spring and temple precinct, she believes the humid atmosphere evokes vibes that are unique to the Pump Room.

Beyond his Pump Room years Alistair Hinton was receiving commissions; one in 1993 was to compose his *Variations for Piano and Orchestra*. In 1994 the current trio recorded a medley of popular Pump Room pieces called *The Pump Room Trio, Bath* – (the programme shared equally between Lorna and Robert on the violin). More recently, one couple from Lincoln wrote in a customer survey 'a CD to take away would be nice – a reminder of pleasant times here. It could also help the musicians, and the establishment's publicity'. Along these lines, the gift shop suggested transferring the cassette to CD format, to include a booklet with the history of the Pump Room Trio, which Robert was given the brief to write. The tape was digitally re-mastered and the history was researched, but consensus among the trio was lacking. Time elapsed and eventually the gift shop decided not to stock it. This early research, however, formed the foundation for this book.

The Festival Club, which, since 1946 had been 'spluttering along barely noticed in the Pump Room,'[394] (and whose members in later years failed to acknowledge the trio) moved to the 1805 Rooms above the Theatre Royal. Unsurprisingly, in Morag Joss's first novel *Funeral Music* about a murder in the Roman Baths, the trio serve as a diminutive backdrop, its music blandly dismissed. When Joss's fictional heroine Sara Selkirk, the glamorised, internationally renowned 'cellist, visited the Pump Room for tea, she 'could hear above the tinkle of teaspoons the trio on the platform, swinging laboriously through a medley of airs from Gilbert and Sullivan'.[395] Later in the novel we find the trio 'pounding out a reduction for piano, violin and cello of the *Trout Quintet*'. Finally, Joss sounds her own death knell – the trio playing 'with unvarying *mezzo forte* . . . its last chords straggled into welcome silence'.

Since his Pump Room days Mike Evans has revisited many musical genres including baroque classical, Celtic folk and swing jazz. In 1999 he fronted the newly formed Stackridge band. They played at the Glastonbury Festival nearly thirty years after the band's first appearance there. But squabbling and management problems allegedly fractured the Stackridge band in this middle phase of its history.

Screen and Stage

BATH has been a film location since the monochrome days of *The Ghost Train* in 1931. The Pump Room became the Moscow Conservatoire in Ken Russell's *The Music Lovers,* released in 1970 and starring Richard Chamberlain and Glenda Jackson. (Prior to a recent screening of this film at Bath's *Little Theatre* cinema, members of the *Goya* chamber ensemble – violinist Robert Hyman, pianist Danny Lloyd and 'cellist Nadija Corcus performed Tchaikovsky's *Piano Trio*).

In the 'seventies and 'eighties it was customary for actors from the Theatre Royal to be invited by the Spa Committee on Thursdays to tour the Roman Baths. Afterwards they would be directed back to the Pump Room for refreshments and to hear the trio.

Mick Jagger with his fiancée Bianca stayed at the Priory Hotel in Bath when the Rolling Stones played at the Colston Hall in 1971. (One teenager who was *there* in Bristol at what turned out to be the Stones' last UK concert tour was this book's co-author Nicola Hyman). On a visit to the Pump Room Mick and Bianca arrived in a cream Bentley.

Chicago's Pump Room proudly acclaims the Rolling Stones icon, along with other rock legends David Bowie and the band Fleetwood Mac, as its guests. Genesis drummer Phil Collins was refused entry for ignoring the dress code; on discovering his identity, the proprietors rewarded his *faux pas* with a new jacket by way of apology. Collins's solo album *No Jacket Required* was released after the incident in 1985. During the shooting of *The Sting*, the late Paul Newman and Robert Redford lunched at the same venue. Michael J Fox, Eddie Murphy, Mel Brooks and Jim Belushi still patronise the famous Booth One. At weekends there is a jazz piano trio and dancing.

Former talk show host Michael Parkinson was having coffee in the Pump Room in Bath with his wife Mary one December morning, when the sight of men straining to put up a Christmas tree clearly amused him. Anthea Turner ran through pursued by her TV film crew, while Kate O'Mara loved its nostalgic atmosphere when she went there during breaks in filming. *Not the Nine O'Clock News* ex-presenter Angus Deayton and *Eggheads* Dermot Murnaghan have also visited the Pump

Mick Jagger and Bianca entering the Pump Room from the Stall Street entrance..
(courtesy of the Bath Chronicle)

Room, while popular pianist and radio presenter Steve Race has played the Pump Room Steinway.

One May morning in 1979 the Hollywood star Elaine Stritch, filming in Bath for HTV's *Sounds of Britain,* was drinking coffee in the Pump Room to the strains of Ivor Novello's *Dancing Years,* when she suddenly tossed her bowler crying 'I take my hat off to Bath!'. Her long-haired dachshund Bridget yapped furiously from her bag, but the trio tenaciously played on. That same year the BBC shot scenes from *Shoestring* starring Trevor Eve in the Pump Room. Gordon Kaye of the TV sitcom *'Allo'Allo* was recognised, and the Pump Room Trio played *Happy Birthday* on Tim Brooke-Taylor's (*The Goodies*) fortieth birthday. Nyree Dawn Porter of the acclaimed TV series *The Forsyte Saga* has also visited. Catherine Morland's carriage drove past the entrance to the Pump Room in the BBC's 1987 production of *Northanger Abbey* starring Robert Hardy. George Takei, *Star Trek's* Sulu, is remembered for his friendliness when he came to the Pump Room.

One spring afternoon in 1989, pop musicians Peter Tork and Micky Golenz had tea there. So impressed were they with the music, the trio was invited to support The Monkees' reunion concert at the

Royal Albert Hall. Violinist Nicholas Barnard, who filled in for Lorna, remembered the Strauss waltz they played as being a surreal warm-up to *Daydream Believer*!

Politicians as well as pop stars have met in the Pump Room, notably John Major and Norman Lamont at the end of the Tory election campaign in 1990. The Tory party's nemesis Bob Geldof was also seen there around the time of the Boomtown Rats concert at the Theatre Royal. A Californian girl, an avid Graduate and Tears for Fears fan, ended her hunt for musician Steve Buck in the Pump Room where he was a lunchtime pianist, and where she contrived a job. When Peter O' Toole came to the Pump Room, the assistant manager Ken Ritchie's policy of maintaining anonymity for celebrities was foiled when she approached the actor for his autograph.

The *Independent* called it an 'intensely dramatic . . . a supremely intelligent piece of television'. The BBC serial *Persuasion*, filmed in and around Bath in 1994, starred Amanda Root, Ciriam Hinds, Corin Redgrave and Samuel West. Austen's characters Anne Elliot and Lady Russell discuss Mr. Elliot while walking around the Pump Room, before taking a glass of spa water at the fountain. Anne greets the Admiral and Mrs Croft as they tentatively enter the Pump Room. Later, in the Sun Lounge next to the Pump Room, Captain Wentworth challenges Anne to reveal her intention to marry Mr Elliot.

In the Pump Room one Sunday morning in early February 2003 pianist Edna Blackwell was surprised by a gentleman, 'with the most intense blue eyes', addressing her with 'Hello Edna, my friends have come from the USA to hear you'. Adam Faith was touring with the play *Love and Marriage*, staged at the Theatre Royal. Sadly, he died a month later from a sudden heart attack while still on the tour. Another great loss to the world of theatre and film that same year was that of Alan Bates. In 1996 Bates had performed in *Fortunes Fool* at the Theatre Royal, and five years later *Bertie and Elizabeth* was filmed at Bath Abbey adjacent to the Pump Room, where Bates stopped for coffee with the crew.

Violinist Matthew Taylor described the bowing action as 'wooden' when the trio mimed to its own pre-recorded music in a scene for the TV detective series *Bergerac*. The same method was used when Robert played with the Ceres String Quartet in an episode of *Respectable Trade*. This 1997 BBC adaptation of Philippa Gregory's historical romance, set in the Bristol slave trade era, was also filmed in Bath.

Drag artists Hinge and Bracket have lightened the atmosphere in the Pump Room with their presence. Other high profile visitors, such as Sebastian Coe and the late Charlton Heston, were more discreet. Sheila Hancock had shared a love of chamber music with her husband, the late

John Thaw. When they went to the Pump Room together, they 'loved the music but they thought the 'waters' were disgusting!'. An episode of *Inspector Morse* was filmed outside Bath's Royal Crescent Hotel. The hotel's co-owner, Jenny Agutter, famed for her superlative performance in *The Railway Children*, also enjoyed coffee in the Pump Room. Other actors who came there were Jack Douglas, Richard Briers, and Paul Eddington – known for his role in the TV comedy *Yes Minister*. Leslie Crowther, who lived near Bath, always chose a time to have coffee in the Pump Room when the trio were playing. In 2000 Edward Fox visited the Pump Room when appearing in Terence Rattigan's *The Browning Version* at the Theatre Royal, and again in 2005 when in Bernard Shaw's *You Never Can Tell*. Fox returned to Bath in 2007 and 2009 to perform in other productions.

One morning, a general outburst of coughing among Pump Room restaurant staff was triggered by a waiter placing an order in the kitchen for 'coughee'! This signalled the recent arrival of a particular TV Quiz cheat, a victim of much media attention.

The film *The Three Tenors of Bath* opens with the waters of the River Avon flowing to the wistful tones of a Schubert String Trio (in B flat D471). The musicians, filmed in the Abbey Churchyard, were Pump Room Trio violinist Robert Hyman, 'cellist Christine Khoo and Ed Burns on the viola – names noticeably absent from Brandnations Productions' credits. Made to launch the opening of the Thermae Bath Spa, the film chronicles the tenors' magnificent concert in August 2003. Schubert never finished his string trio . . . nor at this time did it appear that the Spa would ever be finished. An edited version of the film was premiered on the BBC the following January. John Maguire of BBC Bristol reported on the concert

> Almost 13,000 people sat in a specially-constructed arena, 20,000 watched on video screens in a nearby park, and thousands of others who had been unlucky in the lotteries for tickets crowded around the perimeter fence to listen or to catch a glimpse over the roof of a portable toilet.
> As a perfect – almost too hot – summer's evening darkened, the stunning backdrop of Bath's Royal Crescent was illuminated. And this was a tale of two concerts. The atmosphere in the park where thousands of picnic rugs lay fringed edge to fringed edge in a sea of tartan wool was extraordinary.

Maguire then forebodingly predicted that

They may never sing together in the UK again – Pavarotti is due to retire in two years' time – but if they do, it will be very difficult, perhaps impossible, to top the concert in Bath.[396]

Sponsored by YTL Utilities, owner of the Bath based company Wessex Water, its Managing Director Francis Yeoh – a close friend of the late Pavarotti, had achieved a musical coup.

Clerkenwell Films production of Jane Austen's *Persuasion* in 2006, starring Sally Hawkins and Anthony Head, uses the exterior of No. 1 Royal Crescent to represent Sir Walter Elliot's Bath residence, 'the finest in Camden-place'. Protagonists stroll around the Pump Room where Anne Elliot and Lady Russell are deep in conversation. In the scene at Molland's tearooms, Anne Elliot informs Captain Wentworth that there is to be a concert that night 'at the "Pump Rooms"'. (The concert was actually filmed in the Assembly Rooms – generally referred to as 'the rooms' in the novel).

Trio members Lorna Osbon, Keith Tempest and Derek Stuart-Clark melodramatically expired in a cloud of noxious gas during a scene about Queen Boudicca and the Roman Baths for the TV series *Bonekickers*. Their supposed 'death' was in vain as that particular clip hit the cutting room floor!

The expansive Royal Crescent is featured in the film *The Duchess*. Filmed in 2008, it starred Keira Knightley and Ralph Fiennes and was awarded an Oscar for its sumptuous costume design. Knightley's character, the Duchess of Devonshire, had been a pupil of the eminent Bath dance teacher Anne Fleming.

Tom Conti directed and starred in Neil Simon's *Last of the Red Hot Lovers* in 1999, and performed in Tom Stoppard's *The Real Thing* in 2005 at the Theatre Royal. In March 2009 he was in Bath to film a new TV drama, *The Four Seasons*, with Senta Berger. During the two days of filming, Tom Conti found time to relax and enjoy coffee, while listening to the trio at the Pump Room.

The Pump Room and the Pump Room Trio have appeared in dramas, documentaries and international travel footage filmed by Canada TV, NDR (West Germany), Fuji TV (Japan), the BBC, ITV and many more.

Into a Fourth Century

MUSICAL Director of Bath Cantata Choir and Operaletta, and founder of Soirée Musicale, Edna Blackwell has deputised for the Pump Room Trio for over thirty years. With her love of Bath, she deems playing in the Pump Room a 'privilege' and has forborne many changes there; the sedan chairs, 'temporarily' removed for repair – now in the Assembly Rooms; the absence of the large round table with its welcoming newspapers, briefly replaced with a diminutive one; and the two elegant Chippendale benches, designed to fit snugly into the curved rear wall of the east apse – more recently coveted by the restaurant. Traditionally the public could sit at the back of the Pump Room to enjoy the ambience and the music. These adjustments, apparently made in the interest of the restaurant, collide with Edna's assertion that 'the Pump Room belongs to the Public. To see the Tompion clock and listen to the music is their right.'[397]

Miss Forbes Fraser, the daughter of Bath's distinguished surgeon Mr Forbes Fraser (who attended Pump Room events in the 'twenties) exercised this right until her death in 1999. Wearing the ubiquitous maroon pop socks and huge desert boots come 'rain or shine', she would occupy a bench at the back of the Pump Room with her glass of water; her regular request to hear *My Fair Lady* kindly relayed to the trio by the restaurant staff. Donna Griffiths was one of those staff and has since returned to work in the Pump Room. Donna's own family history is curiously connected to the 'Bath buns' that over the years she has served there.

Bath's oldest coffee house and bakery, Sally Lunn's on North Parade Passage, was named after the French refugee who arrived in Bath when Beau Nash was a boy. The 'original and very secret recipe'[398] for the Bath buns is 'passed on with the deeds'[399] to her house. In 1922 Donna's grandmother Mrs J E Griffiths, a grocer, occupied the Sally Lunn's premises, using 'the ground floor of the bakery as a general store and [rented] out the rooms above. The building became run down and in desperate need of restoration.'[400] Family anecdotes record Mrs Griffiths throwing out the drunken, gambling father of her six children.

The youngest child Montague was aware that his siblings gave money to a tramp frequently outside their house, only to discover later that the man was his father. By 1929 Mrs Griffiths was a wealthy woman, owning property in Bristol and Bath, and co-owning Sally Lunn's with her eldest daughter Ida. It was to this daughter Mrs Griffiths chose to leave her estate, believing Ida was past marriageable age and that the other five siblings would eventually inherit from their sister. However, after Mrs Griffith's death, Ida, at fifty years old was courted by an Australian 'conman', employed by the Horseman's Gear Company on Newbridge Hill. Ida was persuaded by her new husband to have the large goitre on her neck removed, but, less than two years after her wedding, died on the operating table.

A mysterious Marie Byng-Johnson is credited with having 'preserved both the house and its romantic associations after she took over in 1937 [carrying out] extensive restoration, during which time Sally Lunn's recipes were discovered in a secret cupboard in the old panelling which can still be seen today'.[401] By 1940 she owned Sally Lunn's with her violinist daughter but struggled towards the end of her life 'showing people round for 'donations' and making tea for them so they would buy [her] postcards'.[402]

Montague Griffiths, Donna's father, still speaks of the Australian who married his sister Ida, and particularly of the day the conman jubilantly flaunted a two thousand pound cheque in The Dolphin on Locksbrook Road, which Montague ran. This was the proceeds from the sale of Sally Lunn's that only served to hasten the Australian's death from drink.

A quip from one of Donna's more jocular restaurant colleagues landed precariously when Neil Armstrong was in the Pump Room with a group from Aerospace. It was suggested to the astronaut that the words most associated with his moon landing 'One small step for man, one giant leap for mankind' were actually 'No way did that cow jump over here!'.

Two million dollars were spent in 2001 on restoring the Pump Room in Chicago to its former glory with the purchase of, among other items, a quartet of chandeliers, wood panelling and fine porcelain. In the same year, at the Pump Room in Bath, on the morning of the third day after 9/11, a minute's silence followed the trio's playing of *The Star Spangled Banner*. That the violinist was from New York lent the occasion an added poignancy.

On her Golden Jubilee tour a year later, the Queen visited the Pump Room where waltzes and light pieces were played by the trio, and where she met volunteers among Bath's residents.

It was the classical music that lured a lady from Maryland, USA, to the Pump Room, where she enjoyed tea and cheddar scones one morning. This differed from her previous visit when, to her dismay, 'show tunes were playing . . . the atmosphere was more like that of a cruise ship! Pretty dreadful, in an otherwise beautiful and gracious room.' One of her fellow countrymen was of the same opinion

> I was extremely disappointed that the trio, while obviously talented, chose to perform the worst sort of simple, sentimental, schlock pop music instead of something of substance and, dare I hope, of the period – viz. any decent classical chamber music.

British Light Music author Philip Scowcroft, after watching a TV clip of the trio in a feature on 'Bath as Spa City' in the summer of 2003, was delighted to hear Elgar's *Chanson de Matin* when he came to the Pump Room. 'Live music – piano trio – Haydn and Strauss – the ultimate in civilisation. Unique – keep it going' enthused another classical music lover who went to the Pump Room that month. More recently, a small note was left on a table 'in appreciation of the wonderful music from tourists from the Netherlands, Sweden and Malaysia'.

Seven years after its relocation to the Pump Room, the Steinway donated by the Rosenbergers was in need of some remedial work to restore it to its former glory. The decision to replace it did not meet with the approval of all the musicians who played in the Pump Room. Pianist Edna Blackwell was 'very, very sad to see [this piano] with its exceptionally beautiful tone go' and not at least see it transferred to another Bath venue. The Steinway's ornate music stand and solid legs were reproduced in a watercolour by artist Michael Aubrey. Of his visit to the Pump Room and the trio Aubrey wrote

> I was amazed at their ability to maintain the freshness in the music . . . I particularly liked the fact no attempt had been made to modernise either the ambience or the repertoire, and that the audience evidently loved it that way. Long may it last – one of Britain's National Treasures!

Procured with proceeds from the sale of the Rosenberger Steinway, the Rosenberger Trust and the B&NES public appeal fund, a new Steinway piano took up residence in the Pump Room in early 2004. Stephen Clews, Manager of the Roman Baths and Pump Room, reminds us that 'the piano sees more use, played for six hours a day for seven days a week, than almost any other instrument in the public domain'. In addition to its daily use during Pump Room Trio sessions, a solo pianist plays during lunchtime throughout the year and also on winter afternoons. Tom Clarke's Recital Artists' Trust concerts take place monthly and the piano is further used for gigs.

One of the solo pianists at lunchtime is Steve Buck, whose mother danced with friends in the 'seventies Roman Rendezvous, 'in the murky green water of the Great Bath . . . their swimming costumes turning a brownish hue' while musicians played by the side. Steve was the keyboard player and flautist with the Bath band Graduate, formed in 1979 by local musicians Roland Orzabel and Curt Smith. That band was the nucleus of the later, more successful Tears for Fears. Orzabel and Smith still occasionally visit the Pump Room for tea to catch up with Steve. Having survived pop music's own 'murky green waters' Steve now arranges the Pump Room lunchtime pianists' schedule. He recalls being approached by the oldest Titanic survivor and her request for him to play *My Heart Will Go On* from the film. During another session, the Pump Room was evacuated due to a bomb scare triggered by an unattended music case. Inadvertently the culprit secured a free lunch for those who did not return to pay their bill! Another eruption followed when it was discovered that a certain pianist had undercut the group's agreed rate when the role was put up for tender by Milburn's, the Pump Room caterers. Steve was among the group of pianists rendered temporarily redundant, before it transpired the successful bidder was unable to sustain seven days playing in the Pump Room.

Called 'the world's largest – and strangest – piece of chamber music'[403] Alistair Hinton's *String Quintet* was described in 2002 as

> a major work that impresses by its obdurate refusal to embrace the obvious and the threadbare and by its sincerity, its subtlety and its lyricism.[404]

Another critic believed

> The most important part of this work is also a fugue – an antique style fugue that is a kind of minimalism and is of radiant, supernatural beauty . . .[405]

Geoff Brown in *The Times* called it a

> remarkable recording of a remarkable work![406]

and the *Strad* wrote that the String Quintet

headed skyward into a shimmering halo.[407]

The work was broadcast on BBC Radio 3's *British Music Focus* programme in December 2005, and Andrew McGregor, the long-time presenter of the channel's Saturday morning CD Review programme, interviewed Alistair.

The Pump Room has been redecorated and refurbished multiple times throughout its history. This includes the restoration of the gold leaf on the ceiling rose and musicians' gallery balustrade. The columns, whose fluting was originally gilded, have been stripped and repainted white. New chandeliers have been hung and various sets of curtains replaced. Efforts have been made to use 'authentic' Georgian paint colours and styles. All these changes have been met with varying levels of appreciation or disapproval. Michael Forsyth, a lecturer in Architectural Conservation at the University of Bath, deems the rout benches, with their 'centre-back reflecting the oval windows' of the Pump Room 'important pieces of architectural interest'.[408] Two of these benches have recently been placed at a right angle to act as a barrier and starting point for the queue in the restaurant.

The silk brocade curtains and the gold leaf on the columns are still missed by Christine Stoughton, who celebrated her eighty fourth birthday in the Pump Room during a Jane Austen Festival. As part of this Festival ladies wearing 'high waisted dresses with a short jacket known as a 'Spencer', finished off with hat and gloves',[409] drift around the Pump Room, take tea, and then disappear. While outside the Pump Room at any time of the year, entertainers such as the 'thonged, acrobatic performers in the Abbey Churchyard defiantly exposing their nether parts against the glass', intrude upon this 'tranquil and elegant interior'.[410]

For just over a month in early 2006 the trio and catering staff were relocated to the classically designed Tea Room at the Assembly Rooms while the Pump Room was being restored to its 'original splendour'. This was in anticipation of Bath Heritage Services celebration of the tercentennial anniversary of the Pump Room. A timely visit of a young composer, the great grandson of former Pump Room Orchestra violinist Otto Heinrich, was the catalyst for a concert that would celebrate the three hundred year history of the Pump Room Orchestra.

Richard Barnard's new composition *Otto*, with words written by poet and playwright Peter Spafford, pays homage to its namesake – the German born violinist and well-known Bath violinmaker. The story of his alienation by the authorities, when war broke out in 1914, was narrated to digitally manipulated sounds of a violinmaker's workshop. In the audience was Steffen Nowak, the highly skilled maker of Robert's superb violin. Steffen sensed 'the passion of this man, making and repairing stringed instruments and the anguished alienation Otto and his family experienced during the First World War'. In the packed Pump Room, a very elderly gentleman was overheard claiming personal acquaintanceship with Otto Heinrich! Richard Barnard's new composition *Otto* was premiered by Robert, Keith and Derek following pieces by Strauss, Elgar and Gurney performed by Lorna, Keith and Derek. Guests in the interval enjoyed refreshments in the torch-lit Great Bath below the Pump Room.

Deputy musicians have played a vital role in the history of the Pump Room orchestra and trio. The professionalism of the 'deps' has been exceptional. One violinist in the early 'seventies, invited to 'come over to Bath' by his friend Ray Miller, eventually became Sid's deputy for several years during his holidays. Dennis Cole had been Matthew Taylor's first violin teacher. In 2009, at the age of sixty-nine, Dennis was awarded an MBE for his services to music, especially for his fifty years with the Western Youth Orchestra, which he still directs.

Violinist Peter Schreker, who never ceased to be amazed at the endless photos of the Pump Room taken by Japanese tourists, was a stalwart deputy in the 'eighties.

After a short break from the Pump Room, Matthew Taylor returned to deputise in the trio. Of the view that the Pump Room Trio should be 'the jewel in the Council's crown', Matthew also maintains that it ought to feature in the Bath Music Festival. Furthermore, he describes the 'inferiority complex of the West Country'. That if neither in the Festival nor a household name, Bath musicians, even when trained at the best conservatoires and with international experience, 'will often only attract a limited audience to their concerts' – a familiar scenario!

After narrowly missing out on the 'cello position vacated by Shena Power, Sara Lovell was soon asked to 'dep' in the Pump Room Trio. During Sara's first session her role as a 'cellist and future career as an air pilot inadvertently converged. In an enthusiastic upward flourish, Sara's bow flew from her hand and landed on the Bath buns of an American couple seated near the stage! Years later, again 'depping', Sara's strong playing was praised by Robert's good friend Ken Mirkin, a violist in the New York Philharmonic Orchestra, on a visit to the Pump Room. Another excellent 'cellist, Christine Khoo (a former member of the Ceres String Quartet), was also a favourite in the Pump Room and has deputised for over eighteen years. She has more recently developed a supplementary career as a civil funeral celebrant.

Pianist Geoff Ditcham turned pages for Yehudi Menuhin's accompanist at the Edinburgh Festival. Menuhin, arriving promptly for rehearsal, discovered he had left his shoulder rest at the hotel. Geoff, who had been tasked to assist Menuhin as well, offered to contact the hotel. His detailed description of the shoulder rest eluded hotel staff and unleashed a flurry of fruitless activity among them. So Geoff rang the nearest music shop for Menuhin's preferred type. But the only one available was the Yehudi Menuhin brand (marketed for students). Would this be acceptable to the maestro? Definitely! Geoff now turns his own pages when 'depping' in the Pump Room.

Katy Rowe started playing the violin at five and a half so when her grandmother took her to the Pump Room two years later she was already playing in the National Children's Orchestra. Recognising the music being played (Strauss's *Radetsky March*) Katy approached the stage and looking up at the violinist, chatted with him and the other musicians. That was the moment she set her heart on one day playing in the Pump Room and so wrote of her wish to Jimmy Saville on *Jim'll Fix It*, the popular TV programme of the time. Years later it was Robert Hyman who fixed it for Katy to deputise! Her first session was well received and especially emotive for one lady that morning in the restaurant; Ruth Dowling from Bradford on Avon was there to see her granddaughter finally play in the Pump Room.

In the past, the Pump Room Trio's library was inadequately stored – above the kitchen, in the piano and even under the stage. During the 'eighties, Mike Evans, Shena and Alistair each purchased from Sid on his retirement a one third share in this collection of music. This set a precedent for future members of the trio to have equal shares in its ownership. Since Mike's departure, issues regarding the violin share have never been resolved. More recently, several additional music collections have been purchased by individual members or donated to the trio collectively.

The present Pump Room library consists of over three thousand pieces of music. There are numerous piano conductors' scores (with separate violin and 'cello parts) of overtures, symphonic works, ballet suites, character pieces and marches. Additionally there are waltzes by Strauss, Waldteufel and many other composers. There are selections from operas by composers such as Mozart and Rossini and shows by Ivor Novello, Jerome Kern, Irving Berlin, Frank Loesser and the ever popular Gilbert and Sullivan. Numerous songs, baroque and classical trios, as well as arrangements of ragtime and pop music, complete the library. On any day a visitor to the Pump Room is likely to hear an obscure or favourite piece of music when the trio is playing.

Conclusion

Today 'the band' still plays in the Pump Room. A modern trio with four members! It performs every day of the year apart from Christmas and Boxing Day (twice daily during the summer season). On one Boxing Day, however, Radio Bristol brought 'the sounds of the trio into listeners' homes', proclaiming the Pump Room one of the most visited buildings after the Tower of London. Perhaps not quite as bloody as the Tower's past, the Room's history is certainly no less intriguing.

The Pump Room for Francis Fleming, Joseph Bossi, Jan Hurst and Sidney Jones signified the core of their life's work. For William Herschel, Edward Dunn and Maurice Miles it became a launching pad to more distant pastures and broader prospects. With respect to the Pump Room, Thomas Linley's ambitions were somewhat thwarted. William Salmon's displacement, after years of service, was echoed by that of Frank Tapp whose musical compositions endured well beyond his interlude in the Pump Room. Max Heymann's tragic suicide plunged the orchestra into a period of bleakness, further deepened by the humiliation of Otto Heinrich at the start of the Great War.

The Pump Room has borne witness to the struggles, joys, tragedies and ambitions of the 'forgotten army' of musicians, whether in the early Pump Room Band, Pump Room Orchestra, or Pump Room Trio. For three centuries the public has enjoyed their music, often reciprocating with loyalty and affection. It is an awesome legacy to inherit, a musical and cultural tradition that demands to be protected for the next three centuries.

Sources

Anstey, Christopher *The New Bath Guide*
Austen, Jane *Northanger Abbey*
Austen, Jane *Persuasion*
Bath Case Notes *The Trial of Mrs Leigh-Perrot*
Bath Chronicle Archives *Bath: The Golden Years* edited by Theresa Ford and
    Karen Birch
Bath Chronicle microfilm, Bath Reference Library
Bath Histories, Volumes II, III and XI
Bath Spa Committee Minutes
Bath Council Minutes
B&NES County Records Office Archives, The Guildhall , Bath
Black, Clementina *The Linleys of Bath*
Borsay, Peter *Image of Georgian Bath*
Borsay, Peter *Bath 1700 to 2000*
Bradley, Ian *Water Music*
Brown, Frank *William Herschel Musician and Composer*
Bullamore, Tim *Fifty Festivals*
Chaplin, Charles *My Early Years*
Clarke, Andrew *The Bath Messiah, The Celebration of 250 Years of a Provincial
    Choral Tradition*
Cook, Faith *Selina, Countess of Huntingdon*
Defoe, Daniel *Letters*
Dickens, Charles *Pickwick Papers*
Dodd, Dudley 'Bath Assembly Rooms: architect John Wood the Younger',
    National Trust Magazine, Spring 1979
Fawcett, Trevor *Bath Administer'd*
Fawcett, Trevor *Bath Entertain'd*
Fawcett, Trevor *Music in Eighteenth-Century Norwich and Norfolk*
Fawcett, Trevor *Voices of Eighteenth-Century Bath*
Fawcett, Trevor *Georgian Imprints: Printing & Publishing at Bath 1729-1815*
Fawcett, Trevor 'Selling the Bath Waters: Medical Propaganda in an 18th
    Century Spa', *Somerset Archaeology and Natural History*
Fawcett, Trevor 'William Herschel at the Octagon Chapel, Bath' *The Speculum,
    the Journal of the William Herschel Society*
Fiske, Roger *English Theatre Music in the Eighteenth Century*
Fleming, Francis *The Life and Extraordinary Adventures, the Perils and Critical
    Escapes of Timothy Ginnadrake (that Child of Chequer'd Fortune)*, Vols I – IV
Forsyth, Michael *Bath: Pevsner Architectural Guides*
Gasquin, Anthony *Postscript to the New Bath Guide*

Georgian Newspaper Project B&NES
Guide to British Theatres 1750–1950 edited by John Earl & Michael Sell
Hatton, John *Pump Room Programmes 1922-1944*
Harding, Steward & Lambert *Parks and Gardens of Avon*
Haydn, Joseph *First London Notebooks*
Hembry, Phyllis *The English Spa 1560-1815: A Social History*
Hinde, Thomas *Tales from the Pump Room*
Hogwood, Christopher *Handel*
Hogwood, Christopher *Music in Eighteenth Century England*
Hoskin, Michael *The Herschel Partnership*
Hoskin, Michael *Vocations in Conflict: William Herschel in Bath 1766–1782*
    (Hist. Sci., xli, 2003)
James, K E *Concert Life in Eighteenth-Century Bath*
Joss, Morag *Funeral Music*
Life and Letters of Sir Charles Hallé edited by Michael Kennedy
Lowndes, William *The Theatre Royal at Bath*
Lowndes, William *They came to Bath*
Hornsey, Brian *Ninety Years of Cinema in Bath*
Mackerness, E O *A Social History of English Music*
Manvell, Roger *Sarah Siddons, Portrait of an Actress*
'*Musical Times*' Journals
Old, Terry *Bath as Jane Austen knew it*
Pepys, Samuel *Diaries*
Piggott, Patrick *The Innocent Diversion: Music in the Life and Writings of Jane
    Austen*
Plomer, William *Kilvert's Diary Selections*
Reynolds, Brian *Music While You Work*
Robbins Landon, H C *Collected Correspondence and London Notebooks of Joseph
    Haydn*
Robbins Landon, H C *Haydn, Chronicle and Works*
Royal Society and Royal Astronomical Society Selected Scientific Papers:
    Herschel's Life and Works
Sitwell, Edith *Bath*
Smithsonian Journal, November 1984
Smollett, Tobias *Humphrey Clinker*
The Journeys of Celia Fiennes edited by Christopher Morris
Tomalin, Claire *The Life of Jane Austen*
Turner, A J *Science and Music in Eighteenth Century Bath*
University of Bath Archives and Library
Victoria Art Gallery Exhibition: *Bath in the Eighteenth Century*
White, Giles *Hot Bath, the Story of the Spa*
Williams, Marjorie *Lady Luxborough Goes to Bath*
Windsor, Diana *The Dream of Bath*
Wood, John *Towards a Description of Bath* (1742-3)
Woodfield, Ian *The Celebrated Quarrel between Thomas Linley (Senior) and
    William Herschel: an episode in the musical life of 18th Century Bath*
Wroughton, John *Stuart Bath: Life in the Forgotten City 1603-1714*
Young, Kenneth *Music's Great Days in the Spas and Watering Places*
Young, Percy M *A History of British Music*

Notes

1   The Bath Critic, March 1952 p.108/109 by kind permission of the British Library

2   Stephen Bird and Barry Cunliffe *The Essential Roman Baths* 2006 p. 46

3   Trevor Fawcett 'Selling the Bath Waters...' *Somerset Archaeology and Natural History* vol. 134_p. 193

4   Phyllis Hembry *The English Spa 1560-1815 A Social History* 1990 p. 61

5   Diary entry 12 June, 1668

6   Phyllis Hembry *The English Spa 1560-1815 A Social History* 1990 p. 89

7   John Wroughton *Stuart Bath: Life in the Forgotten City 1603-1714*

8   Francis Fleming *The Life and Extraordinary Adventures, the Perils and Critical Escapes of Timothy Ginnadrake (That Child of Chequer'd Fortune)* 1770 vol 3 p.18

9   Pindar *Olympian Odes*

10   Trevor Fawcett 'Selling the Bath Waters..." *Somerset Archaeology and Natural History* vol. 134_p. 195

11   Bath Corporation Minutes

12   Frances Fleming *The Life and Extraordinary Adventures* vol 3 p. 23

13   Ibid p. 23/24

14   Trevor Fawcett *Bath Entertain'd: Amusements, Recreations &*

Gambling at the 18th-Century Spa 1998 p 84

15   K E James 'Concert life in Eighteenth-century Bath' (unpublished thesis), University of London, 1987

16   Frances Fleming *The Life and Extraordinary Adventures* vol 3 p. 23

17   T R Robinson & R J Bossi 'History of the Equation Long Case Clock made by Thomas Tompion London A.D 1709' *Horological Journal* December 1952 p. 791

18   Francis Fleming *The Life and Extraordinary Adventures* vol 3 p. 26

19   Trevor Fawcett *Bath Entertain'd* 1998 p. 29

20   K E James 'Concert Life in ...' vol 1 p. 97

21   Francis Fleming *The Life and Extraordinary Adventures* vol 3 p. 31

22   We are grateful to Trevor Fawcett for this information

23   Trevor Fawcett *Bath Entertain'd* 1998 p. 81

24   Ibid p.6

25   Ibid

26   K E James 'Concert life in ... vol 4 p. 605

27   Francis Fleming *The Life and Extraordinary Adventures* vol 1 p 76

28   Ibid p. 77

29   The term *Company* refers to the

gentry who were in Bath at any one season

30 Trevor Fawcett *Bath Entertain'd* 1998 p.29
31 Ibid p.84
32 Thomas Hinde *Tales from the Pump Room* 1988 p. 50
33 Bath Corporation Minutes
34 K E James vol 4 p. 610
35 Wesley (c.) *Journal* vol 1 p. 286 entry for 11th July 1741
36 Edith Sitwell *Bath* 1932 p. 136
37 Trevor Fawcett *Bath Entertain'd* p. 20
38 Ibid
39 Trevor Fawcett *Bath Administer'd: Corporation Affairs at the 18th-Century Spa* 2001 p. 14
40 Marjorie Williams *Lady Luxborough Goes to Bath* 1946 p. 5
41 Ibid p. 20
42 K E James vol 1 p. 89 'some pieces of Corelli [were] admirably performed by the Pump Room Band in 1778' the year Fleming died.
43 Marjorie Williams *Lady Luxborough Goes to Bath* 1946 p. 31
44 K E James vol 4 p. 648
45 Ibid vol 2 p. 158
46 Ibid p.164
47 Ibid p. 163
48 H. C. Robbins Landon *Handel and his World* 1984 p. 242
49 Ibid p. 232
50 Ibid p. 243
51 K E James vol 4 p. 508
52 Trevor Fawcett *Bath Administer'd* p. 132
53 Ibid
54 Trevor Fawcett 'Eighteenth Century Shops and the Luxury Trade' *Bath History* 1990 vol III p. 67/68
55 K E James 'Concert life in ...' vol 5

p. 815
56 Thomas Hinde *Tales from the Pump Room* p. 128
57 Ibid
58 Trevor Fawcett *Bath Administer'd* p.76
59 Francis Fleming, *The Life and Extraordinary Times* vol 3 p.128
60 Ibid vol 3 p. 98
61 Ibid
62 K E James 'Concert Life in ... vol 2 p. 171
63 Clementina Black *The Linleys of Bath* 1911 p. 16
64 Ibid p. 15
65 Rev. John Penrose *Letters from Bath* 1983 April, 25th 1766
66 K E James Vol 2 p. 179
67 Francis Fleming vol 3 p. 99
68 K E James vol 4 p. 758
69 Francis Fleming vol 3 p.103
70 Ibid p. 102
71 Ibid vol 3 p. 88
72 Ibid p.100
73 Ibid p. 97
74 Ibid p. 98
75 K E James vol 2 p.179
76 Ibid vol 1 p. 90
77 Ibid vol 1 p. 93
78 Royal Society and Royal Astronomical Society Selected Scientific Papers: 'Herschel's Life and Works'
79 Ibid
80 K E James 'Concert Life in ... vol 2 p. 176
81 Ibid
82 Trevor Fawcett 'William Herschel at the Octagon Chapel, Bath' *The Speculum, the Journal of the William Herschel Society* Winter 2006/7 vol 5 No 2 p. 13
83 Frances Fleming *The Life and Extraordinary Adventures* vol 3 p. 104
84 K E James 'Concert Life in ... vol 2 p. 181

85 Trevor Fawcett *Bath Entertain'd* p. 82
86 Dodd, Dudley 'Bath Assembly Rooms' *National Trust Magazine*, Spring 1979
87 *Bath Chronicle* 10th May 1770
88 Clementina Black *The Linleys of Bath* p. 16
89 Ibid p. 20
90 Ibid
91 *Bath Chronicle* 26th Dec 1771
92 Ian Woodfield *The Celebrated Quarrel between Thomas Linley (senior) and William Herschel: an episode in the musical life of 18th Century Bath* 1977 p. 3
93 Ibid p. 4
94 Bath Chronicle 9th January 1772
95 Ian Woodfield *The Celebrated Quarrel...* p. 5
96 Ibid p. 4
97 Michael Hoskin, *The Herschel Partnership* 2003 p. 29
98 K E James 'Concert life in ...' vol 4 p. 695
99 Ibid
100 Sheridan *Letters* vol 1 p. 23
101 Felix Farley's Bristol Journal *The Prattler* 23rd January, 1773
102 Ibid
103 Ibid
104 Trevor Fawcett *Bath Entertain'd* p. 8
105 Ian Woodfield *The Celebrated Quarrel...p.* 13
106 K E James vol 2 p. 212
107 Ibid p. 217
108 Ibid p. 220
109 John Tracy Spaight, 'Alexander Herschel as Telescope Maker' 2003 *Science History Publications* p. 96
110 Ian Woodfield *The Celebrated Quarrel...* p. 14
111 Ibid
112 K E James vol 2 p. 223
113 Ibid vol 2 p. 242
114 Ibid vol 3 p. 508
115 Ibid p. 504
116 *Bath Chronicle,* 1st May 1783
117 *Bath Chronicle* 15th April 1784
118 Trevor Fawcett 'Dance and Teachers of Dance' *Bath History* vol II p. 35
119 K E James vol 4 p. 611
120 *Bristol Gazette,* June 1823
121 K E James 'Concert life in ...' vol 2 p. 253
122 Ibid
123 Iain McCalman, John Mee *An Oxford Companion to the Romantic Age: British Culture 1776 to 1832*
124 Kenneth James 'Concert Life in ...'
125 Ibid vol 2 p.259
126 Trevor Fawcett *Voices of Eighteenth century Bath* p. 56
127 Anthony Pasquin, 'Observations in the Pump Room' *Postcript to New Bath Guide* 1789
128 H C Robbins Landon *The Collected Correspondence ...* 1959 p. 275
129 K E James 'Concert life in ...' vol 4 p.680
130 *Bath Chronicle* 17th January 1792
131 Haydn *First London Notebooks* 5th June 1792
132 H C Robbins Landon *The Collected Correspondence...* p. 254
133 Ibid p 255
134 H C Robbins Landon *Haydn, Chronicle and Works* vol 3 p.226
135 *Bristol Journal*
136 Bath Corporation Minutes, 22 April 1795
137 K E James vol 4, p. 779
138 Ibid vol 2 p. 292
139 Ibid
140 Ibid
141 Trevor Fawcett *Music in Eighteenth Century Norwich and Norfolk*
142 *Bath Chronicle* 26th February

1795

143 K E James vol 2 p.300

144 Terry Old *Bath as Jane Austen knew it* p. 7

145 Trevor Fawcett *Bath Entertain'd* 1998 p. 23

146 K E James 'Concert life in ...'

147 Ibid vol 2 p. 314

148 *Bath Herald,* 2 November 1799

149 K E James vol 3 p. 503

150 James Brooks song *The Tambourine* was published in Dublin

151 K E James vol 3 p. 503

152 Trevor Fawcett 'Selling the Bath Waters: Medical Propaganda at an 18th Century Spa', *Somerset Archaeology and Natural History* vol. 134 p. 203

153 Letter to Hester Lynch Piozzi 7th August 1807

154 Trevor Fawcett *Bath Administer'd: Corporation Affairs at the 18th Century Spa*

155 To Hester Lynch Piozzi 7th August 1807

156 K E James 'Concert life in ...'

157 Patrick Piggott *The Innocent Diversion, Music in the Life and Writings of Jane Austen* 1979 p. 124

158 Original Bath Guide 1815 printed by Meyler & Son, p.19

159 Patrick Piggott *The Innocent Diversion, Music in the Life and Writings of Jane Austen* 1979 p. 123

160 Ibid p. 124

161 Bath Corporation Minutes

162 K E James

163 Andrew Clarke *The Bath Messiah, The Celebration of 250 Years of a Provincial Choral Tradition* 2007 p. 22

164 John Skinner, A.M.Antiquary 1772-1839 *Journal of a Somerset Rectory* 1930 (1987 Impression)

p.395

165 *Bath Journal and General Advertiser* December, 12th 1831

166 Ibid

167 Extract from the *Bath Herald,* 1834 provided by Peter Sheppard Skæved

168 Peter Sheppard SkÆved, RAM

169 Percy M. Young *A History of British Music* 1967 p. 473

170 *The Musical Times,* August 1st 1901

171 *Bridgewater Advertiser,* February 1833

172 Augustus B. Granville, *Spas of England* (1841, reprinted by Adams and Dart, 1971) 2:395

173 Ibid

174 Charles Hallé *Life and Letters of Sir Charles Hallé* (ed. By M. Kennedy) re-issued 1972

175 Andrew Clarke 'The Bath Messiah' p. 33

176 Corporation Minutes

177 Kenneth Gregory *Bath Chronicle* 19th July 1985

178 Corporation Minutes

179 Agreement: Pump Room Committee & William Duck 26th Sept 1867

180 Correspondence: B&NES Record Office ac.no 0169/3/1

181 Ibid

182 Ibid

183 Ibid

184 Bath Corporation Minutes

185 Correspondence: B&NES Record Office ac.no 0169/3/1

186 Bath Corporation Minutes

187 Ibid

188 *Bath Chronicle*

189 *Bath and Cheltenham Gazette* 1st October 1884

190 *Ibid*

191 Andrew Clarke *The Bath Messiah*

192 *Bath and Cheltenham Gazette* 'Notes By the Way' 8th October

1884

193 *Ibid*

194 *Bath and Cheltenham Gazette* 15th October 1884

195 *Bath and Cheltenham Gazette* 24th October 1884

196 *Bath and Cheltenham Gazette* 12th November 1884

197 *Bath and Cheltenham Gazette* 31st December 1884

198 Ibid

199 Ibid

200 Ibid

201 Ibid 18th December 1884

202 Cedric Chivers, Mayor of Bath: Plaque: The Corridor

203 Andrew Clarke *The Bath Messiah* p.43

204 Ibid p. 44

205 Charles Chaplin *My Early Years* 1964 p. 40

206 Ian Bradley, *Water Music* 2010 Oxford University Press p.52

207 Letter to Alistair Hinton, 18th September, 1987

208 Ian Bradley *Water Music* 2010 p.53

209 *Bath Chronicle* 6th January 1910

210 Andrew Clarke *The Bath Messiah* p. 46

211 Suzanne Audrey 'An Audience with Dame Clara Butt' University of Bristol 2008

212 *Bath Chronicle* 28th April 1910

213 Ibid

214 *Bath Herald*, Saturday, 10th September 1910

215 *Bath Chronicle* 8th September 1910

216 Ibid

217 *Bath Herald* 17th September 1910

218 Ibid 1st October 2010

219 *Bath Chronicle* 3rd November 1910

220 *Bath Herald 12th November 1910*

221 *Bath Chronicle* 15th December 1910

222 *Bath Herald 24th December 1910*

223 *Bath Chronicle* 'An Appreciation' 19th January 1911

224 Frank Tapp Pump Room Concert Programme 1913/14 Season

225 Frank Tapp *Should Bath Revive the Pump Room Orchestra?* The Critic, February 1951

226 Richard Barnard 'The Last Concert' Programme 2006

227 Tim Foxon *The British Symphony 1880 - 1920*

228 *Bath Chronicle* 15th May 1915

229 Ibid 10th July 1915

230 Ibid 21st July 1915

231 Ibid 31st July 1915

232 Ibid 1st August 1915

233 Frank Tapp Article *The Critic* February 1951

234 the late Kenneth Gregory

235 BBC Written Archives, Caversham Park

236 Ibid

237 Ibid

238 Ibid

239 Ibid

240 Ibid

241 *Bath Chronicle* 18th September 1915

242 Ibid 18th September 1915

243 Kenneth Young *Music in the Great Days in the Spas and Watering-Places* p. 71

244 Notes by W.H.A. Chislett 'The Survey of Bath and District' No 23, October 2008

245 Contracts, B&NES Record Officer ac. No. 0169/3/1

246 Ibid

247 Spa Committee Minutes

248 *Bath Chronicle* 28th Feb and 13th March 1920

249 Ibid 20th March 1920

250 Ibid 13th March 1920

251 Ibid

252 Ibid 20th March 1920

253 Ibid 13th March 1920

254 BBC Radio 4 *Music by the Sea* 1987
255 *Bath Chronicle* 13th March 1920
256 Brian Reynolds www.turnipnet. com/mom/janhurst.htm
257 Ibid
258 Ibid
259 *Bath Chronicle* 17th April 1920
260 Kenneth Young *Music's Great Days in the Spas and Watering-Places*
261 Eric Blom, *Festival Week at Bath, the Musical Times May 1st 1921*
262 Kenneth Young *Music's Great Days ... p. 73*
263 Tony Hatton
264 Courtesy of Tony Hatton
265 BBC Written Archives, Caversham Park
266 *Bath Chronicle*
267 the late Kenneth Gregory
268 BBC Radio Four *'Great Lives'* April 2009
269 BBC Written Archives, Caversham Park
270 Kenneth Young *Music's Great Days ... p.73*
271 Ibid p.72
272 BBC Written Archives, Caversham Park Letter 18th June 1927
273 Kenneth Young *Music's Great Days...p.74*
274 *Bath Chronicle 8th August 1929*
275 Kenneth Young *Music's Great Days ...p. 197*
276 *Bath Chronicle* June 11th 1934
277 *Bridlington Free Press* 30th July 1934
278 Brian Reynolds Author of *Music While You Work* Book Guild Publishing 2006
279 Ibid
280 The first Pump Room was actually completed in 1706 which is when the first musicians would have played there
281 John Hatton 1929 Pump Room Programmes
282 Christine Lucia *The World of South African Music* Cambridge Scholars Press 2005
283 Tim Bullamore *Fifty Festivals* Mushroom Publishing 1999 p.13
284 Pump Room Programmes 1922 - 1941
285 *Bath Chronicle* 'Down Memory Lane' 1st February 1990
286 courtesy of Joe Bossi's granddaughter Pam Hawker
287 John Hatton *The Book of Bath, 3rd Edition*
288 *Bath Chronicle* June 11th 1934
289 Ian Bradley *Water Music* 2010 p. 48
290 Brian Hornsey *Ninety Years of Cinema in Bath*
291 *The Musical Times* October 1935
292 Tony Hatton
293 Christine Lucia *The World of South African Music*
294 *Bath Chronicle*, letter 18th May 1973
295 *Musical Times* December 1st 1932
296 Referred to in Corporation Minutes
297 T R Robinson & R J Bossi *History of the Equation Long Case Clock made by Thomas Tompion London A.D.1709* Horological Journal December 1952
298 Ibid
299 BBC Written Archives, Caversham Park
300 Kenneth Young *Music's Great Days ...p. 206*
301 Ibid
302 Ibid
303 Bath Abbey Newsletter January 1936
304 Tim Bullamore *Fifty Festivals* p. 15
305 *Bath Chronicle* May 30th 1936
306 Kenneth Gregory, Bath historian and journalist

307 *Bath Chronicle and Herald,* May 30th 1936

308 Ibid May 17th 1936

309 Ibid May 30th 1936

310 We are indebted to Ann Somerset Miles for this information

311 Jeff Walden, BBC Written Archives

312 Ibid

313 Kenneth Gregory

314 Nick Sutton, the Ambassador Hotel, Chicago,

315 Ibid

316 Ann Somerset Miles

317 We are grateful to Ivy Brown for this information

318 Kenneth Young *Music's Great Days...*p. 93

319 Ann Somerset Miles

320 Letter John Madigan

321 We are grateful to Madeleine Hayward for this information

322 Courtesy of Julien Chilcot-Monk

323 BBC Written Archives, Caversham Park

324 Courtesy of Julien Chilcot-Monk

325 BBC Written Archives, Caversham Park

326 Ann Somerset Miles

327 Recorded in the fifties at EMI's Abbey Road Studios with Beecham's Royal Philharmonic Orchestra. More recently it has been available in CD Format

328 Bath Spa Committee Minutes

329 *Bath Chronicle* 4th April 1946

330 Ibid

331 Courtesy of Julien Chilcot-Monk

332 Ibid

333 Ibid

334 Tim Bullamore

335 The Survey of Bath and District No 23, October 2008

336 BBC Written Archives, Caversham Park, letter to Kenneth Baynes August 1949

337 *Bath Chronicle* 6th May 1949

338 Tim Bullamore, Jones Obituary

339 BBC Written Archives, Caversham Park

340 Tim Bullamore *Fifty Festivals* p. 28

341 The late Kenneth Gregory

342 BBC Written Archives, Caversham Park, letter 19th March 1953

343 Ibid, Review 13th August, 1953

344 Bath Spa Committee Minutes

345 Ann Somerset Miles

346 Noel Wade

347 Tim Bullamore 'Yehudi Menuhin *and Bath: A Mutual Benefit?* Bath History XI, Bath Preservation Trust 2009 p. 150

348 Kenneth Young, *Music's Great Days* p. 197

349 Kenneth Young *Music's Great Days...*p. 74

350 *Bath Chronicle,* April 6th 1972

351 Julie Miller (Ray Miller's wife) an MOD employee in the seventies

352 *Bath Chronicle,* 31st May 1972

353 BBC Written Archives, Caversham Park

354 *Western Daily Press* 13th November 1980

355 Tim Bullamore, Obituary January 1986

356 Ibid

357 Julie Walker

358 Chris Evans www.allmusic.com

359 *Bath Chronicle*

360 Courtesy of Ann Somerset Miles

361 Kenneth Gregory, *Bath Chronicle* ' City 'sawers and blowers' 19 July 1985

362 Ann Somerset Miles

363 Ken Ritchie, former Assistant Manager of the Pump Room Restaurant

364 Trevor Fawcett *Bath Administer'd* p. 99

365 Bath Corporation Minutes

366 Tobias Smollet *Humphry Clinker*

367 Kenneth James Concert Life in Eighteenth Century Bath
368 Trevor Fawcett *Bath Administer'd* p. 100
369 Christopher Anstey *New Bath Guide 1766*
370 Trevor Fawcett *Bath Administer'd* p. 100
371 Bath Corporation Minutes
372 Trevor Fawcett *Bath Administer'd* p. 100
373 Bath Corporation Minutes
374 Ibid 6 April 1807
375 Ibid 10th July 1811
376 Bath Corporation Minutes
377 Ibid 1831
378 Trevor Fawcett *Bath Administer'd* p. 100
379 Bath Corporation Minutes
380 Ibid
381 Bath Spa Committee Minutes
382 *Bath Chronicle* 17th August 2000
383 Former Head of Museums in Bath, Sam Hunt
384 www.davidpaskett.co.uk
385 Alistair Hinton
386 Wikipedia
387 Pat Dunlop, Commercial Manager, Roman Baths and Pump Room
388 Gordon Spurrell
389 Patrick Michallat-Cox
390 Rare instrument dealers in Bath at that time
391 *Bath and West Country Life* Nov &
Dec 1987 p. 5
392 *Bath Chronicle*, March 1988
393 *Western Daily Press*, 'West's Diary', 1st March, 1988
394 Tim Bullamore *Fifty Festivals* p. 167
395 Morag Joss *Funeral Music* Windsor 2005 p. 135
396 John Maguire BBC Bristol 8th August 2003
397 Edna Blackwell
398 www.sallylunns.co.uk/history, intro.htm
399 Ibid
400 Ibid
401 Ibid
402 Jon Overton, proprietor Sally Lunn's
403 Records International, USA, August 2002
404 Rob Barnett, *Music on the Web*, October 2002
405 Gordon Rumson *Music & Vision* Tuesday, 14th June 2005
406 Geoff Brown, *The Times* (T2), 12 November 2002
407 Philip Clark, *The Strad*, February 2003
408 Michael Forsyth *Bath: Pevsner Architectural Guide* p. 70
409 Jackie Herring, Festival Director, The Jane Austen Centre
410 West Country Life '*Eating Out*' by Chris Rundle

Index

Page references in *italics* refer to illustrations. Streets, buildings and minor locations are in or near Bath unless otherwise identified.

INDEX

Born in New York City, **Robert Hyman** spent his formative years in New Jersey. From the age of seven he made the weekly trip across the George Washington Bridge to study violin at the Juilliard School of Music, where in years to come he was to gain a Master of Music degree. Amongst Robert's most treasured memories there were the tutelage of the Juilliard String Quartet and the art history classes with Margaret Salinger, curator of the Metropolitan Museum of Art. In his eighteenth year with the Pump Room Trio, (at the publication of this book), Robert likes to keep fit, playing and coaching his favourite sport – tennis. He also enjoys time with his family in their home just outside Bath.

Nicola Hyman is originally from Bristol. An early teaching career in Inner London eventually led to community/charity development work, ranging from playbus and disability sports projects to fundraising. Her current freelance work includes administration in sports media and for the University of Bath's Social Policy department. An English and History graduate, Nicola's long cherished desire to immerse herself in a challenging body of research has, with this book, finally been realised. She now hopes to play more tennis and resume a social life!